The Cheltenham Festival

The
Cheltenham
Festival

A CENTENARY HISTORY

ROBIN OAKLEY

To Carolyn, who makes everything possible

First published 2011 by
Aurum Press Limited
7 Greenland Street
London NW1 0ND
www.aurumpress.co.uk

Acknowledgements

Many people have played a part in this book. I am especially grateful to trainers and jockeys past and
present for their time and trouble. Thanks above all to Edward Gillespie, Simon Claisse and Andy Clifton
of the Cheltenham team and to the long-time chairman Lord Vestey. Thanks, too, to Andy Hayward
for his guidance and to Graham Coster, Sean Costello and Barbara Phelan of Aurum for their
encouragement and painstaking care.

A catalogue record for this book is available from the British Library.

ISBN 978 1 84513 636 9

1 3 5 7 9 10 8 6 4 2
2011 2013 2015 2016 2014 2012

Typeset by SX Composing DTP, Rayleigh, Essex

Printed and bound in Great Britain by MPG Books, Bodmin, Cornwall

Contents

Introduction

The Victory They Will Never Forget

The losing jockey called it the best race he had ever ridden in. The winning jockey was almost carried into the weighing room before he'd got to the winners' enclosure by the sheer weight of the crowd, who grabbed at his clothing and the winning horse's tail for souvenir hairs. Festival regulars have never heard a noisier reception for a winner and no clips of any Cheltenham Festival finish have ever had so many replays. If there is one horse the Irish love even more than the imperious Arkle it is Dawn Run, the mare who is still the only horse to have won both the Champion Hurdle and the Cheltenham Gold Cup.

Dawn Run wasn't cuddly or beautiful. She had a mind of her own and it was sometimes a mean one. Coming into the Cheltenham Gold Cup of 1986 she lacked experience over jumps. She had fallen on her only previous outing over the fences on the undulating switchback track and had never tackled the Gold Cup distance before. But she was an indomitable character, owned by another in the same mould, and was adopted by the Irish as a symbol of the nation's fighting spirit. If the Cheltenham Festival had a patron saint it wouldn't be a human being, it would be a horse, and Dawn Run came as near to filling that role as any creature of flesh and blood has ever done. That is why the Gold Cup the year she ran in it has acquired legendary status.

Dawn Run's owner Charmian Hill believed utterly in her mare and she liked to have her own way. Before the race she alienated racegoers and upset her trainer, the quintessential quiet maestro Paddy Mullins, by insisting on him 'jocking off' his son Tony, the mare's partner in many of her victories, and giving the ride in Dawn Run's most important race to a jockey who had never ridden her in a chase. That jockey, the great Jonjo O'Neill, had been so unimpressed with the mare's jumping when he went over to Ireland to school her at Gowran Park that he believed she probably shouldn't even be in the race.

The first time Jonjo rode the mare was in her hurdling days at Ascot and he admits he told Paddy Mullins then, 'She's no Champion Hurdle mare, you know, she's slow!' After riding her in a few more races Jonjo changed his mind about her abilities and he was on board when she won the 1984 Champion Hurdle as the 5-4 on favourite. But hurdles are one thing, fences quite another.

Dawn Run was going for the Gold Cup in only her fifth run over the bigger obstacles and though Irish money had made her the favourite she had never run over as far as three miles two furlongs before. In the autumn of 1984 she had won the Nobber Chase at Navan but injured a leg in the process and was a year off the course. When she returned in December 1985 she won the Durkan Brothers' chase at Punchestown and the Sean Graham Chase at Leopardstown's Christmas meeting before her prep race at Cheltenham itself in January 1986. In that she clouted the last open ditch and gave jockey Tony Mullins no chance of staying in the saddle.

Her opponents on Gold Cup day were equine warriors proven at the highest level. The classy Wayward Lad had three times won the King George VI Chase, Forgive 'n' Forget had won the previous year's Gold Cup and Run And Skip had proved his stamina by winning the Welsh Grand National.

Says Jonjo: 'I never rode her over fences until the Gold Cup because Tony got back on her. I got kicked in the head and I couldn't get my helmet on. They wouldn't let me ride and he won on her.' He wasn't too optimistic about the mare's chances of getting round, let alone winning.

'I only schooled her at Gowran Park and Punchestown, then rode her in public in the Gold Cup. She was desperate. God she was novicey and she was such a moody old devil, a moody old thing to get her going. She was favourite for the race and I said she shouldn't even be in it!'

The atmosphere among the horse's connections before the Gold Cup of 1986 was therefore uncomfortable. They all knew they had a fine mare. Dawn Run had become the darling of Ireland two years before when she won the Champion Hurdle, the first mare to do so since African Sister in 1939. She had won an Irish Champion Hurdle too and the French equivalent at Auteuil, in the hands of Tony Mullins, in June 1984. But as a result of the time she lost after her injury she was in 1986 taking on the best chasers in two countries for the Gold Cup after only four steeplechases.

By implication blaming Tony Mullins for Dawn Run's fall in her prep race at Cheltenham, Mrs Hill had insisted on her trainer using a more experienced rider for the Gold Cup, just as she had done two years before for Dawn Run's Champion Hurdle victory. Mortified at what he then had to say to his own son, Paddy Mullins reckoned she had just been looking for an excuse to make such a demand. Some felt there were deeper psychological reasons for the owner's decision, nothing to do with the young jockey's ability. After herself riding Dawn Run to win a bumper, a Flat race for National Hunt horses, Mrs Hill had resented finally being 'grounded' by the Irish Jockey Club, who ruled that at the age of sixty-two she would no longer be granted a licence.

Colleagues reckoned that the feisty Mrs Hill, who was barely civil to Tony Mullins when she came to ride out twice a week at Paddy Mullins's Doninga yard, simply could not bear watching her beloved and, in her mind unbeatable, mare in the hands of a twenty-year-old youngster.

But despite that rancour in the background, despite the mare's lack of chasing experience, the 1986 Gold Cup proved to be one of the greatest races of all time. The partner of the second horse home, Graham Bradley, who himself had ridden the Gold Cup winner three years before, called Dawn Run's race the best he had ridden in. Nobody who was at Cheltenham that day has ever forgotten the character and courage that Dawn Run demonstrated.

If you want to know what the Cheltenham Festival is all about, then listen to her jockey, Jonjo O'Neill, tell the story. Twenty-five years on it remains vivid in his memory.

'At the end of that Gold Cup, I thought coming down the hill we were after going a right gallop. I missed the water jump and that kind of messed us up a little bit. There were three or four front-runners. There was Cybrandian, herself, and Run And Skip and I think another [Forgive 'n' Forget] all going for the lead, all good horses. We were going so fast I missed the water and I couldn't give her a breather when I wanted to. Then she got headed by another horse. She didn't like being headed and I had to motivate her out of it, motivate her from every angle.

'We were going some lick. She missed the fence after the ditch going up the hill – she walked through that one – and then I was in trouble trying to get her back as the race was really on at that stage. I was lucky enough that Run And Skip missed the one at the top of the hill and so I got upsides – we were back on top again.

'We were flying down the hill and I could hear them coming behind us. I thought we'd gone a right gallop and couldn't believe they were so close to us. We jumped the third last and they were jumping up my backside and I thought, 'Jesus, if we don't ping the second last we're going to get beat.' She did ping the second last but they passed me as if I was stopped. I couldn't believe it. I thought, 'Oh, we're beaten', so I left her alone for a few strides. Then, just between the second last and the last I could feel her filling up [he gives a huge intake of breath], and I thought, 'We ain't done yet.'

'We rallied to the last and we were flying and she picked up, she picked up outside the wings herself, in fairness to her. Wayward Lad [with Graham Bradley on board] was in front of me and he hung in across. I thought, 'He won't get home', because I'd ridden him the year before and Forgive 'n' Forget had had enough of it at that stage. I just kept going across the track on her now, and the more on her own she was, the better she was. She came up the hill like a tyrant. The funny thing was that half-way going down to the last I knew I was going to win. I just knew she'd keep going once I'd got her motivated. I know it didn't look that way but I knew she'd get up the hill.'

Wayward Lad, who had that season won his third King George VI Chase, was probably a better chaser than Dawn Run. He had the experience and the ground to suit and a jockey who knew all about winning Gold Cups. What he and his rider hadn't reckoned with was the iron will of a mare who was prepared to dig to the very depths of her being in answering her jockey's call to glory. Dawn Run came level with Wayward Lad in the last forty yards and went by to win by a length. Their epic contest was a test as much of character as of racing ability and Dawn Run had that in bucket-loads. No horse has ever appeared so beaten in a big race and yet got up to win. Peter O'Sullevan's vivid commentary that day captured every nuance of the occasion and at the moment he declared, 'The mare's going to get up', a small nation rose to its feet.

Says Jonjo: 'Afterwards the weight of the crowd nearly took us into the weighing room. They were so pleased and so delighted. There was no nastiness, it was just over-exuberance, but I had an awful job hanging on to my weights and my saddle trying to get back in to get weighed. I was worried that I was going to lose the lead weights because they were grabbing everything. They were grabbing hairs from her tail.

'It was a magical day. It was fantastic. The whole of Ireland wanted her to win and knew she could win. It was great that she did it and it was great how she did it. I've met a lot of people since who've told me what inspiration it gave them at times when they were down in their lives. She gave a lot of people inspiration.'

One former champion jockey, in company with an ambulance man and a fence attendant, had his own unique perspective on the proceedings. Up on the hill, Richard Dunwoody's mount Von Trappe, still going well, had fallen at the fourth last. 'It was almost a surreal experience. After I'd thrown away my helmet in disgust and beaten my stick into the ground I was there up in the Gods, watching from afar, peering down on the finish. I saw the horses heading into the straight, then they were hidden by the people on the bank. There was a huge cheer as they turned in and I thought, 'That's it. Dawn Run's going to win.' Then suddenly it was as if somebody had turned a switch. Everything went quiet and I thought, 'Obviously she's beat.' Then they jumped the last and suddenly there was this huge roar rolling back from the stands . . .'

Wayward Lad's partner 'Brad' was the man who won the Gold Cup the year Michael Dickinson trained the first five home but he still called Dawn Run's Gold Cup the best quality race he had ever ridden in. After the race, hats were thrown and trampled. Charmian Hill, significantly, was wearing a red coat and a black belt which matched her rider's colours. As an exultant green tide rolled around the winners' enclosure she and Jonjo O'Neill were chaired by their supporters. Jonjo, aware of the big part Tony Mullins had played in developing the mare's ability, tried to carry the young jockey to the rostrum to share in the glory. To this day he declares: 'I always said she ran sweeter for Tony than she did for me. He had his own way of doing it and he knew her very well.'

When he dropped Tony Mullins off his back the youngster nearly fell on the Queen Mother . . .

Tony Mullins later told reporters: 'Dawn Run was not the quiet lady that some people believe. She was a savage. She was a demon to get a cover on or off. You would literally have to have a lad holding her while you were doing it, unless you knew her really well. She wasn't the lovely little Irish mare that some people think she was – she was a big masculine type of mare . . . From the back she had that big square backside with the second leg as they call it, the extra muscle coming down that only colts or geldings have. I would imagine that she was half masculine.'

Whatever her gender mix, Dawn Run had her own way of doing things. And what she had in bundles was courage. Says Jonjo, 'If you hit her before she was ready to be hit she'd pull up, and she would let you know. But if you got her motivated and motivated then once you had her up and running she'd go through fire – no problem.'

Go through fire she did in that 1986 Gold Cup. It was the finest recovery from an apparently down-and-out position most of us will ever see in a championship race. The sequel however was a sad one. Dawn Run did not go to the paddocks to breed foals with her fighting qualities. A few weeks later Charmian Hill insisted, against her trainer's advice, that the mare should be sent back to Paris to run over hurdles once again. Tragically, at Auteuil she fell and was killed. But she is never forgotten and her statue at Cheltenham remains a favourite meeting point, especially for Irish fans.

Cheltenham's Festival is all about heroes like Dawn Run and it provides them for every generation. Whatever the weather, spring arrives for millions in Britain and Ireland at precisely 2 p.m. on a Tuesday in mid-March, as the crowd spontaneously opens its lungs to roar off the runners in the first race of what has become a four-day extravaganza.

The helicopters of the rich will have clattered in over Cleeve Hill. Numb fingers will have wrestled with car park hamper chicken legs and currant cake (surely only the British could picnic before April). The first few thousand of the 220,000 pints of Guinness which will be drained at the four-day festival will have been sunk, and revved-up younger jockeys, struggling into the tights they wear beneath their breeches, will be dreaming the dream that this year they will ride their first Festival winner.

More than 50,000 people a day will participate in the first true rite of the British spring, confident that this is some of the best fun you can have with your clothes on. The sound that erupts as the runners for the first race set off, a tradition invented by the Cheltenham crowd, encompasses a whole range of emotions. There is excitement that winter is over and the 'jumping Olympics' has come around once more. There is the camaraderie of 50,000 people who share a passion and are prepared, in some cases, to bet their houses to underline their convictions. For trainers, work riders and stable staff there is relief after months of unrelenting graft and occasional heartbreak that they have got their charges to Cheltenham at the peak fitness required to give them a chance. Racegoers, competitors and Cheltenham staff alike are exhilarated at the thought of the four days of effort, drama, heartbreak, achievement and excess that lie ahead, testing both wallets and livers.

The Cheltenham Festival offers the simplest of sporting spec-tacles, taken at a pace. There are no pauses to enquire why the referee has blown his whistle, just the drive to be first past the post, an achievement which will reflect raw courage, tactical nous, stamina and speed – man and beast in perfect synchrony. At Cheltenham, the temple of the jumping horse, the spectators don't just crowd around the parade ring to take a look at the equine stars, they pack ten deep around the pre-parade ring too, watching the competitors being saddled, the lads and lasses who know their charges by shorter, more familiar names than their race card titles sponging their mouths and giving their burnished coats a final brush down.

You don't often hear a racing crowd applauding a 2-1 favourite whose race has ended after only the second obstacle. But that was what happened when Istabraq, the three-times Champion Hurdler trained by Aidan O'Brien, was pulled up at the Festival in 2002 as he sought a fourth title. From the start of the race something was patently amiss with the horse and although the crowd was full of racegoers sporting 'Gimme Four' green and gold rosettes in owner J.P. McManus's colours, nobody wanted to see a great horse humbled, or pushed to the point where he could have harmed himself.

The same spirit was there in 2010 when the crowd loudly applauded the return after the race of beaten Gold Cup favourite Kauto Star in grateful relief that he had not been hurt in taking a spectacular fall four fences out.

There is no more thrilling sporting sight than a huge field tearing down the hill in the Triumph Hurdle jostling for a gap at nearly 40 miles an hour, or the jockeys in the Queen Mother Champion Chase driving their mounts into the last fence, asking for one final effort as they seek precious momentum for the lung-draining climb back up to the finishing post, all the time enveloped in a wall of partisan sound.

The crowds are drawn by the assurance of quality, the knowledge that the best horses will be in competition with each other. 'It *is* the Olympics of racing,' says Ryanair chief Michael O'Leary, who is both a prominent owner and, through his company, a race sponsor at the Festival. 'You will see the best jumps horses from England, Ireland and France. You know that every owner, trainer and jockey is busting a gut to win. There's that, and a very challenging course and the whole carnival atmosphere.'

Cheltenham is rich too in the history of the great moments of the sport it hosts. The ghosts of past champions are forever in the minds of the *aficionados* urging on their would-be successors. They earned their place in the pantheon through class, speed or courage, sometimes a combination of all three. The images of

Dawn Run's victory will never be erased in the memories of racing folk. Nor will the spectacle of Arkle, ears pricked, striding clear of Mill House in 1964. Nor will racegoers forget John Francome's cool swoop as Sea Pigeon took his second Champion Hurdle in 1981 or Night Nurse's slog through the mud which didn't suit him to achieve the same feat in 1977.

More recently Cheltenham crowds have thrilled to Best Mate's three successive wins in the Gold Cup and to the battles for blue-riband supremacy between the athletic Kauto Star and Denman, 'the Tank', the occupants of adjoining boxes in the all-conquering Somerset yard of Paul Nicholls.

The ups and downs at Cheltenham of National Hunt racing, still a sport as well as a business, keep dreams alive. When the 100-1 shot Norton's Coin won the 1990 Gold Cup, his Welsh farmer-trainer Sirrell Griffiths had begun his day by milking a herd of cows. And for jumping folk the Festival is the pinnacle. It took the great Cotswold trainer David Nicholson, 'the Duke', eighteen years before he scored his first Festival success, although he then collected fifteen more. When he finally scored his first Festival win in twenty-two years of trying, Irish trainer Noel Meade bent down and fervently kissed the Cheltenham turf.

People are drawn to Cheltenham from city and country alike, every section dressed as it pleases, there to appreciate technique and talent. They are there to relish the keen but friendly Anglo-Irish rivalry and, in many cases, to bet their socks off and marvel at the scale at which the big punters operate, with bundles of readies in their back pockets. What they all have in common is a true love of the sport and a relish for a champion. 'Simply the Best' should be Cheltenham's theme tune.

There may be argument about what constitutes the greatest racing experience, or the true racing championships, on the Flat: Royal Ascot; the Epsom Derby and its Kentucky equivalent; the Breeders' Cup series, which moves around a cluster of US racetracks; or the richly endowed Dubai World Cup – all have their supporters. But over jumps one pinnacle soars above the others. Aintree's Grand National meeting and Ireland's Punchestown meeting also host top-class championship racing. But Cheltenham, with the Festival meeting including the Gold Cup, the Champion Hurdle, the World Hurdle over three miles and the pell-mell Queen Mother Champion Chase over the minimum two, is acknowledged by the whole jumping community as the supreme event over obstacles.

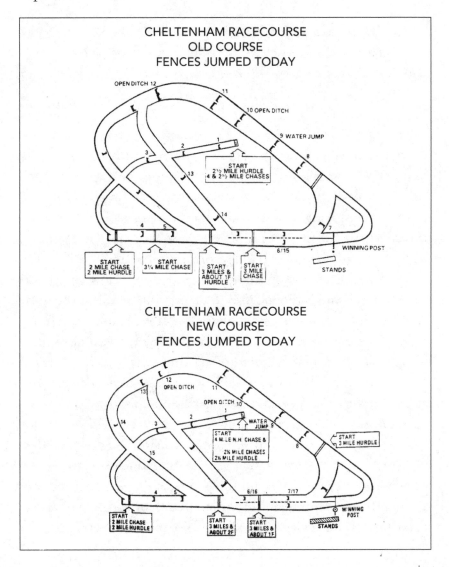

Chapter 1

The Horsemen of Prestbury

'The year centres on Cheltenham. All roads lead to it. You're always looking for a horse for the Festival or even for one for the year after that.' (Owner J.P. McManus)

To unravel the story of how Cheltenham has become the pinnacle, the Olympics of jump racing, we have to go back more than a century and a half and join a few fine sportsmen enjoying a pint in the King's Arms at Prestbury, the nearest village to the course. There wasn't then a Cheltenham racecourse as we know it today or anything like it. The only steeplechase most non-sportsmen would have heard about was the Aintree Grand National, itself then in its infancy. But the spirit of competition, the sense of exhilaration at what man and horse can achieve together, was already in the Cheltenham air. In the village closest to jump racing's natural amphitheatre was a nucleus of keen, tough and able horsemen whose careers and ambitions were to prove crucial to Cheltenham's history.

No formal meetings in the King's Arms are recorded. We cannot be sure who was there on any single occasion. But we do know that a group of regular patrons shared a passion which was to lay the foundations for today's jumping extravaganza, particularly through the development of the National Hunt Chase which was for so long its centrepiece. The successes of the Cleeve Hill cavaliers on a national scale helped the sport of racing to survive in a difficult time and to see off a powerful adversary. In some cases they bred descendants whose lives have been interwoven ever since with the Cheltenham Festival story.

In the 1850s and 1860s, the landlord at the King's Arms, a popular meeting place for the racing fraternity in the Cheltenham area, was William Archer. Those who drank at his hostelry included one Dr Fothergill 'Fogo' Rowlands, the poet Adam Lindsay Gordon and William Holman. They would have been joined on occasion by other locals 'Black Tom' Olliver, Tommy Pickernell and George Stevens, not least because the last trio rode eleven Grand National winners between them, the landlord had ridden another and William Holman trained three of them!

William Archer, whose father had been a Cheltenham livery-man, ran away from home in his early teens, weighing only four stone, and joined the yard of a Birmingham trainer. For a year he worked for Alderman Coupland, his reward being £6 and a suit. Then he joined Thomas Taylor, who was buying horses for the Russian government. The young Archer went to Moscow to help manage Tsar Nicholas I's stud and ride his racehorses for a fee of a hundred guineas a year, all found. On his return to England in 1844 he rode as a jump jockey for a few years for owners like Prince Baratzky, and in 1858 he won the Grand National on Little Charley, trained in Cheltenham by William Holman.

William Archer married Emma Hayward, daughter of the previous licensee of the King's Arms in 1849. One of their sons was the famous Fred Archer, thirteen times the champion Flat jockey in Britain and five times a Derby winner. It used to be recorded on a plaque in the King's Arms that Fred used to sustain himself on 'toast, Cheltenham water and coffee'. The plaque also declared 'The shoe of his pony hangs up in this bar, where they drank to his prowess from near and afar.' Driven mad by personal grief and the poisonous purgatives he took to reduce his weight, Fred killed himself before the age of thirty.

Best man at William Archer's wedding was 'Black Tom' Olliver, another Prestbury resident, who was one of the most renowned professional riders in the country. Olliver was the son of a Spanish smuggler and got his nickname from his swarthy gypsy looks and, some say, his wheeler-dealing. He won the Grand National in 1842 on Gay Lad, in 1843 on Vanguard and in 1853 on Peter Simple, after which victory he declared, 'I was born and bred hopelessly insolvent.' That was true. Despite the high riding fees he could attract, he was several times imprisoned for debt. Having been born Tom Oliver he added the extra 'l', he once explained, because 'l' represented the £ 'and it was always good to have an extra £ in hand'. After his riding career Tom Olliver trained both horses and dogs, though not always in the best of company. It was said that at his funeral the only respectable figure present was his hound.

Among those whom Olliver coached in riding skills were George Stevens and Adam Lindsay Gordon. As a jockey, George Stevens won the Grand National five times; celebration bonfires were lit on Cleeve Hill by the locals every time he did so. His Aintree victories came on Freetrader in 1856, Emblem in 1863, Emblematic in 1864 and on The Colonel in both 1869 and 1870. The 1870 Grand National saw a great duel between Stevens on The Colonel, who prevailed by a neck, and The Doctor, who was ridden by George Holman and trained by his father William.

Emblem Cottage, where George Stevens lived at the top of Cleeve Hill, was said to have been built with funds accrued from his successful bets on the 1863 race. In that year Emblem won the Grand Annual Chase too, a race which continues today on the Festival programme. It is the oldest contest in the jumping calendar and pre-dated the Grand National by several years.

Stevens rode in the Grand National fifteen times, and amazingly, not one of his mounts fell. He never had a serious injury in his career as a jockey. It was ironic therefore that he died in 1871 at only thirty-eight from a freak riding accident. Stevens was riding up Cleeve Hill to his cottage when a gust of wind blew his hat off his head. As a passer-by handed it back the gesture spooked his horse, which turned and bolted down the hill. Nearly at the bottom, where the road forks to Southam, the horse stumbled in a culvert and Stevens was fatally injured as his head crashed against a stone gutter.

Adam Lindsay Gordon, whose father taught oriental languages at Cheltenham College, was no academic himself, being far more attracted to the sporting life, in which he became Olliver's protégé. Expelled from the Royal Military Academy at Woolwich for stealing a horse to ride in a race, Adam preferred riding and boxing in pub bouts. He was, however, a skilled versifier who wrote the famous poem 'How We Beat the Favourite', immortalising the 1847 running of the Grand Annual Chase in which William Archer was one of the riders. In the end, his parents packed him off to better himself in Australia, where he became a champion amateur jockey, an MP and the national poet, though he too took his own life in 1870.

Yet another of the quality riders clustered around Cheltenham and Prestbury was Adam Lindsay Gordon's school friend Thomas Pickernell, who won the Grand National in 1860 on Anatis. He won again in 1871 on The Lamb and in 1875 on Pathfinder, on every occasion using the *nom de course* of 'Mr Thomas' because his family were clerics and did not approve of his horse-racing career. Since the 1875 contest was Pickernell's eighteenth National he can perhaps be forgiven for admitting to having taken a little drink 'to provide jumping power', although perhaps it was unwise to have taken enough to make him enquire of a fellow jockey at the start which way the horses should be facing. Pickernell later became the first inspector of courses under the National Hunt Committee.

William Holman, who on Cleeve Hill, overlooking today's course, trained Freetrader (1856), Little Charley(1858) and Anatis (1860) to win the Grand National, was the first man to send out three winners of that great race. He was also twice placed in the National as a rider on Sir Peter Laurie in 1852 and 1853, and three of his six sons rode in the race. As a rider he dead-heated in 1841 for the Grand Annual. In the next two years he won it with his own horses Dragsman and The Page. Holman won again on Stanmore in 1847 and 1852 before training his three Grand National winners. His son George, reputed to be the best rider in the family, went on to equal his father's feat of riding the winner of the Grand Annual on five occasions.

Still more important in the history of the Cheltenham Festival was one of the Prestbury set who never won the Grand National, although he rode in it twice as an amateur. Abandoning his medical practice in Monmouthshire, Dr Fothergill, or 'Fogo' Rowlands, had come to Cheltenham to enjoy the sporting and racing community around Cleeve Hill and to become a trainer and amateur rider. At first he had his horses trained by Tom Olliver. When he was training in his own right his patrons included the Prince of Wales, the Duke of Hamilton and Baron Queenborough. It was Fogo Rowlands, who used to ride in white gloves, who urged on the others over their drinks in the King's Arms that as an encouragement to the breeding of horses to continue the sport so dear to them all, there should be instituted an annual race for farmers and their horses.

In 1860 Rowlands's brainchild became reality. Starting as the Grand National Hunt Steeplechase, the race which was to become the National Hunt Chase was funded by twelve different hunts with £500 added to an entry fee of £10. It was run for the first time at Market Harborough, attracting thirty-one starters. The four-mile contest was restricted to amateur riders and to maidens (horses which had not won a race). Its organisation became a byword for efficiency, and Rowlands was also successful in pressing for the creation of the National Hunt Committee (originally the Grand National Hunt Committee) to run and regulate jump racing as the Jockey Club did Flat racing. From 1863 onwards the National Hunt Chase was run under the auspices of the National Hunt Committee. Sadly though, as Peter Stevens's detailed history of the race has noted, the aim of stimulating the breeding of good jumping horses by farmers was compromised because, when race conditions were changed to bar horses from public training establishments, it became dominated by the land-owning élite who could afford private trainers.

The National Hunt Chase and the fixture at which it figured became acknowledged over succeeding years as the emblematic centrepiece of National Hunt racing. For years it was something of a 'gypsy' race, moving from one course to another. It was staged at Cheltenham in 1904 and 1905, and at Warwick from 1906 to 1910. But in 1911 the Steeplechase Company (Cheltenham) Ltd agreed terms with the National Hunt Committee for the National Hunt Chase to end its life as a touring attraction and to be held from then on at Prestbury Park, Cheltenham. So was born the Cheltenham Festival, owing a significant debt to the enthusiasm and foresight of Fogo and his fellow drinkers back in those early Prestbury days. A debt was owed also to George III and the dedicated followers of fashion.

Chapter 2

Keeping the Sport Alive

'Steeplechasing is a bastard amusement which no true sportsman
who values his horse would countenance and the sooner it is out of
fashion the better.' (Sporting press letter, 1831)

There had been racing of one kind or another at
Cheltenham since the early nineteenth century. Pigeons,
still depicted in the town's coat of arms, had relished the
salt deposits left by a small spring in Bayshill, surfacing in a field
which has long been part of Cheltenham Ladies' College. When
George III began patronising the spa town to take its restorative
waters the followers of fashion joined him. Soon a town of 3,000
people had 2,000 seasonal visitors and added attractions for their
custom were soon developed. Among them, naturally, was horse-
racing.

Historians differ over precise dates and places but there
seems general agreement that while there had been racing
nearby at Tewkesbury and Minchinhampton Common, the first
Cheltenham race meeting was held on Nottingham Hill in 1815. A
more formally constituted event took place on the heights of
Cleeve Hill, overlooking the present-day Cheltenham racecourse,
on Tuesday, 25 August 1818. On that occasion there were five races
and the first recorded winner was the five-year-old bay mare Miss
Tidmarsh, owned by the main organiser Mr E. Jones of the

Shakespeare Inn in the Lower High Street.

Local enthusiasts then set out a racecourse on the West Down of Cleeve Hill. The Duke of Gloucester, who attended every meeting, was among those subscribing 100 guineas. A three-day event was held from Aug 23–25 1819 with two major races. The first of these was the Gloucestershire Stakes over 2 miles, which was won by Champignon, owned by a Mr Calley. Then on 24 August a Cheltenham Gold Cup was won by Mr Bodenham's Sceptre, who had finished second to Champignon the day before. I call it 'a' Gold Cup because this event for three-year-olds and upwards, like all the other contests, was a Flat race, not one over obstacles.

Looking at some of the old posters which have survived, there seem to have been various bodies involved in organising contests, which were sometimes advertised as 'Cheltenham Races', sometimes as 'Cheltenham and Cotswold Races' and even as 'County of Gloucester Races'.

Jockeys who complain about tough racecourse discipline these days might like to look at the rules and regulations for the County of Gloucester Races at Cleeve Hill on 20 and 21 July 1841. These announced: 'The bell for each race will ring a quarter of an hour before the time appointed for starting, at which time the race will be run without waiting for such horses as are not ready.' Trainers were to be fined if horses were not saddled in front of the grandstand and walked or cantered past the grandstand crowd. Before the start all horses were to be taken back a hundred yards.

> Any jockey presuming to start or even to put his horse into a trot or a canter with a view to take advantage of his fellows before the [starting] flags are dropped, or wilfully turning his horse round or refusing to obey the command of the starter in any respect whatever will be fined £5 for such misconduct and will not be allowed to ride again at the County of Gloucester Races until such fine shall be paid and the stewards will listen to no evidence but that of the starter and will admit no excuse

on the part of the delinquent jockey.

It was an age of greater deference, but there were sanctions for the officials too. The regulations insisted: 'The Clerk of the Course will regulate his watch by the town hall clock of Cheltenham and will be made to pay 10 shillings for every minute he is behind time in ringing the bell for saddling for the respective races.'

Racing soon proved its crowd appeal and by 1825 the crowds flocking up Cleeve Hill were estimated at 50,000. Sideshows and gambling booths proliferated, soon accompanied by pickpockets, prostitutes and other camp followers. A grandstand was erected which was visible from Cheltenham's Promenade. Some locals were far from pleased. Among them was the handsome young orator appointed in 1825 as curate of the Church of the Holy Trinity, the Reverend Francis Close. His tirades and pamphlets excoriating racing and gambling (he also saw tobacco, alcohol and the development of railways as pernicious influences!) soon attracted a powerful following in a Cheltenham beginning to fret about its image.

Close (who later became Dean of Carlisle) was soon promoted to be incumbent of St Mary's parish church and his adherents regularly staged demonstrations against the races. In 1829 mobs hurled bottles, stones and abuse at some of the riders and their horses, disrupting the meeting. In 1830 the grandstand was burned down, although whether that was an act of God or an act of sabotage by anti-racing zealots could not be determined. Thousands bought printed copies of Close's fire-and-brimstone sermons like *The Evil Consequences of Horse-racing*.

Racing enthusiasts were initially undeterred. Lord Ellenborough offered the race stewards use of three fields at his Prestbury Park, north of the recently opened Pittville Pump Room, and a new stand to hold 700 was erected. On 19 July 1831 Confederacy became the first Prestbury Park winner when he took the Gloucestershire Stakes. But the first steeplechase under the label of Cheltenham races, in 1834, didn't actually take place at Cheltenham at all. That year there was Flat racing on Thursday, 3 April at Prestbury Park with the participation of the famous Captain Becher, whose name was later immortalised in one of the Grand National obstacles. Becher, who used to roam the country in search of rides, sometimes sleeping in stables, won a two-mile contest on Mr C.W. Codrington's Conservative. Events then moved on to Andoversford where the first Grand Annual steeplechase on 4 April was won by a Mr d'Oyley on his own horse, Fugleman, despite the presence in the field of the formidable Tom Olliver, who was to win his first Grand National in 1842.

At that time, perhaps the best-known steeplechase in the country was the St Albans Chase, although that became defunct in a few years. According to the honours board at Aintree the first two 'Grand Nationals' were those won by the Duke and by Sir Henry in 1837 and 1838, although their names are followed by a note that 'The above two races were run over a course at Maghull.' That statement is itself disputed by some racing historians, although the two races cannot have been a huge spectacle anyway, attracting fields of only four and three competitors. The commonly accepted date for the first Grand National is the 1839 contest won by the great Lottery and the key is probably that that was the first year Liverpool could be reached by train both from London and from the steeplechasing counties of the Midlands, thus encouraging the arrival of many more horses, spectators and journalists.

It was not until 1847, however, that the race pioneered by William Lynn, the proprietor of Liverpool's Waterloo Hotel, bore the official title of Grand National. Previously it had been known as the Liverpool Grand, the Liverpool Steeplechase or the Liverpool Great Steeplechase. It took a good few years to establish its pre-eminence as jump racing's most favoured national spectacle.

The Grand Annual, which was destined to become a Cheltenham

Festival fixture, was next run over a three-mile course starting near the Kilkenny Arms, going past Foxcote village and finishing by the London Road above the Frog Mill. Captain Becher won it in 1838 on Vivian.

In 1840 the Grand Annual was won by Lottery, the year after his Grand National victory. Because they feared that Lottery's participation would frighten off other entries and lower attendances, the Aintree authorities shamefully stipulated in the conditions for the 1841 race that the Grand Annual winner was to carry a penalty of 18lb extra. That raised Lottery's weight to a ridiculous 13st 4lb over the big obstacles. Such was the public faith in his prodigious jumping that he was still made 5-2 favourite for the race, but he was pulled up on the second circuit. Sadly, after a spell as his Epsom trainer's hack, the first Grand National winner ended up as a carthorse on the streets of Neasden.

William Holman certainly had his admirers on the *Cheltenham Examiner*. In 1845 most of those watching reckoned him the winner of the Grand Annual chase, that year run at Withington, on the hunter Zeno. But the judge called it a dead heat with Tom Olliver on Greyling. The *Examiner* reported: 'A finer race was never witnessed . . . the riding of all engaged in the contest was fine in the extreme. The judgment and nerve displayed by our townsman Mr Holman was the admiration of every person who witnessed this most satisfactory sporting event.'

The Grand Annual became an established fixture, and on 14 April 1847 it moved back to Prestbury Park on a course mapped out by Colonel Berkeley (later Earl Fitzhardinge). This stretched from a perry orchard near Knoll Hill House to Noverton Farm, over 'a stanked brook, having gorse plants on the taking-off side'. That was the year William Holman won on Stanmore, with William Archer finishing second on Daddy Longlegs – the contest which was immortalised in Adam Lindsay Gordon's popular poem, 'How We Beat the Favourite'.

During the evening of 21 May 1852, according to the *Cheltenham*

Examiner of 26 May, 'a party of tradesmen and others, interested in the sports of the field, dined together at the King's Head in the Lower High Street in honour of William Holman and in the course of the evening presented him with a silver tea service and a tankard 'as a mark of respect for his honest and upright conduct as a trainer and steeplechase rider.'

It was just as well that jumping was taking a hold in local hearts. The Cleeve Hill stand had been rebuilt with three storeys and in 1836 the summer meeting had gone back up the hill. But Francis Close and his anti-racing followers were having an effect: Cheltenham craved respectability and the once fashionable and well-patronised Flat races declined sharply over the next decade. After a brief revival between 1851 and 1855 there were no further race meetings on the hill. It fell to the jumping fraternity to keep racing alive through the traditional country sport of steeplechasing.

These contests, mostly matches between two horses literally using church steeples as landmarks for the riders' routes, had originated in Ireland and became popular with the hunting squires of England from the 1830s. Hunting was a vital influence on the British rural scene in those days; Thomas Assheton-Smith, the Master of The Quorn, who was described by Napoleon as 'Le grand Chasseur d'Angleterre', insisted: 'Pursuit on horseback gives hardihood and nerve and intrepidity to youth and confirms and prolongs the strength and vigour of manhood.' But Assheton-Smith was one of those who regarded steeplechasing as 'rough riding' which came a poor second to the pursuit of foxes. Other hunt enthusiasts remained sniffy; one complained in the sporting press in 1831: 'Steeplechasing is a bastard amusement which no true sportsman who values his horse would countenance and the sooner it is out of fashion the better.' He would still be waiting for the 'fashion' to fade and the sporting camaraderie it engendered has remained unrivalled. The wife of one leading rider commented in those early days: 'If I were to begin life again I would go on the Turf to get friends. They seem to be the only people who really hold together, I do not know why. It may be that each knows something that may hang the other . . .'

Through the 1850s and 1860s the jump racing fraternity held together around such fixtures as the Grand Annual and the National Hunt Chase, but there were plenty of ups and downs. Chases were held at Prestbury Park until 1853, but when the land was sold that year for £19,600 the new owner wanted nothing to do with racing.

The Grand Annual, now losing importance, took on a nomadic existence. One year it was run at Bibury, another beside the old Gloucester Road in Cheltenham, another at Andoversford. At Kayte Farm, Southam, in 1866 the grandstand collapsed and 200 spectators fell into a restaurant below. No one was killed but some of those injured sued the organisers and won £2,500 in damages between them.

Johnston's Sporting Publications, an illustrated but undated booklet which covered Cheltenham and West Country meetings when there were still courses at Pershore, Newport and Beaufort Hunt, said that the races were run for four years at 'Kete Farm', a mile to the north of Prestbury Park, and from 1867 to 1885 at a site described as 'back of the cemetery', about a mile to the south east of the Park.

But in 1881, along came the man who was effectively the founder of Cheltenham racecourse as we know it today. Mr Baring Bingham bought Prestbury Park for £30,000. At first he used it mostly as a stud farm, but he was a true racing enthusiast and wanted to revive its former glories. He railed off the course and built a grandstand. It was at this point that the present-day racecourse began to evolve, a left-handed track set in the undulating Gloucestershire foothills between the majestic Cleeve Hill and the main road from Cheltenham to Evesham. (In fact there have long been two tracks to preserve the turf and, since 2004, a cross-country course too, of hedges, ditches and banks within the outer perimeter.)

Against a verdant Cotswold backdrop of honey-coloured stone mansions, paddocks, sheep pastures and woods, different races begin at different points but most take the runners early past the main stands. They then swing left in front of the cheaper Best Mate enclosure and go up the long back hill which includes the water jump. From there, as jockeys seek to estimate how much their mounts have left in the tank, it is on to the last open ditch before the turn at the top. They come thundering back down the hill, fighting for position and hoping for an opportunity to fill their lungs before they reach the lowest point on the course. Then it is round the bend into the finishing straight to face up to the final obstacles as the horses, accompanied by a wall of sound from supporters cheering on them and their jockeys, are on a steady climb once again to the finishing post.

With all races at the Festival run at real pace, the course is a true test of stamina, though, thanks to the curves and hills, it is not a conventional 'galloping track' like some flatter parkland courses. At Cheltenham you need the athleticism to maintain a high cruising speed and the agility and nous to be able to seize the gaps when they appear. Rarely, at Cheltenham, is a race won by a sub-standard horse.

As jump racing fought for survival in Victorian times, the increasingly glamourised Grand National, with far more prize-money on offer than other races, became the dominant feature of the jumping season. But it wasn't entirely unrivalled. In 1889 the Grand Annual at least was revived at Cheltenham. And one other stalwart distinguished the programme too. As *Johnston's* commented: 'Prestbury Park is probably best known as the home of the National Hunt Steeplechase – the blue-riband event of amateur riders and a spectacle second only to the Grand National.'

Aided by the better organisation now being provided by the National Hunt Committee, there were Cheltenham meetings in 1898 and 1902. In 1908 the Cheltenham Steeplechase Company was formed and a building programme was launched. Those seeking to develop the Cheltenham course included Frederick Cathcart, a man with a vision of turning Cheltenham into the centre of jump racing as Newmarket was of Flat racing, and one Alfred Holman. There we see again the links with the Prestbury set.

William Holman's record as rider and trainer has already been discussed but he set his stamp on Cheltenham racing dynastically too. His son, Alfred, after pursuing his own career as rider and trainer, became clerk of the course at Cheltenham under the Cathcart regime. His brother, William Holman, junior, had been Cheltenham racecourse secretary in 1866 when the course was in Bouncer's Lane, Prestbury.

William Holman's youngest son Frederick, who owned a stud farm, was to father Diana, who married Herbert D. Nicholson, known to all in racing as 'Frenchie' Nicholson. With a yard adjoining the Cheltenham course at Lake Street, Prestbury, Frenchie Nicholson, after becoming champion jockey became champion trainer too and, even more famously, the tutor of a generation of jockeys like Walter Swinburn, Paul Cook, Pat Eddery, Mouse Morris and Michael Dickinson.

Frenchie's sister Bobby married trainer Willie Stephenson, who was to train the three-time Champion Hurdle winner Sir Ken. William Holman's great-great grandson, Frenchie's son David Nicholson, added further lustre to the family tradition. Known to all as 'the Duke', he capped a successful career as one of Britain's top riders by becoming champion trainer in 1993–94 and 1994–95. For long one of the most recognisable Festival figures with his sheepskin coat and red socks, he achieved his successes despite suffering from a total of thirty-two allergies, which included horses!

Frederick Cathcart had joined John Pratt of London in 1894 in a business which the latter had set up in 1860 providing inspectors and secretariats for racecourses and acting as agents for trainers and jockeys. Cheltenham in 1902 was being run by a small private company under the chairmanship of Herbert Lord, then Master of the Cotswold Hunt. By 1907 they felt the event was becoming too big for them, and the Cheltenham Steeplechase Company was formed with Cathcart as chairman. Pratt's were brought in in 1908 to take over the practical aspects of running the course.

Meanwhile in 1904 the National Hunt Steeplechase had been run for the first time at Cheltenham racecourse, roughly as we know it today, with Ivor Anthony riding W.B. Partridge's Timothy Titus to victory in a field of eighteen. The course laid out in 1904, however, took the National Hunt Chase runners off the racetrack at one stage. They went behind an orchard, through the car park and past the stables before they reappeared on the racecourse to the right of the stands. There were twenty-four obstacles at heights ranging up to five feet and a water jump reputed to be twelve feet deep.

In another significant development in 1906 the Great Western Railway opened a small station on the north-eastern corner of Prestbury Park to handle race traffic.

Pratt's remained secretaries of the Steeplechase Company until 1978. In May 1908 a new stand was completed which was to last for seventy years. In 1911 a new course was set out and the stands building programme was finally completed for the 1914 Festival. By then the National Hunt Chase and the Grand Annual were accompanied as established elements in the Festival programme by the Foxhunters' Challenge Cup, the Gloucestershire Hurdle, the National Hunt Handicap Chase over three miles, the County Handicap Hurdle and the National Hunt Juvenile Chase.

Admission fees for Cheltenham meetings in those days were: Public Stand, 2s 6d; Grandstand, 4s; Reserved Enclosure and Paddock, 14s. In addition 'Motors or Carriages' were charged at 5s, plus each occupant 1s. The racecard listed owners' and horses' names but did not identify trainers or jockeys. But bigger events were looming then, and the racecard for Cheltenham's meeting on Monday, 9 November 1914 declared: 'The whole amount raised by the sale of the Race Cards will be handed to the *Daily Telegraph*

Christmas Gift to King Albert for his people.'

The First World War, of course, put an end to all plans and soon after the 1914 Festival the grandstand and administration buildings were requisitioned, with the Red Cross taking them over as a troop hospital. Beds were set up for the first patients in the ladies' drawing room and more were then nursed in what had been the members' dining rooms. The jockeys' changing room became a storage room for the patients' kit.

Old Cheltenham hands later remarked on the evidence of the R & R for those recuperating at the course: beside the great fireplace in the Tommy Atkins Bar, a series of small indentations, created as the soldiers 'chalked up' their billiard cues. The brickwork relics have been preserved in the current Tommy Atkins bar at the bottom of the grandstand where a plaque notes: 'This building was used as a hospital for sick and wounded soldiers during the Great War. It was manned by Gloucestershire voluntary aid detachments Nos 14 and 18 and was open from 28 October 1914 to 28 February 1919, during which 3,169 cases were treated.'

Some meetings survived the war, with one in December 1914 and six days' racing in 1915. But jump racing was essentially confined initially to the racecourses at Gatwick, Hawthorn Hill, Lingfield, Windsor and Colwell Park. Such programmes as there were were only permitted provided there were no extra trains and no use of cars and taxis.

There was intense debate about whether any racing should be permitted. Some saw it as a way of 'keeping the home fires burning' and maintaining the breeding industry, at least where the Flat was concerned. (The cavalry horses of the day were mostly sired by thoroughbreds.) Others regarded racing as a frivolous and rather unpatriotic activity while those in the armed forces were making the ultimate sacrifice. The Board of Trade, for example, backed a total ban on racing in the North of England for fear that it would cause absenteeism among munitions workers. The cheap rings remained closed at jumping meetings as a disincentive to the working man to take time off work to attend. Within government there was little joined-up thinking on the subject, with periodic attempts to confine Flat racing to Newmarket. At one stage the Cabinet was on the point of announcing a total ban but instead left it to the Jockey Club to announce a suspension.

Against such a background there was clearly no scope for Cheltenham's further development until the great conflict was over.

Chapter 3

Frederick Cathcart Gets Things Going

'Here there is something that Ascot cannot show nor any other fixture through the length and breadth of England – the real love of racing for its own sake and the embodiment of that much-abused phrase "the sporting spirit".' (The Sporting Life, 1935)

Until the First World War, National Hunt racing had been essentially a sport for amateurs, of whom the most talented were often the dashing, hard-riding young officers of the cavalry regiments. Many of those were killed in the war and many regiments were afterwards reduced and amalgamated. Over the next three decades a new breed of tough young farmers' sons developed as professional horsemen alongside the military contingent, although until the Second World War the prizes for the big prestige steeplechases for amateurs remained higher than the top jumping prizes for professionals (and higher than for many Flat races too).

In the early post-war years, jump racing was still largely a sport confined to an in-crowd for whom the victory alone was enough. It often had to be, since the financial rewards were so tiny. You would be lucky to find more than one race worth more than £100 on the average card, and by the time a successful owner had paid trainers' and jockeys' 'percentages', rewarded the stable staff and paid the horses' travelling costs, there was little profit left. That was why Sydney Galtrey, one-time 'Hotspur' of the *Daily Telegraph*, wrote in 1934 of the previous ten years or so: 'Only the brave and the faithful – some have cynically described them as the needy and the greedy – were followers of the winter sport.'

Life was hard, too, for those who sought to bridge the prize-money gap by betting. While there was heavy wagering on the Flat, many of the big bookmakers at that time took little interest in jump racing. With few big players travelling to the winter meetings, the betting market was weak and it was hard to get 'on' with significant stakes. For many races there would be two short-priced favourites at little better than even money and nothing much over 4-1 for the rest. Eric Rickman, who was 'Robin Goodfellow' of the *Daily Mail* from 1929–49, noted in his memoirs that betting was often limited to two runners in a race.

You could not entirely blame the bookmakers. In the post-war decades the manipulation of form was blatant and widespread, and the sport's integrity suffered. There were too many stories of stewards failing to penalise non-triers, instead merely making a note in their diaries to back them next time out.

Despite those difficulties the arrival of the Cheltenham Festival as a permanent fixture in 1911 helped to build a growing sport. The tribe of true enthusiasts who went to watch riders like Arthur Nightingall, Tich Mason, Jack Anthony and Ernie Piggott compete for tiny prizes at Cardiff, Chelmsford, Tarporley and Torquay gradually swelled in number. Bigger tracks like Cheltenham, Hurst Park, Sandown Park, Manchester and Gatwick brought in bigger crowds.

Part of the trouble in developing jumping's appeal had been the dominance of the Grand National, with a prize on a totally different scale to other races. Good horses rarely had any other objective in their season. They would be fielded semi-fit for one or two engagements in November and December and then rested until the National meeting in the spring. It was a risky strategy. The National, like most other races of any prestige at the time, was a handicap designed to give no-hopers as much chance of winning as established stars. With huge fields attracted by the best prize-money in the country, there was always a heavy risk of being brought down or impeded by inferior horses put in the race with little chance on their previous record by owners treating it as a lottery.

Frederick Cathcart and his colleagues therefore hit on the idea of holding a contest to identify a genuine champion over normal courses (not the more extreme fences at Aintree) and with all the entrants carrying the same weight. The Cheltenham Gold Cup, a steeplechase run over three miles and a quarter for a trophy valued at 200 sovereigns, with added money, was therefore instituted as a weight-for-age chase (that is, with all horses of normal racing age carrying the same weight but with a small allowance given to juveniles and mares). It was run for the first time on Wednesday, 12 March 1924.

The first running carried a prize of only £685, compared with the £1,285 for the amateurs' National Hunt Chase. Indeed, even through the five years of Golden Miller's victories it was worth only around £670 to the winner. It was to be some years before many trainers and owners regarded the Gold Cup as anything more than a prep race for the Grand National. But from that very first contest in 1924 it provided drama, excitement and intrigue.

Many of the major racing figures of the time were involved in that first Gold Cup: Conjuror II, who had finished third in the previous year's Grand National when ridden by an inexperienced amateur, was trained by Tom Coulthwaite. After the National, Conjuror's owner had arranged for Harry Brown, the best amateur in the country, to become his permanent pilot. The Old Etonian Mr H.A. Brown was so good, in fact, that he had beaten the redoubtable professional Dick Rees for the riders' champion-ship in 1919, making him the only jockey from the unpaid ranks ever to hold that title. But Brown had broken his ankle early in the 1923–24 season and did not ride for the whole of January. That he got himself right in time for his Gold Cup ride was no surprise to those who had noted his hardiness the previous year. Then he had fallen two out in the Grand National on his own horse The Bore, breaking his collarbone. But Brown had taken a substantial bet that he would finish in the money and so, remounting with the aid of a bystander and with both reins on one side of the horse, he jumped the last to finish second and collect on his bet.

Red Splash's owner Major E.H. Wyndham confided to friends over dinner the night before that first Gold Cup in 1924 that he and trainer Fred Withington were planning to pull the five-year-old out of the race because they could not secure the services of a jockey with enough experience to give the young horse a decent chance. They did not think either that he stood much of a chance at level weights against the probable favourite Alcazar, especially because Alcazar was to be ridden by F.B. 'Dick' Rees. Rees was unquestionably the best rider of his day and was that year to become the first National Hunt jockey to ride a hundred winners in the season (108 from just 348 rides). But when Fred Withington arrived at the course on Gold Cup morning he learned that Alcazar was not running and quickly engaged Rees to ride Red Splash.

That inaugural running proved to be an absolute cracker of a race, with three horses coming to the last together and battling all the way up the hill to the finish. Forewarned, trained by Aubrey Hastings and ridden by Jack Anthony, was the 3-1 favourite but on a balmy spring day it was Red Splash, the youngest horse in the race (as a May foal, he was not even five) who was immediately taken to the front by his rider. After two and a half miles Red Splash appeared to tire and dropped back a little but a crack from Rees's whip got him going again and he was still in charge over the last two fences, though being challenged by Gerald L. Just behind was Harry Brown on Conjuror II.

Those three had drawn clear of the field. They rose together at the last fence and stormed up the hill, with Red Splash bravely responding to Rees's urgings as Conjuror II got the better of Gerald L and came at him. The three were still locked together as they crossed the line. The judge gave it to Red Splash by a head, with Conjuror II just a neck behind the second. It was a wonderful start for the new race and a fine performance by such a young horse.

The early Gold Cups provided a taste of the Anglo-Irish battles to come; the second in 1925 was won by 'the Sligo mare' Ballinode, trained by Frank Morgan on The Curragh, and the next year's contest was won by Koko, trained in County Meath by Frank Barbour. Frank Morgan had four sons who became steeplechase jockeys. It is typical of the family links with stud Festival history that one of them was Tom Morgan, who rode Yahoo to be second to Desert Orchid in his epic Gold Cup victory and who was champion jockey at that 1989 Festival.

It was only in 1923 that the Cheltenham Festival had become a three-day event. Its growing importance as the main focus of jump racing and a true test of excellence saw the introduction of the Champion Hurdle in 1927. Success was starting to breed success, and a growing acknowledgement of the entertainment which the sport provided was being reflected in greater professionalism among trainers and riders. At the same time a steady increase in prize-money helped to draw in rich sporting owners from home and abroad who added to the quality and the glamour. Jump racing was catching up with the Flat. Stewarding was improving and despite the requirement of jumping obstacles, punters began to realise that 'a certainty over fences was surer than one on the Flat'.

Those who were becoming Cheltenham regulars got a pretty good deal. In the 1920s the annual subscription for members was £5 16s including tax. For that you could enjoy eight days racing through the year and could bring in three friends, though if you were to bring in the wrong kind there was always the danger you could be blackballed. Becoming an annual member was easier for some than others; it was virtually automatic for those who were already members of London clubs like Boodles, the Reform, and the Naval and Military.

There were some seats provided on the lawn in front of the Members' Stand. In the 1920s you paid a guinea a year for a seat in the open, three guineas for one under cover. It was announced one year that 'in order to meet the wishes of those members who desire to secure private seats the committee have sanctioned the hire of seats provided that the names or initials of members are printed on them. Also the committee reserve the right to arrange the positions.' So clearly nobody could hope to grab the best vantage points with a pre-breakfast run with the towels, package-holiday style.

By 1935 Arthur J. Sarl, 'Larry Lynx' of the *People*, was writing in his reminiscences of thirty years of racing, *Horses, Jockeys and Crooks*: 'Cheltenham is an example of what can be done to arouse public interest in National Hunt sport. It is the jumping fixture de luxe. Messrs Pratt, who control Cheltenham, leave no stone unturned in their endeavours to cater for the casual racegoer at the National Hunt Festival.'

When Frederick Cathcart died in 1934, the obituary in the *Sporting Life* declared: 'He was indefatigable in his efforts to increase the popularity and public appeal of the race meetings with which he was associated. Much of the success of the chasing at Cheltenham was due to Mr Cathcart's energy and enterprise.'

The sport was also acquiring its heroes. The riding stars of the decades between the two world wars included several from famous riding and training families. In the 1920s F.B. 'Dick' and Bilby Rees, Ted Leader, Billy Stott and Billy Speck were leading lights in the saddle. In the 1930s Danny Morgan, Gerry Wilson and Ron Smyth rode in company with famous trainers-to-be Fred Rimell, Fulke Walwyn and 'Frenchie' Nicholson, the latter a true son of Cheltenham, with family links back to the early days. Fred Rimell and later Fred Winter are the only two men to have been both champion jockeys and leading trainers.

Dick Rees we have already encountered. His elder brother Bilby was a fine rider too, who won the Grand National on Music Hall in 1922 and the 1928 Champion Hurdle on Brown Jack, but Dick was five times the champion jockey. He won the Gold Cup both on Patron Saint (1928) and on Easter Hero (1929), the Champion Hurdle on Royal Falcon (1929) and the Grand National on Shaun Spadah (1921). A natural horseman and a fine tactician, he was also known as a bon viveur. Junior jockeys were on occasion sent out to bring him a Scotch before a race, and he famously overdid it on one occasion in Paris. He had travelled to ride Easter Hero in the French National, the Grand Steeplechase de Paris. Unfortunately Easter Hero ejected him at the water jump, whereupon Rees picked himself up, gestured rudely to the crowd and relieved himself in full view of the stands. The spectators were undaunted, some apparently encouraging him with shouts of 'Vive l'anglais!'.

Billy Speck and Billy Stott lived close to each other in Bishop's Cleeve. They always seemed to be thought of as a pair, though the former drank tea and the latter preferred champagne. Speck, who had started as a Flat jockey, rode with leathers remarkably short for his time and was famous for his ability to galvanise a horse into a last-fence leap. On Thomond II he figured in the famous duel with the crowd's favourite Golden Miller in the Gold Cup of 1935.After the tight finish that day he congratulated Gerry Wilson, who had ridden the winner, and whose exploits are covered in the chapter on Golden Miller. Speck told him: 'When we are old and grey, sitting back and enjoying a drink, we can tell them how we did ride at least one great horse race one day in our lives.' Tragically that moment of contemplation never arrived. Speck broke his back in a fall in a seller (a race where the winner is for sale afterwards to the highest bidder, if there is one) at Cheltenham's next meeting and died six days later. He had become a local hero, and Cheltenham folk turned out to honour him with a funeral procession that was two miles long. His saddle, whip and colours were buried with him.

The cheerful, talkative Stott was another denied the chance of reminiscing about his exploits in old age. Tutored like Billy Speck by Stanley Wootton at Epsom, he won the jockeys' championship from 1927 to 1933 and achieved the rare distinction of winning the Gold Cup and the Champion Hurdle in the same year on Dorothy Paget's Golden Miller and Insurance in 1933. He fell at the last when leading in the 1933 Grand National and was then forced by heart trouble to give up riding. He died later that year in a car crash.

Racing over hurdles was gaining in prestige and a new expertise was developed in riding over the smaller obstacles. The first great specialist was George Duller, who for decades had a race named after him on the Cheltenham Festival card. 'The Croucher', as he was known, revolutionised the style of riding over timber, keeping his weight well forward in the saddle and not shifting his position on take-off. Horses ridden Duller's way quickly recovered their cruising speed as the hurdle was jumped. Speed was clearly impor-tant to Duller; he was not only a first-class jockey but flew his own aeroplane and later became a motor-racing driver at Brooklands. In the First World War he had joined the Royal Flying Corps.

Duller had a great sense of pace, derived, some said, from his father 'Hoppy' Duller having trained trotters, and he liked to dominate races from the front. He seemed almost impossible to dislodge, with contemporaries agreeing that however hard his horse hit an obstacle Duller never budged an inch in the saddle. He had been champion jockey in the restricted season of 1918 with just 17 winners and in 1922 he won 97 of the 239 races in which he rode. His seven Imperial Cups at Sandown (the premier hurdle race until Cheltenham launched its championship) included three on the great Trespasser.

It was sad that the Champion Hurdle was founded too late for Trespasser to get his name on its roll of honour. An entire horse (that is, one who has not been gelded, like most jumpers), he was unbeaten in his six races over hurdles and his successes included a treble from 1920–22 in the Imperial Cup, despite his having to carry the burden of 12st 7lb on the last two occasions. He did, however, with Duller aboard, win the County Hurdle at the Festival in 1920.

Even allowing for the fact that he took few rides over the bigger obstacles, Duller's strike rate was phenomenal. In the seven years leading up to the first Champion Hurdle in 1927 it was an incredible 26.8 per cent, and it was not surprising that Duller's chosen mount for the race, Blaris, was made favourite in a small field of four.

Trained at Epsom by former champion jockey Bill Payne, Blaris was owned by Mrs H. Hollins. She was known for chasing amateur Tuppy Bennett around the paddock, seeking to bludgeon him with an umbrella after he had several times remounted a horse of hers that had fallen in the Grand National. The Frank Hartigan-trained Boddam kept Blaris company until the second last but after that Duller urged on Blaris and he went away to win by eight lengths. Blaris was good, but as quality increasingly became Cheltenham's keynote, it was the second winner of the Champion Hurdle in 1928 who provided the stardust factor. This was the great stayer, Brown Jack.

Spotted by Irish trainer and bloodstock agent Charlie Rogers grazing on a lawn when his then owner gave him a lift, Brown Jack was bought by trainer Aubrey Hastings, who knew that one of his owners, Sir Harold Wernher, was looking for a future Champion Hurdle winner.

Despite early sickness, Brown Jack soon proved himself a wise buy and though only four horses lined up once more for the 1928 Champion Hurdle, the *Sporting Life* reckoned that Blaris, Brown Jack, Zeno and Peace River were probably the four best timber-toppers in the land.

Zeno made the running until Brown Jack took him on at the second last. Blaris could not go with him and it was Peace River who joined him in the air at the last. Once on the Flat, however, Brown Jack had the better speed and won by one and a half lengths in a time eight seconds faster than the previous year. Another star had placed himself in the racing firmament and another big Cheltenham championship was up and running.

The Champion Hurdle was also now on its way, but Brown Jack was not to figure again on its honours board. His future lay elsewhere. Before sending him out on the track Aubrey Hastings had asked the champion jockey Steve Donoghue if Brown Jack might prove a winner on the Flat, receiving the emphatic reply: 'Yes, he will win on the Flat and I will ride him.'

How right he was. Brown Jack went on to win the Queen Alexandra Stakes at Royal Ascot for six consecutive years. He also won an Ascot Stakes, a Goodwood Cup, a Doncaster Cup, an Ebor Handicap and a Chester Cup, proving himself one of the greatest stayers of all time. Not surprisingly, his run in the Champion Hurdle was his last over obstacles.

Cheltenham was however establishing itself as the home of excellence, and as a sporting venue with a unique camaraderie. As the *Sporting Life* put it in Blaris's year:

> The fact that so many people look forward each year to the meeting is not in the least surprising for, try how you will, you can find no parallel to this fixture through the racing year. There is nowhere quite like Cheltenham. It has been called many names and perhaps the most common term is 'the Ascot of steeplechasing'. Though meant as a compliment the phrase does not go nearly far enough and certainly misses in its wording all that is really most charming about Cheltenham. Here there is something that Ascot cannot show nor any other fixture through the length and breadth of England – the real love of racing for its own sake and the embodiment of that much-abused phrase 'the sporting spirit'. At Cheltenham nothing matters quite so much as the sport.

Indeed so. But we were moving into an age of glamour. Could racing produce the personalities to keep pace?

Chapter 4

A Hero for a New Age

'The best horse never to win the Grand National.'
(A common contemporary assessment of Easter Hero)

With the Cheltenham Festival providing first-class organisation, focus and top championship races, the two further ingredients the growing sport needed were equine heroes to capture the crowd's imagination and colourful owners with money to spend. Both turned up on cue. The arrival in the owners' ranks of the likes of Dorothy Paget and John Hay 'Jock' Whitney helped to give jump racing a new patina, while the money they spent aided the discovery of true jumping stars. One potential hero, Brown Jack, had been snatched away for a glorious and profitable career on the Flat. But we were moving swiftly into the era of Easter Hero and Golden Miller; the latter, some would argue, was the best jumper of all time.

Steeplechasers who have truly gripped the sporting public's attention in Britain have included Golden Miller, Arkle, Mill House, Desert Orchid and Best Mate. But the first true equine superstar in the Cheltenham firmament was Easter Hero. Until his arrival chasers had mostly been big and burly – large-framed animals built for endurance rather than speed. Easter Hero was the first of a new kind of steeplechaser – lighter-framed, agile and athletic.

An elegant chestnut gelding by the well-known jumping sire My Prince, he had class stamped all over him. His style was impetuous, his jumping was spectacular, he had character and he never seemed to be far from a drama. He was what journalists call 'good copy'. It is no exaggeration to say that this one horse put British steeplechasing on the sporting map – and he attracted plenty of Americans too.

At the age of seven, after an indifferent early career which included a win at Manchester, Easter Hero, bred near Dublin, was sold for £500 by his English owner, a Mr Bartholomew, to Frank Barbour, a rich businessman and trainer who was Master of the West Meath Foxhounds in Ireland. Barbour, who had already trained Koko to win the Gold Cup in 1926, moved the next year to Wiltshire and during the 1927–28 season he transformed the former erratic jumper. Although Easter Hero was still seen by some traditionally minded pundits as 'lacking in substance', Barbour won five chases with him, including two at Aintree. Easter Hero had been thought of as a two-and-a-half mile horse but then won Kempton's Coventry Chase over a mile further and was suddenly hailed as a potential champion.

However those looking forward to his appearance at the Gold Cup in 1928 were disappointed. Before the meeting opened, Easter Hero was purchased by a mystery buyer who wanted him trained for the Grand National and had him pulled out of the Cheltenham Festival. It turned out that the new owner was a millionaire Belgian financier called Captain 'Low' Lowenstein, who kept a stable of top-class hunters in Leicestershire. He paid Barbour £7,000 for the horse with a contingency of £3,000 should he win a Grand National. It was a clause which later came tantalisingly close to being invoked but in that year's Grand National Easter Hero, carrying a massive 12st 7lb, was at the centre of a different kind of story. He was sailing along ahead of the field in his imperious style when he reached the open ditch at the Canal Turn. Taking off much too soon, Easter Hero landed on top of the fence, straddling it and, in his struggles to free himself, baulking many of the other runners. It caused a massive pile-up like that occasioned by Popham Down in 1967 when the outsider Foinavon won. Only nine horses escaped the 1928 melee and only two reached the last fence. When Billy Barton fell there the race was left at the mercy of the 100-1 outsider, Tipperary Tim.

Easter Hero was somehow never out of the news. He figured in stories a few months later when Captain Lowenstein, flying back to Brussels, disappeared from his private plane over the North Sea. No trace of him was ever found. When Lowenstein's executors put his horses up for sale the purchaser of Easter Hero was the American millionaire Mr J.H. 'Jock' Whitney, who transferred him to Jack Anthony's yard at Letcombe Regis to be prepared for the next year's Gold Cup.

Whitney, who was once listed as one of the ten richest men in the world and romantically linked at different times to actresses like Tallulah Bankhead, Paulette Goddard and Joan Crawford, was a co-owner of the oldest venture capital company in the US. Indeed it was his partner who first coined the term. Interested in show business – Fred Astaire was a good friend – he was the publisher of the *New York Herald Tribune*, and his help in funding Dwight D. Eisenhower's campaign for the presidency was rewarded by his appointment as US Ambassador to Britain from 1957–61.

In earlier days Whitney was an outstanding polo player with a four-goal handicap and he and his sister ran his mother's Greentree Stables. In 1928 he became the youngest member of the Jockey Club ever elected, and he owned some of the best horses seen out in Britain before the Second World War.

The 1928–29 winter was a terrible one in Britain. Continuous frost and snow saw the 1929 Festival delayed for a week. Partly thanks to the weather, Easter Hero's run-up to the Gold Cup consisted of victories in four hurdle races in each of which he was partnered by George Duller. He was also worked on the sands at Tenby in Pembrokeshire.

In that year's race, wearing Whitney's colours of pink, black and white striped sleeves and white cap, and ridden by Dick Rees, Easter Hero dominated his field with his high cruising speed and swift fencing. The 7-4 chance was well clear after the first circuit and, when most in the stands expected him to stop after showing such pace, he simply flew again and won on the bridle (the racing term for still going well within himself with a firm grip of the bit), twenty lengths clear of Lloydie. It was the first time a favourite had won the Gold Cup and it meant that in the first six Gold Cups Rees had ridden the winner three times and been second on another occasion.

Just ten days later Easter Hero ran for a second time in the Grand National. In what was acknowledged as one of the bravest efforts ever seen in the race, he finished second of the sixty-six runners. With the plate (racing horseshoe) on his near fore twisted, broken and hanging loose all the way from Valentine's, Easter Hero was in no condition to resist the late surge by Gregalach, who passed him to win by six lengths.

Easter Hero won his second Cheltenham Gold Cup in 1930, again as the favourite but this time odds-on at 8-11. Crowds flocked to the course because they anticipated a keen duel between Easter Hero, who was essentially being aimed at the National and whose trainer would have left a little to work on, and the rising young star Gib, who had given Gregalach 6lb and beaten him, carrying 12st 9lb, in a handicap at Lingfield. Gib was not entered in the National and would be fully tuned for Cheltenham.

This time, because Dick Rees had been claimed for Gib, Easter Hero was ridden by Tommy Cullinan. The horse, who seemed to have a nose for drama, gave the crowds a shock by diving at the roots of the first fence and then making an almost equally severe blunder at the second. Cullinan managed to steady him and by the end of the first circuit he led by ten lengths. Gib seemed to struggle to keep up with Easter Hero's cruising speed down the back but then drew level at the top of the hill. They came to the second last fence together but Gib, perhaps feeling the pressure by then, hit it and toppled over, leaving Easter Hero to stroll home once again by twenty lengths. In second place was Grakle, who had been third the year before and who was to go on to win the Grand National of 1931 with Gregalach in second place.

Easter Hero had cut himself with an overreach in the Gold Cup and could not go on to run at Aintree in 1930. He then developed tendon trouble and missed most of the rest of the year. At the 1931 Festival it was planned to run him in the shorter Coventry Chase rather than the Gold Cup but the whole meeting was abandoned due to the weather.

In his preparations for the 1931 Grand National, Easter Hero won three races and was made favourite for the Aintree spectacular but he was knocked over at Becher's second time around. He was then pulled out the very next day to contest the two-mile Champion Chase. By modern standards that is incredible. It is a bit like asking a human athlete to compete in the 1500 metres and the 400 metres on successive days, but Easter Hero still managed a share of victory, earning a dead-heat verdict with Coup de Chateau. Fortunately his sporting owner took that as a sign of declining powers and, reckoning that Easter Hero had done enough racing, let him end on that winning note. He was shipped over to the US and spent the rest of his days hunting with his owner over the Virginia countryside, living on in retirement to the age of twenty-eight. Contemporary racing writers commented on his passing that Easter Hero was the best horse never to have won the Grand National. The British racing public meanwhile did not have to wait long for the new superstar.

Chapter 5

The Greatest Jumper of All Time?

'I doubt if I ever experienced a worse day's mount. We went through the roots of every fence he jumped and, try as hard as I could to coax him to take an interest, my efforts were all in vain.' (Trainer Basil Briscoe on early days with Golden Miller.)

The second great chaser to be lionised by the British racing pubic was Golden Miller. Whether or not his achievements make him the superior of Arkle has been the subject of endless debate. No one can give a conclusive verdict, but such inter-generational debates are an essential part of the fun for sports enthusiasts. We will look later at Arkle's career, but for some old-timers the Irish champion's undoubted brilliance never quite equalled Golden Miller's incredible consistency through a seven-season career.

Basil Briscoe, Golden Miller's trainer for most of his career, bought the horse unseen. He did so because the Leicestershire bloodstock dealer Captain Farmer, who had found him good horses before, sent him a telegram offering him for £500 'a good-looking three-year-old out of Miller's Pride'. Briscoe already had a decent horse, May Crescent, out of the same mare and so he said yes. But when a gangly, morose and mud-spattered dark bay was coaxed out of his horsebox Briscoe took one look and protested to Farmer that he was not the sort he wanted. Farmer offered to take him back but Briscoe chose to persevere with his equine ugly duckling.

At first it seemed he had made a mistake in doing so. So bad was Golden Miller's response to early training efforts that Briscoe took him for a day's hunting with the Fitzwilliam, only to declare despairingly, 'I doubt if I ever experienced a worse day's mount. We went through the roots of every fence he jumped and, try as hard as I could to coax him to take an interest, my efforts were all in vain. Not only that – he appeared to me so slow that we could not even keep up with the hounds.' Head Lad Stan Tidey's opinion was that Golden Miller was 'a damned good name for a damned bad horse'.

But Golden Miller was a horse who knew what he liked and what he didn't. Two of his dislikes, it seems, were hunting and Aintree. That 'damned bad horse' was to go on to win an unrivalled five Cheltenham Gold Cups, including one gained in an epic struggle with Thomond II in 1935 which rates as one of the greatest-ever Festival races. To this day, only L'Escargot has equalled Golden Miller's feat of winning both the Gold Cup and the Grand National, and L'Escargot only won two Cheltenham Gold Cups.

Golden Miller proved to be a kindly and intelligent horse and as he grew into his frame and began to look the part, one of Briscoe's owners, Philip Carr, bought him for £1,000, despite his trainer's honestly expressed doubts about his ability. Golden Miller won a few hurdles and was second in a chase, but then sadly Carr learned that he had a terminal disease and instructed Briscoe to dispose of his horses. Briscoe, a self-confident Old Etonian who was by now getting a far better tune out of Golden Miller at home, told the eccentric owner Dorothy Paget, who was just switching her attention from motor-racing to horses, that he could sell her for £6,000 the best chaser and the best hurdler in England, who would win her a Gold Cup and a Champion Hurdle. The deal was done and for that sum Golden Miller and Insurance passed into the hands of one of the most remarkable characters ever to play a part on the British Turf, certainly one who would afford a field day to modern psychoanalysts.

Dorothy Paget, the daughter of Lord Queenborough, had been a fine horsewoman in her youth: eventing, hunting, showing and riding in point-to-points. Once she had been beautiful but she grew so obese that she looked twice her age. She was the owner of a vast chain-store fortune inherited from her maternal grandfather William Whitney, and it was racing's good fortune that she diverted much of it into buying horses, having been fired with enthusiasm for the sport by her cousin Jock Whitney's success with Easter Hero.

A partly tragic figure despite her riches, Dorothy Paget suffered from a chronic shyness and an aversion to men. In the days when she used to make regular visits to the racecourse, clad in a thick, shapeless tweed coat and a beret or blue felt hat, wearing no make-up and with her cropped hair unstyled, she would be accompanied by a posse of protective female secretaries. Contemporaries say she would lock herself in a lavatory until most racegoers had left and then summon her trainers for a debrief.

Apart from the huge sums she spent on buying horses, even more went on betting. She often put £10,000 on her own horses, serious money in those days. Later, when she lived a reclusive life in Chalfont St Giles, the floors of her house stacked with yellowing copies of the *Sporting Life* mentioning her horses, she would sleep by day and work at night, telephoning her trainers at all hours. The garden became unkempt because she would not allow Hall, the gardener, to use the lawnmower during the day. Aware of her strange habits, bookmakers would allow her to bet long after races had been concluded, trusting her not to have found out the results. She kept a retinue of cooks and would demand gargantuan meals to be cooked in the middle of the night, only to pick at a few crumbs and waste the rest. She drank only Malvern water.

When she spent winters in Germany her trainers would be

deluged with telegrams containing questions about the horses, some of them pages long. She worked her way through a long list of trainers and many stories circulated about how they dreaded her ire. One day she asked the jockey who had ridden one of her horses down the field where the trainer Fred Darling was. 'I'm not too sure, Miss Paget,' came the reply, 'but I rather suspect he might be on the grandstand roof, cutting his throat.'

Dorothy Paget herself cannot have been without a sense of humour. She had nicknames for the few men she could bear to have anything to do with. Her racing and stud manager Charlie Rogers she used to call 'Romeo'. Sir Gordon Richards, who rode and trained for her for more than thirty years, was 'Moppy'. And what did she call herself? 'Tiny'.

Many who worked for 'D.P.' would not hear a word against her, although that number did not include Basil Briscoe. He once declared: 'Training horses is child's play but it's a hell of a bloody job trying to train Miss Paget.' By contrast, Sir Gordon Richards said: 'I never want a better owner and she was the best loser I have ever known.' But there were plenty of winners in the famous blue colours with the yellow hoop – 1,534 of them in all – to go with the losers by the time D.P. died in 1960. Her successes included the Cheltenham Gold Cup seven times, the Champion Hurdle four times and a Grand National. One day at Folkestone she, trainer Fulke Walwyn and jockey Bryan Marshall won the first five races and were only just beaten in the last, for which she castigated the trainer. She was three times leading owner over jumps and once on the Flat, where she won a wartime Derby with Straight Deal.

Basil Briscoe more than lived up to his sales patter. Golden Miller won his first steeplechase in Dorothy Paget's colours, beating the future Grand National winner Forbra at Newbury and landing a stable coup, although the horse was subsequently disqualified for carrying the wrong weight. He then won two of his next three chases as he prepared for his first effort in the 1932 Cheltenham Gold Cup. There he was not given much chance against Grakle, being sent off at 13-2 while Grakle, trained by the great Tom Coulthwaite, was an odds-on favourite at 10-11. In the event, Kingsford fell a mile out and in swerving to avoid him Grakle lost his jockey. Golden Miller, ridden by Ted Leader, was left to win his first Gold Cup easily from Inverse. Later that same afternoon Insurance won the Champion Hurdle, delivering the second half of Basil Briscoe's promise.

Golden Miller was given a good summer's rest with a Great Dane for company and, reflecting the race programme of those days, was not seen out again until December. He won chases at Kempton, Lingfield, the now defunct Hurst Park and Lingfield again before defending his title at Cheltenham on 8 March 1933, this time ridden by Billy Stott, with the jockey's great friend and rival Billy Speck on the 11-4 second favourite Thomond II, owned by Jock Whitney.

The growing popularity of British steeplechasing with the international set, especially American owners, was underlined by the presence in the field also of Kellsboro Jack, a fancy for that year's Grand National who was owned by Mrs F.A. Clark. Her husband Ambrose had been trying to win the National for years. Reckoning that he was jinxed, 'Brose', as he was known, sold the horse to his wife for £1 to run him in her name instead.

Golden Miller, now a six-year-old, was an odds-on 4-7 for the Gold Cup. Despite his consistency, Basil Briscoe's charge was still not receiving much praise in the media, perhaps because he lacked Easter Hero's exuberance and panache. In fact he was a lazy horse who did not do more than he had to and usually had to be niggled throughout his races to keep his place. His jumping was economical rather than spectacular. What he did have was a high cruising speed and a big stride. He was the epitome, say those who saw him, of the horse who 'gallops his opponents into the ground'. He was also a strong horse; he not only survived mistakes that would have felled others, he did not even seem to lose momentum in recovering from them. Golden Miller may have had to be asked a lot of questions in a race but he always answered them, and there was no doubt about his courage.

On heavy ground, the running in the 1933 Gold Cup was made by Delaneige. Thomond II jumped the third last fence in front but that was the end of the race. At that point Stott let Golden Miller take command and he simply strode away from his field to win as he liked by ten lengths. It seemed to take no more out of him than an exercise canter. The correspondent of *The Times*, one of the previous doubters, recorded: 'Galloping with ease, resolution and obvious enjoyment, he went on by himself and in his glory to win without being challenged. It was done in the style of a great horse. At last he must be admitted to be that.' Insurance won a second successive Champion Hurdle at the same meeting.

The priorities of the times though still showed in a front page report by J.L.T. in the *Sporting Life* recording that remarkable double: 'Tomorrow when the "Amateurs' Grand National", the National Hunt Steeplechase, will be run is *the* day, but to the regular racegoer today provided equally as good a feast with the reappearance of the crack hurdlers and steeplechasers in the Champion Hurdle Challenge Cup and the Cheltenham Gold Cup.'

J.L.T. did however add:

> I feel sure that if all those thousands who follow racing at home could be made to realise how enjoyable, invigorating and thrilling is such a day's outing at picturesque Prestbury Park, the Great Western Railway would not be able to run sufficient trains to cope with the rush.
>
> Any sportsman who would like to take his wife for a day's outing could not choose a more ideal venue than Cheltenham. Ascot and the Derby are regarded by most southerners as the two 'outings' of the year but both of them are equalled by what Cheltenham provides on a clear day.

Golden Miller went on to run in the National at Aintree but did not figure in the finish. At Becher's second time round he hit the fence and gave his jockey Ted Leader no chance of staying in the saddle. The race was won by Kellsboro Jack, Ambrose Clark's £1 sale to his wife seemingly having done the trick.

His grateful owner, who had himself buried next to Kellsboro Jack when he died, determined that his horse should not be asked to face the rigours of Aintree again, but he did line up against Golden Miller once more for the Gold Cup in 1934, the year Dorothy Paget and Basil Briscoe had decided to make the Grand National their main target. He was not the only high-class competitor. Jock Whitney's Thomond II had beaten Golden Miller in a shorter race at Kempton, and Southern Hero, owned by another millionaire, Mr J.V. 'Jimmy' Rank, had also bested him, although in receipt of two stone when doing so. Jock Whitney had another top-class horse in Royal Ransom and the international flavour was also reflected by the presence of the French horse El Haljar, who was made second favourite.

Not surprisingly, Golden Miller, now a seven-year-old and being ridden by Gerry Wilson, was favourite, not odds-on this time but at 6-5. The story of the race was of one pretender after another taking him on and all being rebuffed in turn. First El Haljar, then Kellsboro Jack and finally Avenger sought to match strides with him but each was seen off and once again the champion, ears pricked, galloped up the hill alone to the cheers of the sporting crowd. This time the margin was six lengths although it could easily have been more.

The sequel to that year's Gold Cup was played out before the adoring crowd at Aintree. Carrying the welter weight of 12st 2lb and with Southern Hero and Thomond II among his rivals, Golden Miller was among the leaders all the way. Delaneige, an old rival from Cheltenham, jumped the last ahead of him but on the flat Golden Miller motored away to win by five lengths in a then record time of nine minutes and twenty seconds. His long-time rival Thomond II was third. The crowds were delighted and three cheers were raised for the painfully shy Dorothy Paget in her usual misshapen tweed coat, utility stockings and squashy hat. She did however stay on until midnight, dressed in red velvet, at the party thrown at the Adelphi by her father, Lord Queenborough, where Jock Whitney proposed the toast to her and Golden Miller. Then she slipped off through the staff lifts to avoid any public contact.

This time the *Sporting Life* was in no doubt. Its banner headline read:

FINEST CHASER OF THE CENTURY
Wins Grand National in Fastest Time
Champion Golden Miller

Its correspondent described the result as 'The most popular victory since Ambush II won in the Royal colours in 1900.'

That Grand National victory by a horse who was to demonstrate that he really did not like Aintree was a superb achievement. But Golden Miller's greatest race was not there. It was at Cheltenham, where in 1935 he won his fourth successive Gold Cup in one of the most exciting contests ever seen at the Festival.

In that Jubilee year Golden Miller, now a public hero, was again being aimed at the Grand National, taking in the Gold Cup contest as a useful warm-up. That, anyway, was the plan with his most dangerous rival Thomond II apparently being aimed instead at the two-mile Coventry Cup, since his owner Jock Whitney already had the useful Royal Ransom in the Gold Cup field.

Whitney flew in for the meeting and saw his Rod and Gun win the National Hunt Chase on the opening day, under a rider whose story was to become typical of the times. The successful jockey was Mervyn Jones, who joined the RAF at the start of the Second World War. In 1940 Jones was offered the ride on Bogskar in the Grand National. When he sought permission from his air commodore, Flight Sergeant Jones was asked if he had passed his navigation exam. When he replied that he had the response was, 'Well, go and navigate Bogskar round Aintree. If you don't we'll give you another navigation exam.' Mervyn Jones accomplished his Aintree mission, winning the National. Sadly, in 1942, he was reported 'missing, presumed dead' on an RAF sortie.

Rod and Gun's success seems to have increased Whitney's competitive urge because when he met Basil Briscoe after the last race he told him that he had changed his mind and that Thomond would now contest the Gold Cup. Briscoe was highly perturbed. He had not been expecting to take on anything of Thomond's ability. With the National in mind he did not have Golden Miller fully wound up and, as he forcefully told the American millionaire, he didn't think a protracted battle on the prevailing firm ground would do either horse any good with the Grand National to come. But Whitney remained adamant and the public, scenting a historic duel, arrived in record numbers to see it. On a glorious sunny day people fought for places on Paddington race trains. Roads were blocked for miles around the course. The emergency supplies of racecards were exhausted an hour before the first race. Racegoers, tired of queuing, burst through hedges to get access to the course. Many failed to get their bets on.

Dorothy Paget flew into Prestbury from Germany just half an hour before the contest in time to see a class-packed field in the parade ring including Kellsboro Jack, Avenger and Southern Hero. It was Southern Hero who set the early gallop. The pace was fast and unrelenting. Basil Briscoe declared afterwards: 'If either horse had hit a fence he would never have stopped rolling.' By the third last Southern Hero could do no more as the two principals passed him, stride for stride, with Kellsboro Jack also making up ground with them.

The brave little Thomond, with Billy Speck on board, was relishing the fast ground, the bigger Golden Miller much less so. Over the second last, with Gerry Wilson driving the Miller for all he was worth, the two were level, but Thomond had the inside and

Golden Miller had extra ground to cover. Coming into the last, Golden Miller's bigger stride had him inching in front but Speck, going for his whip, conjured such a great leap from Thomond that the two touched down together. With everybody in the crowd on tiptoe screaming home their selection, the two great horses battled every inch of the way up that final hill. But though Thomond clung to him the Miller's superior strength just gave him victory by three parts of a length with Kellsboro Jack five lengths away in third.

This time the *Sporting Life* was less restrained. Meyrick Good declared of Golden Miller's fourth Gold Cup: 'There has never been anything like the performance of the Miller on any racetrack throughout the world and Basil Briscoe is to be congratulated on the fine condition of his charge.'

Golden Miller was not distressed but he had never been given a harder race and in a sense it was the turning point of his career. There were victories still to come, but he may never have been quite the same horse again.

Both Golden Miller and Thomond went on to Aintree, with some experts suggesting that they had left their Grand National hopes behind them on the Cheltenham hill. With Golden Miller having been coupled in many spring doubles with the 10-1 Lincoln winner Flamenco there were rumours of a plot to nobble Golden Miller and he was closely guarded. Gerry Wilson told Basil Briscoe and Dorothy Paget a week before the race that he had been offered money to stop the horse.

In the event, coming to the fence after Valentine's, Golden Miller wandered and seemed to want to refuse. Still driven into it by Gerry Wilson, he somehow scrambled over but ejected his jockey. Basil Briscoe, who had allegedly backed Golden Miller to win £10,000 and told his owner weeks before that he was a certainty, took exception to her comments that the horse looked too light and had been over-galloped. He told her that if that was the way she felt she could find another trainer.

Gerry Wilson said he thought the horse had gone lame before the fence at which he tried to refuse but two vets brought in by Briscoe could find nothing wrong and they ran him again the next day in the Champion Chase. He was following in the hoof-prints of Easter Hero but for Golden Miller there was no consolation prize. He galloped to the first, hit it hard, and ejected his jockey, although once again he did not fall himself – he never did come down in fifty-two races.

Dorothy Paget sent her horses to Owen Anthony to be trained and Golden Miller came out the next December at Sandown. He ran third there, won a chase at Newbury and then in February ran out in a three-mile chase intended as his last race before the 1936 Gold Cup. That resulted in a change of rider, with the young Evan Williams taking over.

Racing scribes and public did not know what to expect next. Golden Miller had never failed to win a Gold Cup. There didn't seem to be anything wrong with him physically, but what was going on in his mind? Would a return to what seemed to be his favourite course produce another masterly display or would he repeat his Aintree antics? New rider Evan Williams was in an unenviable position.

When it came to it, Williams proved fully up to the task. So did Golden Miller. With Southern Hero and Kellsboro Jack in the field again, joined by future Grand National winner Royal Mail, Golden Miller jumped with all his old power and authority, moved into the lead three fences out and was fifteen lengths clear at the last. The crowd went silent; many were wondering: would something now snap, would the Miller refuse as he had done at Aintree or run out as he had done at Newbury? The nine-year-old did neither. He took the fence cleanly, though pitching a little on landing. The stands erupted with a great roar of relief and encouragement that echoed back off the hills, and Golden Miller strode on up the hill. At the post he was twelve lengths clear of Royal Mail.

Surprisingly, with hindsight, he was sent again to Aintree that year. Knocked over at the first fence he was remounted and got as far as the fence after Valentine's, where he refused.

In 1937, when Golden Miller would almost certainly have added to his tally of Gold Cups, there was no Cheltenham Festival thanks to bad weather, and once again connections (that is, the horse's owners and trainers) sent him to Aintree. Now ridden by Danny Morgan, he jumped well to begin with. But as soon as his rider came to Valentine's he could sense Golden Miller would refuse at the next, which he duly did. Driven into the fence a second time, said his rider, 'he jumped down instead of up'. Connections finally accepted defeat and Golden Miller was never again sent to Aintree. But his Cheltenham efforts were not over.

Before the 1938 Gold Cup the Miller won a couple more chases, but he was twice beaten by a good young horse called Macaulay. The writing was on the wall. At the Festival this time he was ridden by Frenchie Nicholson, up against old rival Southern Hero, Macaulay and Morse Code, who, in a sign of the increasing importance of the race, was being trained specifically for the Gold Cup with no thoughts of going on to Aintree.

With his age and the very hard ground against him, Golden Miller still gave his all. He mastered Airgead Sios and saw off Macaulay. Coming round the bend towards the last he was still in front, but Frenchie Nicholson was having to work hard to keep him stoked up. Morse Code, ridden by Danny Morgan, had been tracking him through the race and now drew level. He landed half a length up over the last and though Golden Miller drew level with him at the point where the courses crossed, that was his final effort. His courage had got him to the leader, but he no longer had the acceleration to pass him. Morse Code became the first and only horse ever to beat Golden Miller at Cheltenham, drawing away to win by two lengths.

The public still cheered in their old hero who had given all in defeat. Fortunately, after he ran poorly in his only race the next season – at Newbury in February – he was retired with Insurance to The Paddocks, Dorothy Paget's stud at Stanstead. The two old horses seemed to enjoy each other's company and their owner, who visited regularly, ensured they had regular health checks and plenty of apples. Golden Miller, the horse who turned the Cheltenham Festival into a must for all lovers of steeplechasing, was finally put down at the age of thirty in 1957.

For the first time in six years, Golden Miller was not in the field for the Cheltenham Gold Cup of 1939. That was a significant event in racing's own little world. But soon things were to change far more dramatically than that.

Chapter 6

The War Years and the Recovery

*'There were no declared runners. You didn't know what was going
to run in the race. You had to enter three weeks prior. There was
no racecourse commentary. But you just got on with it.'*
(Mercy Rimell on racing in the 1940s)

A few days after Brendan's Cottage won the 1939 Gold Cup
from an unaccountably lacklustre Morse Code, Hitler's
armies marched into Czechoslovakia and the whole world
changed. Horse-racing, like other sports, was severely curtailed.
Cheltenham's 1940 Festival, with part of the National Hunt Chase
course under the plough for the war effort, was trimmed to just
two days, and the course restrictions saw the Gold Cup itself
shortened by two furlongs.

Even so, the growing status of Cheltenham's big fixture and its
feature races was being acknowledged. Racing planners were eager
to keep it going and when thick snow on the Wednesday made the
Cheltenham course unusable the Gold Cup was not abandoned, as
it had been in 1931 and 1937, but rescheduled six days later. That
played into the hands of Dorothy Paget, her trainer Owen
Anthony and Roman Hackle, the horse she had bought in the
hope of replacing the great Golden Miller.

Having the previous year won the Broadway Novices' Chase, in
those days the nursery for future Gold Cup candidates as the Arkle

Chase is now, Roman Hackle was favourite to win. Both Brendan's Cottage and Morse Code had been retired and Royal Mail was past his prime. But Roman Hackle was short of preparation, having had only one run that season. His connections were worried that the front-running Airgead Sios might have the edge over him.

Given the six-day postponement, Owen Anthony took the opportunity of running Roman Hackle in a two-mile chase at Windsor, far too short for him but a good tune-up, and was delighted when he won it. Airgead Sios's connections also went for an extra prep race, in his case at Wolverhampton, but sadly he broke down, injuring a leg so badly that his racing career had to be suspended. When the Gold Cup was eventually run Roman Hackle duly triumphed by ten lengths as an even-money favourite, giving Owen Anthony his second Gold Cup and Dorothy Paget her sixth.

In 1941 jump racing was cut back still further, but while there was no Grand National, partly because the authorities feared air raids on Liverpool, Cheltenham was one of the courses granted dates. That was a considerable boost to the advancing championship course in what had become a key debate in jump-racing circles. Its massive prize-money and colourful history had ensured that the Grand National continued to dominate the pre-war season. However jumping trainers and owners were becoming divided over their objectives. Some wanted the money and the glory available at Aintree and regarded the Gold Cup at best as a prep race for Aintree and at worst as a potential graveyard for National hopes. If horses entered in both big races endured too hard a race at the Festival their Grand National prospects could suffer. Others acknowledged that the conditions of the Gold Cup made it the true test of champions despite the poor prize-money, which was only raised to £1,000 for the first time in 1939. The continued running of the Gold Cup while there was no Grand National could only enhance Cheltenham's status, and the home secretary vetoed the idea of staging a substitute 'Grand National' at Prestbury Park.

Perhaps that was just as well for the horses and riders, given one plan for the race leaked to the *Gloucestershire Echo*. John Saville's history of British racing in the Second World War, *Insane and Unseemly*, notes: 'A four-and-a-half mile race over the gladiatorial National Hunt course would have involved climbing the Cheltenham hill by various routes three times: anything still walking at the end would have won.'

The first years of the war saw a repetition of the debates during the First World War on whether racing should be allowed to continue, particularly after the random bombing of Newmarket High Street in 1941. Was it a distasteful, unpatriotic diversion of key resources or a necessary relaxation for workers contributing to the war effort? Cheltenham's MP Daniel Lipson was one of the more vociferous opponents of racing and the *Echo* published letters saying that people should not be encouraged to rush around the country to race meetings, that there would be food shortages for locals if a Grand National was staged at Cheltenham, and that binoculars could be put to better use by the services!

One of the more entertaining debates raged around the 'horses vs. chickens' question. The *Daily Express* claimed that if the number of horses and greyhounds were halved, there would be ten million more eggs and another million pounds of bacon for the populace. Lord Winterton countered in the House of Lords that if all 6,000 tons of oats allowed to racehorses were fed to hens instead, every member of the public could have an extra egg every four years. As public debate continued, one letter to *The Times* said the Cheltenham executive should scrap its fixture and give the money to Warships' Week instead. The National Hunt Committee only voted to continue staging meetings after a statement from Lord Rosebery that every member of the Cabinet was in favour of racing continuing. But government restrictions were accompanied by a hard winter and the result was to allow only eighteen days of jump racing in Britain in 1942.

Relations between the racing authorities and Cheltenham

locals were clearly not as good in those days as they have since become because Cheltenham Borough Council added its collective voice to those calling for a cessation of horse racing at Prestbury Park while hostilities continued. A major complaint voiced in a letter to Herbert Morrison's Home Office from Cheltenham's acting town clerk was that race days had 'given the town the appearance of pre-war gaiety which . . . the council consider is quite out of place.' Clearly the spirit of firebrand preacher Francis Close was living on, even though Vic Smyth, the owner and trainer of that year's Champion Hurdle winner Forestation, gave the £495 prize to Lady Kemsley's War Relief Fund.

As the war ground on, with Cheltenham's facilities being used first by the British and then the American army, further curtailment of the racing programme seemed inevitable. On 10 September 1942 a notice in the *Racing Calendar* announced: 'The Stewards of the National Hunt Committee have received notification from His Majesty's Government that they are unable to sanction National Hunt Racing during the season 1942–43.' The grounds given were the shipping and foodstuffs situation, petrol supplies and transport difficulties, the low entertainment value of a threadbare racing programme and the unimportance of jumping to the bloodstock industry. So that was it. The Gold Cup and the other Festival highlights did not take place again until 1945 when the end of the war was in sight.

Appropriately it was Cheltenham which then staged the first jumping meeting for nearly three years on 6 January 1945. The pattern soon became clear; punters had to rely on old stagers who had proved their jumping ability in the past, even though some of them were getting somewhat long in the tooth. The owners and trainers who had paid the bills for keeping them through the non-racing years were obviously keen to win back a little of their costs.

In a mood of growing optimism, the sport-starved crowds turned out in huge numbers to welcome back their old heroes at a one-day Festival meeting on 17 March. They were rewarded with the largest-ever field of sixteen for the Gold Cup including the veterans Schubert, Poet Prince, Rightun and Paladin. Poet Prince surged and then dropped back. At the last, Paladin and Schubert were together. But then Red Rower, who had been jumping a little stickily, was driven up to join them and pass them. He won going away by three lengths, an immensely popular favourite because his breeder, owner and trainer Lord Stalbridge had been a great supporter of the sport.

Lord Stalbridge, a member of the National Hunt Committee, is the only man ever to have brought off that triple feat. But just as remarkable is the subsequent career of the man who rode Red Rower to his Gold Cup victory, D.L. Jones. Davy Jones, who had begun his apprenticeship twenty years earlier with local trainer Ben Roberts in Prestbury, was already thirty-seven at the time of his Gold Cup win and he went on riding over jumps for another three years.

For most jump jockeys that would have been enough. Given the injury toll, the normal career path for a jump jockey after reaching that sort of age is to join the training ranks or to find some other employment in horse-breeding, sales or feeding. Davy Jones, who once rode a winner on the Flat, over hurdles and over the big Aintree fences on the same day, chose not to pursue the normal path. He was very light for a jump jockey – on the day of Red Rower's victory he carried 3st of lead in his saddle to bring him up to the required 12st 0lb – and for the next twenty-five years he rode on the Flat, pursuing his career in India, Denmark, the Far East, America and Kenya. Even when he had reached the age of sixty-five and the Kenyan stewards decided that they should no longer renew his licence, he set up an academy for Kenyan riders before returning to a Cheltenham home and regular Festival attendance.

One of the more colourful aspects of Davy Jones's riding, said Tim Fitzgeorge-Parker, who used him as a jockey, was that the lightweight rider could imitate to perfection the scream of an enraged stallion. On the Flat, with huge fields of nervous two-year-olds lining up, Davy Jones would take a position in the second row and yell as he charged from behind when the tapes went up. 'Those little chaps were so petrified that they parted for me just like the waters of the Red Sea,' he used to say.

The Gold Cup, and with it the Cheltenham Festival, had emerged from the war years with undiminished prestige. But status was one thing, prize-money in wartime another altogether. In 1941 and 1942 the Gold Cup winner's connections received just £495, and in 1945 the prize-money dropped to only £340. That was a problem to be addressed as the popularity of racing soared in peacetime.

Fortunately for racing, as well as the veteran horses who came out to contest the 1945 Gold Cup, a number of major racing figures spanned the war and provided continuity. Prominent among them were three top riders who were to prove themselves equally skilled at training horses: Frenchie Nicholson, Fred Rimell and Fulke Walwyn. The first two shared the jockeys' championship in the brief 1944–45 season with fifteen winners apiece.

Fred Rimell took out a trainer's licence as well in 1945, reasoning that by doing so while still in strong demand as a jockey he would be sent horses to train by people who wanted to ensure that he rode them. He finally retired as a rider after breaking his neck for the second time in the Gold Cup of 1947 when Coloured Schoolboy dived at the roots of a fence and 'buried' him. The list of training successes he went on to share with his remarkable wife Mercy, a fine horsewoman who later went on to train big winners after his premature death, was a formidable one, including a record four Grand Nationals and two Cheltenham Gold Cups with Woodland Venture and Royal Frolic.

Fred and Mercy were steeped in racing. He had ridden his first winner under rules at the age of twelve, she rode a point-to-point winner when she was only fourteen. 'You couldn't do it now, all these bloody silly rules and regulations,' says Mercy, now in her forthright nineties. Initially she did the entries and the organisation and he did the training. And it was a different world to today. 'There were no declared runners. You didn't know what was going to run in the race. You had to enter three weeks prior. There was no racecourse commentary. But you just got on with it. I remember the day my son Guy was born, Fred went to Aintree to ride a horse called Atco for Dorothy Paget. It was second.'

Mercy says that one winner who gave Fred particular pleasure was Brains Trust, the victor in the 1945 Champion Hurdle, who was trained by his great friend and brother-in-law Gerry Wilson. Gerry Wilson thus became the first man both to have ridden and trained a Champion Hurdle winner. Fred rode three other winners on the Festival card that day. Another of his successes she doesn't forget is the year Poor Flame won the National Hunt Handicap Chase. The horse was jumping badly to the right on the left-handed track and in his efforts to straighten him Fred lost his whip. When he saw fellow-rider Nicky Pinch had no chance on his mount Fred grabbed the whip from his hand, shouting, 'You won't need that, will you?' and then rode a powerful finish to win by a head. Mercy confirms that he compensated the deprived Pinch with a fiver in the weighing room. Not a bad recompense for a loser because, as she points out, jockeys were then getting just £3 a ride, less than a pound a mile for risking life and limb.

Racing is studded with dynasties and family connections, and one of the Festival victories which Mercy recalls with special relish is that of Three Counties in the Christie's Foxhunters' Challenge Cup in 1988. The rider was her grand-daughter Katie. Mercy had bought the horse in Ireland out of a field of calves and she trained it while Katie's other grandmother paid the fees. The combination had actually been second in the Foxhunters' the year before and Mercy says that Katie blames her grandmother for that. 'I said, "Over the third and second last keep hold of his head." She says that if she had kicked on she would have won, and she was probably right.'

For all their Grand National successes, the Rimells were among those who pioneered the lighter-framed, classier style of jumper. Says Mercy: 'If you have those great big horses they have so many problems, wind problems, leg problems. You're much better to have a nice 16 or 16.1 horse that's got quality.' But she admits that their great favourite Comedy of Errors, who won two Champion Hurdles and was second to Lanzarote in another in between, was an exception to their normal rule. 'Normally we didn't like big horses, but he would have won any lightweight hunter class on his looks. He was a very good-looking horse who would have won in the show ring.' When Comedy's racing days were over she kept him on as her hack. 'I kept him until he died. I used to ride him every day. When he gave up, I gave up.'

Comedy of Errors was bought from trainer Tom Corrie, or rather his owner. Tipped off that there was a quality horse for sale, the Rimells approached Corrie. He insisted the horse was not for sale. But when they approached Comedy's owner he readily cut a deal for £10,000.

As for Woodland Venture, recalls Mercy, he belonged to a Dorset farmer, Harry Collins. 'He bred the horse. We didn't really know him but we went down to see him. Harry Collins was a big milking man and he had an alcove in the corner. "What are you going to put in that alcove?" asked Fred. Back came the reply: "The Gold Cup, when you've won it for me." At that point the horse had run in two point-to-points, fallen in one and pulled up in the other.

'Harry Collins's greatest friend was Harry Dufosee, who owned Stalbridge Colonist [a horse who, given lumps of weight, once beat Arkle], and it was Stalbridge Colonist whom Woodland Venture beat in the Gold Cup. I think that pleased Harry Collins more than anything.'

She calls Woodland Venture a troublesome horse. 'He used always to follow me, he wouldn't go with the string. I think he'd been spoiled in his point–to-point days. But he was genuine in a race,' says the woman whom stable staff used to refer to as

'Mother'. She saw Woodland Venture's Gold Cup rider much the same way. The irrepressible Terry Biddlecombe, a man who rode hard and played hard, is recalled by a smiling Mercy as 'Difficult – Terry was the best jockey we ever had but of course he was a playboy. If you could make him behave he was a very good jockey.'

The Rimells' other Gold Cup winner was Royal Frolic, the first leg in 1976 of a Gold Cup/Grand National double for them and rider John Burke who also took the big Aintree prize on Rag Trade. Royal Frolic was owned by the old and ill Sir Edward Hanmer, whose objective with the horse, duly achieved, had been the Greenall Whitley Chase at Haydock Park.

Mercy Rimell, unimpressed by the likely opposition of Bula and What A Buck, felt they must run the comparative youngster, still really a novice, in the Gold Cup. 'Fred rang Sir Edward and said, "I would like to enter him in the Gold Cup." Sir Edward's reply was, "Don't you think it's a year too soon?"' Not knowing quite how to put it to the ailing 86-year-old, his trainer responded, 'Don't you think we're running out of time, Sir Edward?' There was a quiet chuckle and he was told 'Go ahead and enter him.'

They ran Royal Frolic and he won. Although Sir Edward died soon after the race, which he was too ill to attend, he died with a Gold Cup winner to his name. Mercy Rimell not only collected the owner's trophy for him, she had a nice little pick-up from the bookies, too, having been incensed to find that Royal Frolic was at 500-1 ante post and invested £5 each way.

After Fred Rimell's death in 1981, Mercy took over the licence and won a Champion Hurdle in her own name with Gaye Brief in 1983.

There was great camaraderie between jump-racing people, says the ever-forthright Mercy. But in their case it didn't extend to Fred Rimell's one time riding rival, 'Frenchie' Nicholson. 'We didn't see much of Nicholson. Fred didn't like him, I didn't like him. He didn't enter our lives, really, except to annoy us.' Nevertheless Nicholson, who long had a training yard adjoining the course at

Lake Street, Prestbury and whose son David 'the Duke' Nicholson became a top jockey and then champion trainer, is another jumping hero and another key link in the Cheltenham story.

Married to a descendant of William Holman and the rider of Golden Miller in his last race in the Cheltenham Gold Cup, Frenchie also figured on the lengthy list of Dorothy Paget's trainers after he took out a training licence in 1946 – like Fred Rimell, while he continued to ride. David Nicholson rode the last of all D.P.'s winners, and Frenchie's sister Bobbie married trainer Willie Stephenson who trained the three-time Champion Hurdle winner Sir Ken.

Frenchie Nicholson, whose real name was Herbert, acquired the nickname by which everybody knew him from being apprenticed to a French trainer in Chantilly when his father was Master of the Pau foxhounds. Later he transferred to Stanley Wootton's yard at Epsom, a famed academy for young riders. An early big success came with a stylish all-the-way victory in the Champion Hurdle on Victor Norman in 1936. It was therefore entirely appropriate that in 1942 it was Frenchie Nicholson who won the last of the Gold Cups to be run before the Festival was suspended for two years at the height of the Second World War. His victory on Medoc II, trained by Reg Hobbs and owned by Lord Sefton, was a particularly popular one locally because the rider had told the whole village that he was going to win.

The meeting was split over two Saturdays that March and several of the Gold Cup runners used the running of the Grand Annual chase on the first Saturday as a practice effort before the Gold Cup the next weekend. In the Grand Annual on 14 March, Red Rower won, beating Medoc II with Broken Promise in third. The Gold Cup itself, run on 21 March in poor weather in front of a sparse crowd, proved to be a chapter of accidents. At the ditch on the back hill Broken Promise, led at a strong gallop by Solarium, was going well but was brought down when Solarium hit the fence and toppled. Red Rower, moving up at the time, was badly impeded by the two fallers while Medoc II, on whom Nicholson had been riding a waiting race, was able to seize the opportunity and dash into a lead which no one was able to peg back. The French-bred eight-year-old's margin over Red Rower at the line was still eight lengths.

As a trainer in the post-war years, Frenchie Nicholson produced a fair few winners but his true claim to fame was as a trainer of jockeys both on the Flat and over jumps. Would-be champions of the future including Paul Cook, Walter Swinburn, Pat Eddery and Tony Murray from the Flat, and jump riders Michael Dickinson, Brough Scott and Mouse Morris flocked to his Prestbury yard where they encountered firm discipline, careful coaching, meticulous attention to detail and a chauffeur service to the races from his wife Diana. Long-time Cheltenham racecourse chairman Lord Vestey, who had horses with Frenchie (and with David Nicholson from the first day the Duke started training) recalls: 'You would go at 12 noon on Sunday to see the horses and all the boys would be lined up. Frenchie's line was, "They come to me on the top of a bus, they go away in a Rolls Royce." '

Sam Vestey had a horse called Cavalryman whom Frenchie wanted to run on the Flat at an Ascot meeting in May. Cavalryman proceeded to run away with a then unknown youngster called Pat Eddery, who was immediately informed by a gruff Nicholson: 'Right. That's it. No rides for a month.'

The likes of Frenchie Nicholson and Fred Rimell, switching their interests gradually from riding to training, soon recovered their fortunes. However the wartime restrictions and cancellations hit harder for some of those with four legs, especially the best horse in Ireland.

Chapter 7

A Prince Denied His Throne

*'Had he been able to contest Cheltenham Gold Cups as a
younger horse there is no telling where he may have ranked in the
history of great chasers.' (Cheltenham historian Stewart Peters)*

The true racing victim of the war years was Prince Regent, a big strong bay who might have proved himself another Golden Miller if he had been born a few years earlier or later. Millionaire flour magnate Jimmy (J.V.) Rank was a great admirer of Prince Regent's sire My Prince, who had already been responsible for Easter Hero and Gregalach, the horse who beat Easter Hero in the Grand National. He had been dissuaded from buying another of My Prince's offspring, the subsequent National winner Reynoldstown, by a trainer who didn't like black horses, but in 1937 Jimmy Rank's bloodstock agent Harry Bonner did succeed in securing Prince Regent for him.

At first the horse seemed to be hauling a hoodoo in tow. The young vet Bobby Power, who was breaking him in, was killed while changing a tyre on the way to the Dublin Horse Show. Then, after being schooled by Tom Dreaper, Prince Regent was sent to England to be trained on Salisbury Plain by Gwyn Evans only for Evans also to be killed in an accident. Prince Regent returned to Dreaper, then essentially a farmer with a few horses on the side, who rode him to victory in a bumper in his last public ride.

Wartime restrictions by both racing authorities meant that Prince Regent was forced to make his career on the depleted Irish stage, nearly all the time humping massive weights against inferior opponents. It still did not take him long, however, to stamp his class on the Irish scene. In 1941–42 he won five of his seven races. He was nearly a fence ahead when he fell in another and in the Irish National was only beaten a short head by Golden Jack.

With the world at war it was a strange scene in a small neutral country. Petrol was hard to come by unless you were a doctor, a priest or an undertaker, and the number of deaths seemed to increase shortly before race days. Were those really pall-bearers playing cards on the coffin? British, German, Polish and Italian detainees were circling suspiciously around each other on the racetracks. All that was certain was that it was still a country in which the horse ruled. T.W. Dreaper used to go the fifteen miles to Dublin in a pony and trap. One day a policeman at a crossing asked him if Prince Regent was among the horses he was escorting. When the answer was in the affirmative he replied: 'In that case I'll stop the traffic both ways.'

In the 1942–43 season Prince Regent never carried less than 12st 3lb. He was second to Golden Jack in the Irish National, giving him 33lb. The next year he was again runner-up in the race, that time giving the winner 42lb. In 1944–45 Prince Regent had some time off with an inconveniently placed warble (a nodule caused by a burrowing insect's larvae) on his withers. That meant that he missed the Cheltenham Gold Cup on his first opportunity to run in it. When he reappeared in November he was beaten a short head by Dorothy Paget's Roman Hackle – but only because Prince Regent was giving the Gold Cup winner 3 stone.

It was an astonishing record, and Prince Regent was a horse of such quality that Tom Dreaper wouldn't acknowledge Arkle as his equal until Arkle had won a brace of Gold Cups. The tragedy is that through his prime Prince Regent was restricted to weight-carrying feats against the best that Ireland's small pool could offer, unable to compete in Grand Nationals that were not being run and prevented from running at level weights against the cream of British jumpers at the Cheltenham Festival.

Finally, in 1946, Ireland's powerhouse hero was able to travel over and show the British what they had been missing. The full course had been restored, the contestants were back starting behind the stands and the prize-money of £1,130 made it the richest-ever Gold Cup.

Prince Regent duly collected the trophy in convincing style. The only one to make a race of it with Timmy Hyde on the horse he partnered in 28 races was Poor Flame, ridden by Fred Rimell. Long before Prince Regent sailed majestically over the last and powered up the hill the result was obvious. He won by seven lengths. The sad thing was that Prince Regent was already eleven years old and Hyde said quietly to Tom Dreaper in the winners' enclosure: 'It took me a minute or two to beat that fellow today.' He was acknowledging that the edge had gone from Prince Regent's finishing speed, even against comparatively moderate opposition.

All of Ireland expected Prince Regent to win at Aintree too, but thanks to the war he had had no earlier experience of jumping Aintree's stiff fences and he tried brushing through a few of them as he could have done at home. Twice he was almost brought to a standstill before he got the hang of things. He still made a fight of it but on heavy ground four miles was a bit much for him under 12st 5lb and he could do no better than take third place behind Lovely Cottage and Jack Finlay.

The next year, ducking Cheltenham in the hope of fulfilling Jimmy Rank's dream of winning a National, Prince Regent was still asked to carry 12st 7lb and finished fourth. He had lost his best years carrying weights around Irish tracks which would have broken any other horse's heart and the clock had caught up with him. There was though to be plenty of Cheltenham success to cheer his compatriots in the years to come.

Chapter 8

The Arrival of Vincent O'Brien

'There has appeared an entirely new and eager public waiting to come out and watch the jumping horses. The new generation has found something its predecessors missed.' (The Irish Horse, 1948)

With a clear sight of its fences, National Hunt racing really took off in the post-war decade. People began looking for enjoyment and crowds flocked to the Cheltenham Festival to see a sport which invariably delivered a real spectacle. Horse-feed and tack may have been in short supply and many stable buildings in need of refurbishment as the troops struggled home but new money was soon coming in. Racehorse ownership expanded from a few hundred to 3,500 by 1950, with the old landed aristocratic families giving way to businessmen making the best of rebuilding contracts and supply shortages.

Some of those who were making money and finding the government taking rather too much of it looked to racing, and betting, to find ways of keeping more of it. The big bookmakers, noting the popularity of the winter sport, turned their attention to jumping, strengthening the betting markets. Increasingly prosperous farmers with their point-to-points gave National Hunt racing a guaranteed feeder stream of both horses and riders. Already by 1948 the *Irish Horse* reflected on the Festival: 'The National Hunt meeting, since it became stabilised at Cheltenham, has become the function of the year and there has never been a more successful one.' The next year it noted:

> Steeplechasing in England has in the last few years undergone an almost unbelievable change. For generations during the winter months meetings under National Hunt Rules have been sparsely attended. Now all that has changed and there has appeared an entirely new and eager public waiting to come out and watch the jumping horses. The new generation has found something its predecessors missed.

The other crucial development was the arrival on the scene of a little Irish genius called M.V. O'Brien and two horses he trained called Cottage Rake and Hatton's Grace. Vincent O'Brien's father Dan had been canny enough to win the Irish Cambridgeshire with Solford and Astrometer from a tiny yard at Churchtown, County Cork. But when he died of pneumonia in May 1943 he left his son little more than the equine management skills he had implanted. He had eight sons from two marriages and there was very little for any of them when his assets were divided. Vincent rented the stable and gallops from his stepfather, one of those rare Irishmen not interested in racing, and took out a licence. That very first year his Dry Bob dead-heated for the Irish Cambridgeshire and his Good Days won the Cesarewitch.

There were plenty of good days to come and Vincent's first top jumper was Cottage Rake, a son of the jumping sire Cottage who had the speed to win four Flat races. Cottage Rake's career must have caused a fair measure of teeth-gnashing among those who might have been part of it. Twice he was sold to would-be English owners. Twice the deal was aborted because vets refused to pronounce him healthy enough, finding fault with his wind. On the second occasion the vet told O'Brien that at Cottage Rake's age he didn't think the technical infirmity would affect him. O'Brien rang the only man he knew with any money, Frank Vickerman, told him what the vet had said, and urged him to buy Cottage Rake. Vickerman did so, although he too was on the point of backing out until he discovered his deposit was non-recoverable. That autumn his young trainer won the Naas November Handicap with him, and a year later the Irish Cesarewitch, as well as scoring four victories over fences which induced him to enter him for the 1948 Cheltenham Gold Cup.

Come March 1948 and there was Cottage Rake, the 10-1 Irish unknown ridden by Aubrey Brabazon lining up for the big race alongside the likes of the 7-2 favourite Cool Customer, owned by Major 'Cuddy' Stirling Stuart (the first would-be buyer of Cottage Rake) and Dorothy Paget's Happy Home, ridden by Martin Molony.

Cool Customer fell at the first, the only fall of his career. Second time round, Cottage Rake and Happy Home raced down from the top of the hill and over the last two fences in a duel as thrilling as the 1935 contest between Golden Miller and Thomond II. The crowd then witnessed simultaneously two crucial pieces of race-riding. Martin Molony knew his inexperienced rival had speed from the last so he threw his mount into the final fence in search of a massive jump which might hustle Cottage Rake into a mistake or leave him flat-footed. Aubrey Brabazon, faced with the uphill finish but confident of his mount's finishing speed, needed to play his card late, a risky proposition on Cheltenham's rising run-in. Molony was brave. Brabazon was cool. Both did the right thing, but although Cottage Rake did not land particularly smoothly his rider simply gave him a few strides to collect himself and then pressed the pedal. He sprinted up the rise past Happy Home to win by a length and a half.

Brabazon, who never touched his horse with the whip, said later: 'Martin Molony and I had a tremendous duel for the last mile. He knew as well as I did the only way he could win was to make the then inexperienced Cottage Rake stand off too far at one of the last three fences and either fall or make a bad mistake and I would not have time to get him balanced again before the winning post arrived. But the Rake had such speed that I could afford to ease him up at those last three fences and still pass Miss Paget's good horse half-way up the final hill.'

Asked later in his career about the best race he had ridden, Molony did not point to a victory. Instead he instanced that Gold Cup duel with Cottage Rake and the awesome jump he coaxed out of Happy Home at the last, gaining about a length and a half in the air. He declared 'God gave me great courage.'

There were no big viewing screens in those days and Vincent O'Brien, standing down at the last fence, had no idea which horse had won until he saw Aubrey Brabazon touching his cap to acknowledge the cheers of the crowd as they came back to the winners' enclosure.

It was a remarkably similar story in the 1949 Gold Cup, delayed until April after racing was frosted off on Gold Cup day in March. That in itself was a lucky break for Cottage Rake who had been coughing, and was thus given longer to recover. This time it was Cool Customer who took on Ireland's hope and who led him down from the top of the hill and over the last. It was a real battle but again 'the Brab' was only waiting to play the speed card and went past his rival on the run-in to win by two lengths.

The next winter Lord Bicester's Finnure, receiving 11lb, beat Cottage Rake in the King George VI Chase at Kempton Park, raising English hopes of defeating him at Cheltenham. But in March 1950 it was the same old story summed up in the Irish jingle:

> Aubrey's up, the money's down
> The frightened bookies quake
> Come on, my lads, and give a cheer
> Begod, 'tis Cottage Rake

Only three other English chasers joined Finnure in taking on the two-time champion and this time the result was clear a long way out. Aubrey Brabazon gave Cottage Rake a slap and caught his fellow riders napping with a tactical burst of speed coming down the hill the second time. In no time he was half a dozen lengths clear and the others never looked like making up the deficit. In the end he won what was to be his last Gold Cup by ten lengths. And by now it was a prize worth having; Mr Vickerman's reward that third year was up to £2,817.

For a young trainer, three Gold Cups in a row would have been a remarkable achievement on its own. But Vincent O'Brien did not just stop at that. In 1949, the year of Cottage Rake's second Gold Cup, he took the Champion Hurdle too with a far less imposing individual, the pony-sized Hatton's Grace, who dominated his field from the moment he headed it at the top of the hill and won by six lengths.

Bringing over his contingent, O'Brien had called Fred Rimell asking him to help him find somewhere to stay. The Rimells did so and Vincent and Jacqueline O'Brien, Mercy recalls, brought them an Irish salmon as a thank you. But she was less impressed with the O'Brien horse. 'He was a miserable looking little thing walking round the paddock, and I thought, "I don't think much of that." But Hatton's Grace promptly trotted up and ours finished in the ruck [very much among the also-rans].'

Horse and Hound wasn't any more impressed with Hatton's Grace's looks the next year, describing him as 'a mean and ragged-looking animal'. But he remained an effective one. Four horses took the last abreast in 1950 with National Spirit, who had won in 1947 and 1948, touching down first. But it was Hatton's Grace who then forged ahead on the run-in to win by four lengths.

Team O'Brien was back again at Cheltenham in 1951, this year without Cottage Rake, who had been retired with leg trouble. Hatton's Grace was now ridden by Tim Molony, who had been a schoolfriend of his trainer. Rough and woolly, just trace-clipped, the scruffy little Hatton's Grace, who was now eleven years old, was allowed to start at 4-1 despite his record. The going on

Champion Hurdle day was badly waterlogged and the rest of the meeting was to be postponed. By the turn at the top Hatton's Grace and National Spirit, like him a former champion, had seen off the challenge of two French horses. National Spirit, England's hero, led over the second last but Hatton's Grace, who had had the speed to win on the Flat, was closing rapidly. Timing his challenge perfectly, Molony had him jump the last with great momentum beside National Spirit, who appeared unnerved and who fell without having touched the obstacle at all. The race was over and Hatton's Grace too was a three-time champion, a quite extraordinary feat for his trainer.

Hatton's Grace, who won eleven of his twenty-seven hurdle races, didn't see a racetrack until he was six because of the wartime restrictions. He was owned by Colonel Dan Corry, an international showjumper, and was trained by him and by Barney Nugent before he passed into the hands of O'Brien. He was nine when he won his first Champion Hurdle and less than a month later showed his versatility by winning the Irish Lincoln Handicap over just a mile on the Flat. The O'Brien team were probably rather less delighted by Hatton's Grace's victory that November in the Irish Cesarewitch. On that occasion they had their money down for his stablemate Knock Hard who was backed in from 6-1 to even money favourite.

Incidentally, the capable Flat racer Knock Hard's Gold Cup victory in 1953 was a tribute not just to O'Brien's training skills but to the courage of his jockey Tim Molony. Vincent had discovered that Knock Hard had a heart condition which could have caused him to drop dead at any time but Molony agreed to go on riding him.

He and the Irish racegoers who were starting to flock to Cheltenham in ever-greater numbers had plenty more fun in store.

Chapter 9

It's Special for the Irish

'Cheltenham is the best craic you can have and if you cannot look forward to it you need to have your doctor check you are still alive.' (Bookmaker Paddy Power)

The early post-war years, with the O'Brien raiders in the vanguard, marked the real start of the Irish invasion by owners and trainers, horses and their adoring punter-followers which has made such a colourful contribution to the Festival atmosphere ever since. Five of the six races on Champion Hurdle day in 1946 were won by Irish horses. And, with the English layers (that is, the bookmakers, in those pre-betting exchange days) and punters initially as blinkered in their opinions as they later proved to be with the first Australian sprinters coming to Royal Ascot, the early invaders were allowed a handsome profit too. Before English bookmakers cottoned on to O'Brien's extraordinary talent, Cottage Rake was allowed to start at 10-1 for his first Gold Cup and Hatton's Grace at 100-7 for his first Champion Hurdle victory. Both had been at much longer prices ante-post.

Irish prizes were small; there was nothing on their side of the water to compare with Cheltenham. When bookmaker William Hill told O'Brien at York in 1958, 'I would have saved myself thousands of pounds if I had had you done away with ten years ago,' Vincent replied: 'We had to gamble to survive.' It was indeed a way of life in Churchtown; people who gave the yard petrol in the Emergency (the Irish government's euphemism for their country's neutrality during the Second World War) – or even the Churchtown priest who blessed the horses – would not be given cash directly but 'put on' for an amount on a fancied runner and sent a cheque when they came in.

One of the biggest Cheltenham bets in O'Brien's meticulously maintained ledger was the wager on Ahaburn to win the County Handicap Hurdle in 1952. In all £1,452 was invested – around £37,000 at today's prices. But though the Brab was told, 'I think this one should win', even Vincent O'Brien's 'good things' could come unstuck. He was only cantering at the second last but suddenly the horse stopped as if he had been shot. It turned out from the stone-black droppings collected when Ahaburn was on his way home that he had burst a blood vessel internally. He was injected for the problem and won the Irish Cesarewitch that year.

O'Brien was not just a wonderful trainer and a successful gambler. He was an innovator who was looked at askance when he pioneered the practice of flying in his horses from Ireland. The time and stress saving across the Irish Sea may have been limited by comparison but in 1946 the *Irish Horse* reported the first trans-atlantic flight of horses from Shannon to Burbank, California in a converted bomber. The cost was four times as heavy as the combined sea and rail fares from Ireland to California. But for the journey of 6,000 miles, flying time was twenty-nine hours compared with seventeen days at sea and a five-day rail journey across the US.

Broadcaster Sir Peter O'Sullevan says: 'Vincent was always far-seeing and that was characterised by him flying his horses over in 1949. So many people said, "Getting out of an *aeroplane* and bloody running at Cheltenham?" and wondered what the hell would happen to them but he flew over Castledermot, Hatton's Grace and Cottage Rake.'

O'Brien, he says, changed the whole Irish approach to Cheltenham. 'Before, they couldn't afford to come if they had a potential Cheltenham winner. They just had to sell it. Vincent was the first one who persuaded owners like Frank Vickerman to hang on and have some winners themselves.'

Targeting, he says, was the key to O'Brien's success. 'It was a bit like Francois Mathet training a horse for the Prix de l'Arc de Triomphe. The prep races were good sharpeners along the way rather than gruelling events.'

Vincent O'Brien certainly was a meticulous planner in his quest for Cheltenham Festival victories. His brothers Dermot and Phonsie used to joke about a disease which annually afflicted the stable called 'Cheltenhamitis'. Said Phonsie: 'Not only was Vincent affected by it but everybody working for him was hit with it also. No stone was left unturned in the countdown to Cheltenham to ensure that failure could not be laid at the door of human error. Vincent was totally analytical in his approach to every facet of getting the horses ready for their particular races and he knew, of course, that the money would be going on them'. Said Dermot: 'It would hit us soon after Christmas and there would be no respite until the horses were on their way to Cheltenham.'

O'Brien didn't just win those three Gold Cups and three Champion Hurdles. In the next few years, before he turned his attention to the Flat and started winning Derbies instead, he won the Grand National three years running. He took another Gold Cup with Knock Hard in 1953. He also had an extraordinary strike rate in the Gloucestershire Hurdle which was partly put down to his schooling of horses almost before they were taught to gallop. In all, between March 1948 and March 1959, he trained twenty-three winners at the Cheltenham Festival, an extraordinary achievement. What was his secret? His own verdict was, 'Patience, logic and ambition.'

O'Brien insisted that it was very difficult to train horses to jump after they had begun racing on the Flat. So he ensured that the long term candidates for the Gloucestershire Hurdle had the jumping ability of handicap hurdlers before they were even entered. Once the ground turned soft in September, O'Brien would set out four fences and four hurdles, and all dual-purpose horses were made to jump eight hurdles or eight fences every Tuesday and Friday. The fences, though, were kept smaller than those they would meet on the racecourse, to build confidence and ensure that horses enjoyed their jumping education.

O'Brien did not neglect the amateur races either. One of the biggest winning margins ever seen at the Festival was that of his Castledermot in 1949. He was so far ahead at the end of the four-mile National Hunt Chase that the judges could not estimate the number of lengths by which he won. Though Castledermot was trained in Ireland by O'Brien he was ridden by one of the darlings of the English jumping crowd, Anthony, Lord Mildmay. In those more deferential days, apparently, crowds did actually shout, 'Come on, my Lord.'

Mildmay was tragically killed in a drowning accident in 1950. The *Times* obituary declared of him: 'There was never a harder rider, a better loser or a more popular winner, and although he always valued the race more than the victory and the victory more than the prize, he would not perhaps have disdained the reward he has won, which is a kind of immortality among the English.' One other thing put English racing supporters in Anthony Mildmay's debt. He it was who introduced to the sport Queen Elizabeth the Queen Mother, who became one of its icons. Appropriately both Vincent O'Brien and Anthony Mildmay still have races com-memorating them on the Festival card. But the English and the Irish are divided as well as united by Cheltenham.

The tradition which the O'Brien raiders began has been a vital ingredient of the Festival appeal ever since. The English bring their sheepskins and their car-boot fruitcakes to the Festival; the Irish bring what often looks like a year's supply of betting money and a proper sense of the importance of the occasion. As John Scally put it in his *Them and Us*, a study of the Anglo-Irish rivalry over the years: 'When they bet on an Irish horse at Cheltenham, Irish fans are betting on national property, investing emotional as well as tangible currency.' In 1996 Judge Esmond Smythe postponed a Dublin court hearing so that witnesses could attend Cheltenham. Any other decision, he declared, would have been 'most unpatriotic'. The former Irish Finance Minister Charlie McCreevy, later an EU official, once scheduled his budget speech to the Dáil to avoid missing a big race at Cheltenham.

The Irish Church plays its part too. When the Irish hero Danoli was given a warm-up over the Gowran Park fences as part of his 1997 Festival preparation, a local priest came along to sprinkle him with holy water. Father Sean Breen, who used to offer tips from his pulpit in Ballymore and became a successful racehorse owner and a tipster for the *Kildare Post*, was a Cheltenham fixture. Indeed, he once declared that Cheltenham was a check-list for the Irish, arguing that if your friends didn't turn up at Prestbury Park on the right day they must either be ill or dead. He would hold services for the Irish Catholics present in Gloucestershire and publicly seek the Almighty's blessing for the efforts of the Irish horses, although his congregation did hear him concede one year, 'I know it's difficult for you, Lord, when we have so many runners.' He was even known to pray that the bookmakers would have enough money left to pay out. Not that divine inspiration always works. The first and only tip I received from an Irish priest encountered in the Festival Tote queue fell at the first.

There is something special about the Irish on the Turf. It is not just the demeanour of the wiry, weather-beaten stablemen, the sort who can look in a horse's mouth and tell you its life history when most of us would be hard put to it to tell you what it had for breakfast. It is the way the Irish know how to take their pleasures. Any horse who comes home in front with Irish money riding on it is wafted into the Cheltenham winners' enclosure on a 40 per cent proof wave of boisterous enthusiasm. When Irish equine heroes like Danoli, Florida Pearl or Moscow Flyer triumph at Cheltenham there is whooping and cheering. There are tears and laughter. And the barman's elbow is soon in need of cortisone assistance. When you ventured into the Golden Valley hotel, which used to be the heart of the Irish invasion in Cheltenham week, you would find owners, trainers and camp followers playing cards and putting drinks away until nearly dawn. Says Cheltenham's managing director Edward Gillespie: 'The Irish are at the centre of the party. They take centre stage in the pubs and clubs in town as well as at the racecourse.'

Even Vincent O'Brien and Aubrey Brabazon in their day entered into the spirit of things. The jockey admitted they had been known to slip into a bar before the first race for a port and brandy – not quite how jockeys are encouraged to behave today.

Like some of the English riders who followed him, Brabazon rode hard and well and also knew how to party afterwards. Once he rode a 1-7 shot at the now defunct Hurst Park for Sam Armstrong. Brabazon incurred the punters' and the stewards' ire after 'dropping his hands' when well clear (i.e., not continuing to drive his mount all the way to the post). He was caught by a dogged pursuer who was awarded a dead heat. 'Poor Aubrey,' said Armstrong tolerantly. 'It was the only sleep he had all week.'

Edward O'Grady, who has trained more Festival winners than any Irish trainer still in business, says: 'The atmosphere is different to any other meeting. The Irish come here as a team. It is the only place I know where every Irish trainer is hoping that if he does not win another Irish trainer does.'

Jessica Harrington, Moscow Flyer's feisty trainer, says: 'I was brought up on it. I went to Cheltenham for the first time for the Festival when I was seventeen. It has always been England v. Ireland, the Irish horses getting the better of the English horses. It just is. We really feel it – that we want to beat the English horses. Being beaten by another Irish horse isn't quite so bad.'

While some Irish trainers argue that it is overstating it to say they function as a team since they are all individuals working for different owners, there is certainly a fellow-feeling. Says Jessica Harrington: 'You'll support each other . . . Cheltenham for us is the away game and anyone who wins the away game is great.' O'Grady showed his own team spirit one year when Ireland's favourite Danoli was not eating up well in his Cheltenham box. 'I'd brought some fantastic hay with me which I was happy to give them and which he ate. I like to think we helped along the way.'

Is there a special 'Irish factor' to explain the number of successes by horses trained over the water? Tradition, inherited instincts and the lush green paddocks of a country where it sometimes seems to rain sideways as well as vertically have been responsible for producing much of the best jumping bloodstock, even if they have been rivalled in recent years by the French. Dublin governments which understood racing, breeding and gambling have shown a sensitivity in framing the laws affecting those industries which has not often been matched at Westminster.

The Irish racing scene is one which helps to develop a competitive edge for the Festival. With less racing, you won't get many runs on Irish tracks unless you are producing a certain level of form. Irish horses don't get too many chances for odds-on victories in small fields and tend therefore to be more battle-hardened than their English equivalents when it comes to the Festival hurly-burly. They also seem to produce tougher animals. In 1960 the Irish won fourteen of the then eighteen Festival races. Among them, Albergo was second in the Champion Hurdle and came out again two days later to win the County Hurdle, while Solfen won both the Broadway Novices' Chase and the three-mile Spa Hurdle, ridden by the new star Bobby Beasley who had won the Champion Hurdle on Another Flash. In 1953 Teapot II, who had endured a nightmare journey to Cheltenham, nevertheless finished third to Sir Ken in the Champion Hurdle. He was then pulled out again on the third day in the County Handicap Hurdle, which he won by half a length despite carrying top weight of 12st 7lb.

Irish riders, whether home or British-based, often dominate the Festival and nobody doubts their will to win. Jonjo O'Neill, for many years now a successful trainer too with seventeen Festival victories to his credit, was the epitome in his riding days of the soft-spoken, smiling Irishman. But former rider Steve Smith-Eccles, no softie himself, noted how the gentlemanly Jonjo of the weighing room was transformed on the track: 'Jonjo was granite-hard in a race, no quarter asked or given, but his greatest quality was never knowing when he was beaten. Many was the time I saw him hard at work, out the back and with apparently no chance, only for his horse to inexplicably respond to the urgings and come charging through with a decisive late run.'

Success at Cheltenham needs more than just natural horse-manship; true grit helps. One of Ireland's most popular horse-pilots in recent years has been Paul Carberry, for whom the thrills and spills of racing are not enough without plenty of hunting too. He was injured out in the hunting field before one Festival and trainer Noel Meade, anxious to have him fit to ride his horses, telephoned him in hospital to ascertain the extend of his injuries. 'What did you break?' he enquired. 'A gate,' replied the irre-pressible Carberry.

Another highly focussed Festival trainer is Mouse Morris, who was also previously a successful Cheltenham jockey. When he broke his leg so badly in a race in America that he had to quit the saddle he immediately headed off, his leg still in plaster, to indulge in his other passion. No, not fly-fishing or darts but hang-gliding! Michael 'Mouse' Morris, the son of Lord Killanin, is reckoned by colleagues to have an impressive concentration so far as Cheltenham is concerned. After War of Attrition's win in the Gold Cup, Tony Mullins said, 'Mouse trains solely with Cheltenham in mind and whatever comes beforehand is just a bonus.' But there is no mistaking the Irishness.

A favourite Irish tale is of the occasion in his riding days when Mouse Morris was listed by his trainer for a mount at Sandown

Park's Grand Military meeting. The race conditions required that the riders should have an association past or present with the Forces. The stewards, most of them ex-military types themselves, called him in and quizzed him. Had he been an officer in a military unit? 'Not unless you count the IRA, sir.' It might have gone the wrong way, but they had the grace to chuckle, although he was not allowed to participate.

The era of cheap flights has brought a vast increase in the numbers of Irish folk attending the Festival, upwards of 15,000 on occasion. Some Irish tour operators say numbers have been exaggerated and that the number is often no more than 5,000. It certainly feels more than that. Perhaps Edward Gillespie, Cheltenham's managing director has the best explanation: 'People from the Home Counties will come here and behave as if they are Irish for a week in a way they couldn't if they went to Sandown Park.' Certainly Cheltenham is conveniently placed and they can fly into Bristol or Birmingham, their numbers swelled by the many Irish happy to make a two-hour journey from London. On Cheltenham's own figures, about a third of the Festival racegoers come from within Gloucestershire and a 30 to 40-mile radius, about a third come from London, and the other third come from the rest of Britain and from Ireland.

The importance of the occasion and its prominence in the Irish consciousness is underlined by the descriptive slogan adopted by Tully's Travel, one of the leading companies involved in organising the influx. It summed up their business as 'Pilgrimages and the Cheltenham Festival'. Is there really any distinction in Irish minds?

The Irish passion is well understood by Ryanair chief Michael O'Leary, who has himself tasted Cheltenham success and whose company remains a Cheltenham sponsor. His War of Attrition, trained by Mouse Morris, won the Gold Cup in 2006. At the time O'Leary declared, 'I've died and gone to Heaven.' Later he told me: 'When I look back on life as a doddering old man it is something I will remember along with my marriage and the birth of my children.' If you grow up in a family with an interest in racing, says O'Leary, 'There are two races you remember, the Grand National and the Cheltenham Gold Cup. To win either is a dream come true. Why? Because it's so bloody difficult.'

Edward Gillespie agrees that, 'The Irish help to set the tone. There's a sense of a citadel here. It is a British event but we do have a bit of Irish music. We rely on the health of the Irish horse business and the Irish economy.' He points out, however, that rather more leave Ireland claiming to be heading for the Festival than actually arrive. Make of that what you will, divorce lawyers. Or do some simply lose their stake money in the poker schools on the way over?

One of the best-loved Cheltenham institutions is the 'Guinness village', the temporary grandstand with its music stage and range of food stalls which has been part of the Festival facilities since before Edward Gillespie's arrival as MD in 1980. There was just one year when sponsorship negotiations stalled which, to the dismay of many patrons, meant you couldn't buy a Guinness at the Festival and had to settle for Murphy's or Beamish. However Guinness wisely returned with a new deal the next year and have remained ever since.

As for how much Cheltenham means to the Irish, that is perhaps best summed up by one of their favourite sons, the inimitable Jonjo O'Neill, partner of Dawn Run and chief trainer to J.P. McManus: 'It's the be-all and end-all. It's what you live for, and when it's over you start saving to come back again. Everyone at every level is wanting a Cheltenham horse. That's how magical it is, everyone wants a Cheltenham winner. But it's all so difficult, so competitive, even the handicaps.'

Championship racing, gambling and drinking are all part of the Cheltenham cocktail. But the *craic* is everything at Cheltenham and the intensity of the Anglo-Irish rivalry is an essential part of that. Most of us reckon that these days it is a friendly rivalry. But surprisingly, one man who has seen many more Cheltenham

Festivals than most of us, the commentator-supreme Sir Peter O'Sullevan, thinks it goes deeper still. Partisanship, he says, is at the root of the Festival's success. 'There's quite a bite to it underneath. The potato famine is not a thing that dies easily in the memory of the Irish. It's wonderful all the arms around each other con-gratulating each other on a win, but under the surface there's still that little bit of real, deep satisfaction. The basis of the Festival's unique ambience is deep-rooted in the heart of history.'

Chapter 10

Over the Wall: Walywn and Winter

'It may sound banal, but this is the greatest day of my life. I have kept horses in training over here for ten years with only one objective — to win the Gold Cup.' (Peggy Hennessy, on Mandarin's victory)

I f the 1950s saw a post-war attendance boom at Cheltenham, the course story of the 1960s was a cleverly planned expansion of the facilities for the crowds of the future. It helped Cheltenham's progress that at the same period Aintree, then run by the redoubtable Mirabel Topham, an eighteen-stone former Gaiety Girl and actress who could certainly have auditioned as the role model for the female battleaxe, had become run down, with the quality of the Grand National fields dropping sharply. Soon doubts were being expressed about the continuation of racing at Aintree, while Cheltenham was advancing. Crucially, the action of a far-sighted few safeguarded Cheltenham's future at a time when it could have come under threat of disappearing, as so many other racecourses have done.

The introduction of car ferries on the services from Rosslare and Dun Laoghaire and the boom in coach travel also helped to develop the growing Irish enthusiasm for Cheltenham through the 1960s and '70s. The 1960s also saw jump racing in general and Cheltenham in particular boosted by television. Advertisers soon realised that jump races lasting several minutes offered a better platform than the over-in-a-flash contests on the Flat. It helped too that they were staged during the winter when audiences were bigger.

These were the years of Tim and Martin Molony, of Fred Winter and Fulke Walwyn, of Dave Dick and Terry Biddlecombe, and, of course, of Mill House and the champion of champions who broke the big horse's heart, Arkle – known better to the Irish contingent simply as 'Himself'. Arkle's victory over Mill House in 1964 was the third most viewed item on RTE that year.

Before we celebrate their achievements we should pause and reflect too on the contribution the amateurs have made to Cheltenham's story. Inevitably perhaps, the Festival story has been one of ever-growing professionalism, both in the saddle and back in the yard. Through the 1950s and 1960s that became obvious. But thanks to the tradition enshrined in the National Hunt Chase and in the Foxhunters', the amateurs have always been part of Cheltenham's special appeal and they continue to be.

The amateurs have certainly had their moments. In 1938, for example, the Champion Hurdle winner Our Hope was partnered by the amateur rider Perry Harding, later Major General Sir Reginald Peregrine Harding DSO, who had brought his mount home in second place the year before. It was twenty-five years before another Champion Hurdler was ridden by an amateur – Alan Lillingston, in 1963 – and in 1982 Colin Magnier did it on For Auction, trained by Michael Cunningham. Like some other amateurs of the time, Perry Harding's amateur status was slightly dubious. As an army officer he was not allowed to ride as a professional but nor could he afford to ride regularly without some financial reward. With generous 'petrol money' and other such arrangements, ways have usually been found of bridging that gap for talented amateurs, though some have eventually been given the nudge by authorities that it is time for them to turn professional.

In the year of Perry Harding's triumph, 1938, the National Hunt

Chase, confined of course to amateurs, was won by the Scots Guards officer Captain Bobby Petre, who went on to win the first post-war Grand National on Lovely Cottage at 25-1. His riding career ended after he broke a leg on a breakwater and had to have it amputated. He became a trainer and was later 'warned off' the Turf because one of his horses was found to have been doped. No one suggested he had had any involvement in the malpractice, but in those days such a penalty was automatic for the trainer of a horse discovered to have been 'got at'.

In those early years there were amateur successes too in the Gold Cup itself. The fourth running of the race in 1927 was won by Thrown In, trained by Owen Anthony and ridden by the Hon. Hugh Grosvenor, son of the horse's owner Lord Stalbridge. What was remarkable about that, particularly because he came to the last fence duelling with the professional Jack Moloney and yet showed admirable coolness on the run-in to win by two lengths, was that Hugh Grosvenor was riding in only his ninth steeplechase. Sadly, after riding the same horse in the Grand National he went to Australia and was killed in a plane crash.

Another Gold Cup victory for an amateur was that scored by Mr Richard Black on Fortina 1947. Because Fortina's success was sandwiched between Prince Regent's only victory in the race and the first for Cottage Rake in 1948, it tends to be forgotten that his fast time on the day in winning by ten lengths had many predicting he would be the next Golden Miller. Two other facts made Fortina's success, with Dorothy Paget's Happy Home well beaten behind him, remarkable. Firstly, he was only six years old. More surprisingly, because few non-geldings contest hurdle races, let alone steeplechases, the handsome chestnut was still an entire. When he retired to stud in Ireland Fortina proved a huge success in siring winners, including two of the Gold Cup, despite the trainer-writer Tim Fitzgeorge-Parker's comment that the horse had the smallest private parts of any he had ever seen. Handsome is as handsome does.

Rider Richard Black must have been one of the fitter amateurs of his time. The Gold Cup had been delayed once again by bad weather and was run on Saturday, 12 April, a day tacked onto the next Cheltenham meeting. The sun was out and so were the crowds, causing such traffic problems that, with a mount in the first race, the Foxhunters', Black had to jump out of his car and run two miles to the course to be in time to weigh in. He then rode a vigorous race on Celtic Cross to be second to Lucky Purchase before coming out again for the Gold Cup. This was a headlong contest with Chaka for most of the way which led to Fortina's course record time as he beat Happy Home to the line by ten lengths.

Let us return now to the professionals with the Gold Cup race in 1951. Here was continuity and tradition. One of the biggest supporters of National Hunt racing before and after the war had been Lord Bicester, a man with firm views on the conformation of good jumpers. His big, bold, deep-bodied – some would say old-fashioned – chasers with their hefty backsides had included Roimond, Asterabad, Prince Blackthorn and Finnure, the last three of whom had been placed in Gold Cups. This year his twelve-year-old veteran Silver Fame took the Gold Cup by the shortest of short heads over J.V. Rank's Greenogue, almost certainly owing his victory to the talent and strength of his jockey Martin Molony, who was at the time averaging a win for every three rides in Britain.

The race had been postponed; had it been staged in March, as planned, Molony would have been unavailable as he was in bed with flu. The Champion Hurdle had been run in March and was won by his brother Tim, substituting for him on Vincent O'Brien's Hatton's Grace.

Racegoers at the time reckoned Martin Molony as dominating a talent as Dick Rees had been before the war. Many said no one else could have won the Gold Cup on Silver Fame. But Martin's career was cut short by injury and it was Tim who stayed around at the top for some years, being champion jockey for five years from 1948 to 1952. Unlike his brother, he was so lucky with his falls – until a broken thigh ended his career in 1958 – that they called him 'the rubber man'. In those days there was little racing in Ireland except on Wednesdays and Saturdays, and in the 1949–50 season Martin Molony, based in Ireland, won the title over there. Despite the frequent commuting, he still managed to finish second to his brother Tim in the English championship too. A pity they didn't give air miles in those days!

Although he did not win it, it was the 1952 Gold Cup that first brought the great Fred Winter into the Festival statistics and the public eye with a considerable feat of horsemanship. The favourite for the race, surprisingly, was the Grand National winner Freebooter, essentially an Aintree horse who never liked the pressure of jumping at Gold Cup speed at Cheltenham. Those up against him included Dorothy Paget's Mont Tremblant. Then there was Knock Hard, a horse with Flat-rate finishing speed from Vincent O'Brien's yard, the subsequent Rimell Grand National winner ESB and a gutsy little grey called Shaef, ridden by the young F.T. Winter.

Mont Tremblant and ESB went best through the mud. Knock Hard tumbled at the second last when catching them and in the end Mont Tremblant, trained by Fulke Walwyn, won by ten lengths, giving Dorothy Paget her seventh success in the race. What was extraordinary was that little Shaef battled past ESB too to finish second, despite the fact that at the water jump first time round his bridle had slipped and Winter had had to spend the rest of the race keeping the bit in place with his reins. The next year Fred Winter was to ride 121 winners, more than anybody had ever done before in a National Hunt season.

In anybody's book Fred Winter was one of the giants of his sport. He is the only man ever to have both ridden and trained winners of the Cheltenham Gold Cup, the Champion Hurdle and the Grand National. Only Fred Rimell has been, like Fred Winter, both champion jockey and champion trainer. As a jockey he won two

Grand Nationals, three King George VI Chases, two Gold Cups (on Saffron Tartan and Mandarin) and three Champion Hurdles, having been told after breaking his back in a fall in the 1948 season (his first), never to ride in a chase again. He became Champion Jockey in the 1970–71 season and then won the title in six of the next seven seasons. He was the only jockey able to win co-operation from the talented little chaser Halloween, on whom he won two King Georges and fifteen other races. When he retired from the saddle he had ridden 923 winners and yet, when he applied to the Jockey Club to become an assistant starter, his application was refused. There was nothing for it then but to start training!

In that capacity Fred Winter won three Champion Hurdles, two Grand Nationals, two King George VI Chases and a Gold Cup with Midnight Court. He was champion trainer for eight seasons and he helped to polish the skills of Nicky Henderson, Oliver Sherwood and Charlie Brooks, who all worked with him as assistants. His remarkable score at the Cheltenham Festival was seventeen winners as a jockey and twenty-eight as a trainer. It might have been more had it not been for his bad luck with the talented Pendil, who twice started an odds-on favourite for the Gold Cup and was twice beaten. In 1973 he had to swallow losing both the Gold Cup (with Pendil) and the Grand National (with Crisp) in the last few strides of the race.

To many, Fred Winter's supreme achievement, reminiscent of his ride on Shaef, was not only staying in but winning the Grand Steeplechase de Paris at Auteuil on Mandarin in 1962 after the rubber bit in the horse's mouth had broken as he jumped the fourth fence. With no brakes and no steering, there were twenty-six more fences to surmount, but with some sporting assistance around the bends from the French jockeys, Winter kept his mount in the race and then drove him first across the line. It was not just a feat of horsemanship: it was the ultimate demonstration of Winter's key quality as a jockey – his iron determination. The jockey had been violently sick before the race and virtually had to be carried back into the weighing room afterwards. But he still came out and won the next race on Beaver II.

Winter was not the easiest of men for those who did not know him. Some felt that beneath his gruff exterior lay an equally gruff interior. Once when his then jockey, the sharp-as-nails John Francome, managed to drive him to the wrong destination, Winter stopped his apologies with the declaration: 'That's all right, son. It's not your fault. It's mine. You're so bloody stupid I should have put up a blackboard and written your instructions on it.' But what made him a figure of universal respect in the racing world was the total integrity that was allied to his professionalism, and his bravery. He had terrible luck with injuries. He broke his shoulder on only his fifth ride in public and he broke his back in his first year. No sooner had he become champion jockey than he fell at the first hurdle in the first race of the next season and was out for the year with a broken leg. In 1959 he fractured his skull in a fall at Leicester. Tragically, that ill-luck stayed with him. In August 1987 Fred Winter suffered a stroke after falling downstairs which left him unable to speak or write. He died in April 2004 and is, naturally, commemorated in a Festival race.

Fred Winter was stable jockey first to the controversial and short-tempered Ryan Price, a trainer with a streak of genius who had frequent clashes with authority and who was one of the first to raid French stud farms, paddocks and racecourses to find his potential stars. More than 500 of Fred Winter's 900 wins as a jockey were for Ryan Price. In 1953 they won the Triumph Hurdle at the Festival with Clair Soleil, despite the horse trying to savage an opponent. In 1955, after Fred had spent the previous year out with a broken leg and his mount had suffered leg problems as well as being gelded, the pair were reunited in the Champion Hurdle in a contest that was billed as the best of Ireland – Vincent O'Brien's Stroller – versus the best of England – Price's Clair Soleil. It proved to be a classic.

Ryan Price had told Fred Winter to tuck in behind and to use Clair Soleil's finishing speed at the end of the race to win. He therefore tucked in behind the front-running Prince Charlemagne, but Prince Charlemagne was a poor jumper. After he had clouted a series of hurdles he ran out of steam suddenly and dropped back, leaving Clair Soleil in front. Making the best of a bad job, Winter kept Clair Soleil in the lead but O'Brien's jockey T.P. Burns drove Stroller past him after the last. With every ounce of his considerable strength Winter fought back up the run-in as the crowd thrilled to one of Cheltenham's tightest-ever finishes. At the end the judges gave it to Clair Soleil by a nose. They had won the Champion Hurdle, but it didn't stop Ryan Price giving his jockey a rare bollocking.

Fulke Walwyn, for whom Winter also rode, could just as easily have made his entry into this book a couple of chapters earlier. He rode his first winner at the old Cardiff track before going to the Royal Military Academy at Sandhurst. He rode as an amateur from 1929 to 1936 and as a professional from 1936 to 1939. At the age of twenty-five, as a serving officer in the Ninth Lancers, he won the 1936 Grand National on Reynoldstown. But then early in 1939, riding in a Ludlow hurdle, Walwyn fell at the last and fractured his skull, remaining unconscious for a month. On recovering, he set up as a trainer and sent out his first winner just eight days before the outbreak of the Second World War.

Just about every honour in National Hunt racing was to fall to him. At the start of the 2011 Festival, although Nicky Henderson and Paul Nicholls are advancing and have the advantage of four-day festivals to boost their tallies, Fulke Walwyn still held the record for the number of Festival winners trained at 41.

In 1962, for example, he did the classic double, winning the Champion Hurdle with Anzio and the Gold Cup with Mandarin, who thereby became the highest-stakes winner in National Hunt history. Bred in France by the Hennessys with a pedigree more appropriate to the Derby, Mandarin thrilled Peggy Hennessy, who confirmed the international allure of his prize: 'It may sound banal, but this is the greatest day of my life. I have kept horses in training over here for ten years with only one objective – to win the Gold Cup.'

Just for easy comparison in this chapter with Fred Winter, Fulke Walwyn's training achievements included four Gold Cups, two Champion Hurdles, five King George VI Chases, seven Whitbread Gold Cups, seven Hennessy Gold Cups and a Grand National. He was five times the champion trainer. Apart from Mandarin's Gold Cup, Walwyn won it with Mont Tremblant, Mill House, who will figure in the next chapter, and The Dikler. The story of The Dikler's victory in 1973, and of the ensuing celebrations, is one that has gone down in Cheltenham lore.

In their time, there was no sharper rivalry in the racing village of Lambourn than that between the adjacent yards of Fulke Walwyn and Fred Winter. Walwyn was the established big name in National Hunt training when the former champion jockey, who had ridden for him, set up shop at Uplands next door. There was nothing the two sets of lads liked more than to win a race against what they referred to as 'over the wall' and have the chance to brag about doing so over a pint in their local, the Malt Shovel.

After Walwyn had won the 1964 Grand National with Team Spirit, the Winter yard got off to a great start with two early Grand Nationals, Jay Trump (1965) and Anglo (1966). Fred Winter's stable was soon full of stars like Bula, Pendil, Killiney and Crisp, who occupied boxes in the part of the yard that came to be known as 'Millionaires' Row'.

In 1973 there was huge stable confidence behind the spring-heeled Pendil, one of the most naturally talented chasers seen for years. The odds-on favourite for the Gold Cup at 4-6, he simply exuded class and was unbeaten in eleven races over fences. The Dikler, by contrast, was a big, brave but rather moody horse who pulled hard and was never an easy ride. So difficult had he proved that after the first attempt to train him he had been sent back into the hunting field. He then won a couple of point-to-points and ran off the course when holding a massive lead in another. He had come back into training with Walwyn in 1969 and was being ridden in the Gold Cup by the tough Northern jockey Ron Barry, who was nursing a secret. He had broken a collar bone only ten days before and he was worried that if The Dikler fought him on the way to the start he might not be able to stop him running away with him because of the pain.

They got to the Gold Cup start without incident but because of his injury, Barry could not fight his wilful mount and he said afterwards that he reckoned this allowed The Dikler to 'go to sleep' and relax on the first circuit, though others put that down to his horsemanship. Pendil, ridden by Richard Pitman and fencing with his usual exuberance, hit the front two out and looked to be about to justify his short price. At the last he was a good three lengths clear of his pursuers. But as the crowd cheered him up the finishing hill in anticipation of emptying the bookies' satchels, Pendil began to falter. Ron Barry, driving his mount with every fibre of his considerable strength despite the pain from his collarbone, began reeling him in. About fifty yards from the line he got The Dikler's white nose in front and stayed there.

Barry had been 'wasting' hard to ride lightweights on the Friday after the then three-day Cheltenham. Having eaten nothing, he celebrated handsomely in the cellar behind the Arkle Bar, providing the traditional case of champagne for his fellow jockeys. The next morning, feeling like death and with four rides booked at Uttoxeter, he set off for the Midlands course after a hair-of-the-dog glass of champagne. In the parade ring there, alarmed by his jockey's deathly pallor, trainer Gordon Richards revealed to 'Big Ron' that the yard had gone for a big bet on his first mount Pneuma, a 9–1 shot, and suggested that something else had better make the running. Ron's friend Jonjo O'Neill, who was riding another of Richards' horses in the race, confirms that fellow jockeys were sympathetic. 'Ron had had a rather heavy night. He was not feeling very well. Our instructions from Ron were that one of us was to make the running and one of us was to tell him when the hurdles were coming up and when we'd jumped the last. It worked out somehow and he won the race.' Says Ron, 'Mostly I shut my eyes and the horse did the rest'.

Having done so effectively on auto-pilot, Ron Barry weighed in. Then, with the room still spinning, he confessed to the course doctor that having won the Gold Cup he'd had a great celebration, was now dying of alcohol poisoning, and could not possibly take the rest of his mounts. Could he please just put down that he wasn't feeling so good? – he didn't want to miss the next day's rides. Medical books, the records of jockeys' injuries and ailments which they have to take with them from course to course to prove they are medically cleared to ride, were then in their infancy, and the entry in Ron Barry's read: 'Off colour. Headache. Should be all right tomorrow.' As Jonjo says: 'Good times they were and they were proper people then. They knew the craic. You thought you were pulling the wool over their eyes but they knew. They played along with it, using common sense at the end of the day.'

Fulke Walwyn's other entry in The Dikler's Gold Cup was Charlie Potheen. He was ridden by Terry Biddlecombe, who nurtures fond memories of his trainer. 'He really used to love his horses; he would go round at night and give them carrots after a dinner party. Mind you, he would give you orders then on how to ride the horses the next day. They went straight out of my head that time of bloody night. But it didn't matter because he would tell you again the next day – often a totally different set of orders. Join him in the paddock and there would be another lot of orders. But he was a very good trainer. He only had about forty horses but he was a specialist in those big races.'

It was an era of colourful champions, both in the training yard and in the saddle, and there were plenty more to come.

Chapter 11

How Cheltenham Was Saved for Posterity

*'As a director you meet all the people who've won, not the
miserable ones, and you tend to be happy too. You're with the
winners and it makes the day.' (Long-time Cheltenham chairman
Lord (Sam) Vestey).*

If Fred Winter had the racing crowd's respect, Terry Biddlecombe,
the blonde bomber, had their adoration. A Gloucestershire
farmer's son, the most charismatic rider of his day loved his
public and his public loved him. When a nervous member of
Margaret Thatcher's Cabinet once enquired during some political
crisis: 'What would happen if Margaret were run over by a bus?' her
Foreign Secretary Lord Carrington responded: 'No bus would
dare.' It is the same around Gloucestershire for Terry. To this day
he doesn't need a badge to get into Cheltenham: no gateman
would challenge him. Unfailingly courageous and occasionally
inspired in the saddle, he was the epitome of the 'ride hard and live
hard' set who made the weighing room in those days such an
entertaining place to be.

Says Terry: 'After racing we used to go down to the Cellar
Bar, five or six of us. We'd always get a bottle of Bollinger for
about a fiver and some orange juice – this was after racing,
mind you – and we'd stay there for two or three hours.' At
the Festival every contest matters and the Cellar Bar set would sit

on the champagne cases and talk their way through the day, race by race.

Old traditions die hard, some jockeys live hard and Graham Bradley recalled how they celebrated Graham McCourt's victory on the 100-1 shot Norton's Coin in 1990: 'All the jockeys used to go to a nightclub in Cheltenham called Gas. We were in the VIP area and Graham McCourt put £5,000 behind the bar, which was gone in an hour – bear in mind this was 1990 prices. I don't know how we rode the next day but we always celebrated big winners like that.'

In the 1960s there was plenty of humour – even during races. Terry Biddlecombe recalls in the 1967 Gold Cup approaching the fence which would be the last next time round, alongside David Nicholson. Both were riding big-name horses, Biddlecombe on Woodland Venture and Nicholson on Mill House. 'I said to him, "If we meet this right, Duke, we'll be on the Christmas cards." Unfortunately we both got close and missed it!'

The jump jockeys respected the tough core in each other and perhaps, living with the dangers they did, they needed the humour. 'Tim Brookshaw was the hardest I ever rode against,' says Terry. I was at Fontwell Park with him one day. He had a fall and he drove me back in this Jag and I said, "Are you OK?" He said he had a bit of a headache. I looked and saw there was blood coming out of his ear. He'd got a fractured skull. But it didn't seem to worry him.' Even Terry shudders momentarily when he recalls, gesturing with his fingers, 'I saw him break his back at Liverpool. He went through the wing of a hurdle. I can see it now – over, snap . . .' To watch that and go on riding takes real courage.

Like most of them, Terry can still take you through the important races he rode, as when he won the Gold Cup on Woodland Venture for Fred Rimell, whose number one jockey he was for more than eight years.

'My father stood down by the first fence and Woodland Venture went to the first and he never raised a leg. He broke the take-off board. I don't know how he stood up.

'During the race he was jumping well. We were all happy and then, going to the last ditch on the back, I took on Nicholson on Mill House. I saw a stride and he saw one too but he was half a length behind me and he landed in the middle of the fence.

'About three out Woodland Venture started looking at these cabins at the side of the track and spooking but I gave him a couple of cracks and he ran on. Up the run-in, Stan Mellor on Stalbridge Colonist got to me and actually headed me – I had dropped my rein at the last – but I gave him a couple and he ran on and we won half a length. What A Myth was third with Paul Kelleway. He was flying at the finish but it was too late.

'They were very deep friends, all the people I rode with, like Josh Gifford. David Mould stands out to me even now as a perfectionist, as stylish as anybody riding today. He was a very good jockey. He was always suave and he dressed smart. He was good at dances too. One pop record, a Coca-Cola and he was away. I used to stay with Josh and a lot of the jockeys used to stay with me. Dave Dick one time was riding the next day and had had plenty of champagne. He was taking about five 'physics' every day – they were terrible things [to help to keep the weight down] – but he went in and took half a jar of my mother's pickled onions too.'

Dave Dick was one of Terry's favourite shooting companions. Invited one time to go shooting at the Duke of Norfolk's estate on the Solway Firth, they went up early. Dave Dick had arranged for them to enjoy some driven goose shooting at another friend's home but they could not resist a little poaching the day before when they came across a well-ordered estate. Keeping an eye out for some game, they saw nothing much but suddenly Terry looked around to see Dave Dick being pursued by a gamekeeper. He ran too but they were caught. 'It looked as though we were going to lose our guns, but we managed to talk our way out of it.' The next day they joined their hosts for the shooting party and were introduced to the keeper. 'I believe we've met before,' said the stern individual, the very man who had grabbed them by their shirts the day before. Their relationship with the keeper improved after the three had spent the night together in the pub, and when the pair left for their return journey to London they were carrying not just their guns and equipment but a dozen dead birds as well. Their 'bag' was getting heavier and heavier, and in the end Dave Dick went and presented a couple of the dead geese to the train driver, urging him to get them safely home.

Dave Dick's sense of humour never deserted him during fifteen years at the top of his profession. One year, as the jockeys circled nervously before the Grand National, gastric butterflies fluttering, a religious campaigner displayed a banner proclaiming 'Repent, or your sins will find you out.' 'In that case,' commented Dave Dick, 'I'm unlikely to make it to the first fence.'

It cannot have been too easy for the officials, let alone the WAGS, as we have come to know the wives and girlfriends of much better-paid professional footballers, coping with the top jockeys in those hell-raising days, so how did they manage?

Says Terry, 'Oh, they were proper officials. They'd been in the army, they'd been amateur riders themselves. It was a straight old game then. They were hard men if you abused the rules but there weren't many done for dangerous riding. Nowadays you slap a horse, not hurting it, and you get stood down four or five days. It's a bit of a farce.'

Officialdom certainly had to show its common sense the day Terry won his Gold Cup on Woodland Venture.

'I'd had a fall the day before on Glenn which nearly took my bollocks off and screwed my knee. Next day I couldn't walk. I didn't tell anyone but I saw Dr Bill Wilson who said: "You need cortisone." He talked his way into the weighing room before the Gold Cup – how, I don't know – and gave me an injection into the knee. The pain disappeared and I won the race but when I was coming back into the winners' enclosure the first thing I saw was Doc Wilson waving a syringe and shouting: "This is what won you the race, Terry." I told him to shut up but the racecourse doctor saw it and reported it to the stewards.'

They were called in and asked to account for their actions. Terry explained and they told him he should have asked the course doctor for treatment, to which he replied perfectly accurately: 'If I'd done that he wouldn't have passed me to ride.' Terry had what he calls 'a bit of a scary moment', fearing that he might lose such a big race on a technicality. But in the end, common sense prevailed and it was 'case dismissed' with a warning not to do it again.

With crowd-pullers like Fred Winter, Terry Biddlecombe, David Nicholson, Johnny Haine, Jeff King, Paul Kelleway and Andy Turnell around, not to mention Pat Taaffe and Bobby Beasley from Ireland, National Hunt racing was now sometimes drawing bigger crowds than Flat racing. There were other potent factors at work too, notably the huge expansion in broadcasting, in those days coverage of Cheltenham coming from the BBC.

In 1948, says Sir Peter O'Sullevan, there were 45,000 combined radio and TV licence holders. By 1954 there were 3,250,000 combined licence holders.

The BBC first showed newsreel of the Cheltenham Gold Cup in 1948, four days after the event. The live coverage of the Festival, with the commentary in Sir Peter's distinctive honeyed gravel tones, began in 1954. His immaculate records confirm that the audience figures for the three days varied between 1,165,600 and 1,391,200 and for the ten-minute evening highlights – shown just before the News – 2,800,000 tuned in. Viewing figures exceeded those for *Watch with Mother* and *Andy Pandy*, making it the biggest-ever racing event on TV.

The regular coverage was first shown in colour – a big boost for such a naturally vivid sport – in 1970. Says managing director Edward Gillespie: 'As the big investment was beginning in the 1960s, BBC Television was opening up sport. But what a contrast. Then they were urging us to move Festival races to the Saturday to meet the public interest; now the BBC is hardly in racing at all.'

Sixteen years ago Cheltenham switched the broadcasting contract to Channel 4. For Edward Gillespie it was a deliberate registering of Cheltenham's inclusive and classless self-image. 'It was a strategic decision after we had taken careful soundings and, to a man and a woman, we were told that it would accelerate the development of the business in the way we wanted to. We don't mind upsetting some people to that end and we knew there were going to be cries of "How could you bring in those awful people like McCririck compared with Peter O'Sullevan?" but it was about how we wanted to be seen and how we were to project the sport.

'Of course it was a sadness to lose the likes of Peter O'Sullevan but it was a decision that spoke for our ambition. It was about accessibility. Channel 4 helped us to be centre stage, not just a component in *Grandstand* wrapped around other sports.'

The Cheltenham team were impressed that Michael Grade, head of Channel 4 at the time, personally fronted the bid for the much coveted contract. Andrew Franklin, the director of Highflyer Productions, who has long masterminded Channel 4's racing coverage as executive editor, says that Grade's role was crucial. 'He had set his heart on it and he put all his weight and his formidable negotiating skills behind the effort. You could almost say he did it single-handedly. It was a truly awesome performance, a master-class in charm and professional persistence.'

Andrew Franklin had been with Channel 4 Racing from the start, ten years before, and winning the contract to broadcast Cheltenham was a breakthrough moment for him. He was so excited by the professional prospect before him that when he got home that night he remembers, to his chagrin, totally failing to take the appropriate notice when his son proudly paraded before him in his new prep school uniform.

He says now: 'I was always conscious we could do it better than the BBC. We were inheriting a national treasure – we'd tried for the contract and failed five years before – but it was a treasure not being exploited to the full. The BBC in those days was all powerful in sporting contracts. Sky was only just getting into its stride and Cheltenham was just one of many jewels in the crown for the BBC. The BBC had the doyens of sports broadcasters – the Bill McLarens, the Dan Maskells – and they had trusted templates right across their sporting coverage. They didn't see the need to change much when it had stood them in good stead for forty years. Nothing had broken so why mend it, why should they, but I felt that the rainbow pattern *Grandstand* style was ultimately doomed, particularly with Sky presenting events in their entirety.'

The *Racing Post*'s Alastair Down, a man whose passion for racing shines through every minute he spends on air, is typical of the enthusiasm which the Channel 4 team brought, along with their expertise and added colour. Like his colleagues, he doesn't criticise the BBC's broadcasters; there is a healthy professional respect there for today's BBC team, but he argues that in the old days the BBC didn't make enough of Cheltenham. 'There is, for example, that great shot at Cheltenham as the horses come back down the horse-walk after the race, the shot with the horses and jockeys between you and the cheering crowd as they applaud. The jockeys play up to the reception. But the BBC didn't use that. In our coverage we have always been determined to put across the atmosphere as well as the action.

'I remember the stink kicked up when the BBC ceased to provide Cheltenham's coverage. People said Channel 4 would vulgarise it but the whole crew, especially at the Festival, are energised by being there. It is in my water. I am paid to follow my passion. Channel 4 strikes a chord with everybody. A duke can stand next to a dustman at Cheltenham and they have something to talk about. I can't think of any other sport where there is such an excess of passion.'

The broadcaster has reflected the variety of the audience. The Channel Four team through the years has included experienced horsemen like John Francome, Brough Scott and (Lord) John Oaksey, one of the most respected pillars of the Injured Jockeys

Fund, along with polished and practised commentators like Derek Thompson, Lesley Graham, Mike Cattermole and Nick Luck and from the expert Jim McGrath, each of them with their own style but united by that passion for the sport.

Cheltenham is theatre, says Alastair Down: 'No other sport is so drenched in emotion, and Edward Gillespie is an impresario.' No other sporting venue, he argues, has gone from strength to strength the way Cheltenham has done and TV has played a huge part in that. 'We don't fool ourselves that TV is as important as the thing we are televising; we are servants bringing the drama into people's front rooms. But we know there are things which Edward provides that we cannot and vice versa.' Andrew Franklin too uses the impresario word about Gillespie, saying that he is the ultimate example in racing. 'He understands entirely the value we bring. It is a fantastic hand-in-glove relationship.'

There may be upwards of 50,000 a day at the Festival but for many hundreds of thousands more the Cheltenham Festival is an experience that they enjoy most years through the theatrics and the distilled wisdom of 'Big Mac' John McCririck and the canny Tanya Stevenson (presented originally in his adopted male chauvinist terms as 'the Female'), the incisive McGrath, the colourful Down, the coolly elegant Mike Cattermole and the wittily informative John Francome. The partnership between them and Cheltenham has, says Edward Gillespie, been 'a massive success'. Both teams are about accessibility, and the association has worked to mutual advantage. Andrew Franklin's assessment is that 'You can trace back the steep rise in the popularity growth of the Festival to roughly the time we took over. When we began, the combined attendance at Cheltenham's open meeting in November was around 42–43,000; now it is 70,000.'

There is one other key contribution which Channel 4's racing coverage makes to the success of the Cheltenham Festival. The fashionable word these days as racing agonises about its finances, its crowd appeal and its public image is 'narrative', and as Channel 4 reports on the other jumping meetings across the country it feeds weekly into the Festival build-up. Trainers, jockeys and commentators all provide that narrative naturally as they discuss earlier performances in terms of Festival potential. They show the horses weekly on their way to the Festival so there is almost no need to advertise the event itself.

Back in the 1960s as Cheltenham began to spend with an eye on the future, a new commercialism took root in what had once been an almost private sport for countrymen. The first race sponsorship on the Cheltenham course was that by Messrs Hennessy for their Gold Cup in November 1957 (though they were later to opt for Newbury instead). Mackeson soon followed. Jump racing was becoming a business, and fortunately for Cheltenham those concerned with its welfare had business acumen too.

In 1951 membership of the Cheltenham Steeplechase Club was a pretty good deal. There was no need to be proposed and seconded if you were already a member of any of these clubs: Brooks, the Turf, the Carlton, the Cavalry, the Reform, the Oxford and Cambridge, the Guards, Pratt's or Boodle's. Or, of course, of the Jockey Club. Entrance was £9 9s. 0d. (including £3 16s. 8d. tax) and the annual subscription was £9 17s. 1d. (£3 17s. 1d. tax). That gave the member admission to the club stand and enclosure and to the paddock at all meetings. Ladies could only join the club as honorary members.

In 1960 the first stage of a rebuilding plan was completed. At a cost of £125,000, a second new stand was provided in the Tattersall's enclosure to cope with growing numbers and the Members' Lawn was extended. In a rolling programme of developments, the main grandstand was completed in 1979 and extended twice in the 1980s, with the top two floors devoted to private boxes. In 1982 the weighing room, parade ring, and winners' enclosure were rebuilt behind the stands, with terraces opening the emotional scenes to far more racegoers. That resulted in a little less intimacy but even more passion.

In 1997 the original Tattersall's Grandstand was demolished and replaced with tiered terraces, a betting hall and more food outlets. In 2003–2004 the Best Mate enclosure was constructed in the centre of the racecourse, offering a new perspective on the action, along with the Centaur, also used as a conference centre with a capacity of 4,000, the Hall of Fame and more restaurants. One welcome improvement was the bedding down of wire mesh in the grass car parks to stop so many cars getting stuck in bad weather. A crucial development was planning and siting a New Course to ease the strain on the cherished turf of the Old Course. In the early 1980s they were able to do away with the section of the National Hunt Chase course which used to go round the back of the stands through the car parks. The sixties investment was crucial, and from then on there was been continual development.

The most important move came at the instigation of then Cheltenham chairman Johnny Henderson, father of Lambourn trainer Nicky Henderson. He and a few friends saw the danger that with Cheltenham's population growing and sprawling to the north, developers and councils might become greedy for more building land. Courses elsewhere had been lost to developers, so they formed a consortium and purchased Cheltenham, forming a tax-advantageous trust in the process. That became Racecourse Holdings Trust which was then sold on to the Jockey Club to preserve racing at Cheltenham in perpetuity.

Lord Vestey, the popular and forward-looking chairman of the Cheltenham board for twenty years until 2010, says that the course was 'ripe for development' but fortunately was owned by the Holland-Martin family who were pro-racing. 'Johnny Henderson was a director of Barclays and also a senior partner of J.H. Cazenove. He devised a scheme putting what the Jockey Club already owned — Newmarket, the Newmarket Heath gallops and so on — together with money he borrowed from Barclays. It was extremely tax-effective. There were no dividends to be had and all the money had to go back into racing in some form. What we have now is fourteen racecourses owned by the Jockey Club. Racecourse Holdings Trust still exists because it is so tax-efficient.'

Just how much of an immediate threat there then was to Cheltenham is uncertain. Sam Vestey stresses: 'The Holland-Martins were very much on side. They were racing people. They were desperate to see Cheltenham stay as a racecourse.' But precautionary action was wise nonetheless.

The Jockey Club is the sole owner of RHT, and Johnny Henderson's initiative has proved crucial to Cheltenham's continued development, even if it came from small beginnings. Philip Arkwright, who became clerk of the course in 1977 and stayed in office for twenty-three Festivals, blesses its creation: 'The main problem faced in those days was financial. There was no money about. I was employed at the same time as the new manager Alan Morris. Chairman Sir Randle Feilden introduced us to the annual members and said: "The bad news that I have to report is that I can see no sign of any significant development at Cheltenham in the foreseeable future." That was in 1977. But by 1979 we had the new grandstand. Money became available, how or why I was never privy to. RHT suddenly found the money.

'When I joined in 1977, RHT consisted of Johnny Henderson, Tommy Wallis and Kate, the secretary. Tommy had a second-hand Rover, there was a kettle in the office and that was RHT. Cheltenham used to cough up £300 to keep them going and Warwick fifty or sixty quid a year. It was a tiny little operation. It hasn't half developed.'

Indeed it has. The Jockey Club's subsidiary, Jockey Club Racecourses, these days owns fourteen racecourses. But Cheltenham was responsible for more than half the Jockey Club's operating profit of £17 million in 2009.

The shrewd Sam Vestey is himself a key figure in Cheltenham Festival history. The word genial might have been invented to fit him and he treats everybody from the royals down to the ticket touts with the same good humour. Lord Vestey has embodied the friendly ethos which distinguishes Cheltenham from some other courses, and as a steward since 1971 and a director of the course since 1976 he has clearly enjoyed his role. 'As a director you meet all the people who've won, not the miserable ones, and you tend to be happy too. You're with the winners and it makes the day.'

Sam Vestey acknowledges the other name which has to figure on the roll-call of Cheltenham's heroes. Racecourse managements have not always been famed for their youth policies or their readiness to embrace the future. He says: 'The bravest thing Johnny Henderson did was to put [managing director] Edward Gillespie in at whatever age he was, certainly under thirty. It was through him things started to move, with Johnny getting the money.'

As Lord Vestey says, in what might be taken as Cheltenham's motto over recent decades: 'You can't stand still, you've got to develop', and if one man has driven Cheltenham forward it is Edward Gillespie. A constant live-wire presence ever since, always ready to experiment and combining a media-friendly approach with sharp commercial antennae, he has made Cheltenham not just a racecourse but a business model. It is unquestionably first in its field but has never taken that position for granted, and as I have found in putting together this volume, there are few modern enterprises with so many satisfied customers.

It was apparently an advertising agency which some years ago came up with the strapline 'The home of National Hunt racing' to describe Cheltenham's role. But that was also Frederick Cathcart's dream a hundred years ago. Gillespie has cemented its realisation: Cheltenham *is* the spiritual home of the sport. And no one can doubt the racing credentials of a man who could write of one monsoon-style Sunday on the Cheltenham track: 'Jockeys came and went from the weighing room with the determination of fighter pilots on a vital mission. On the face of each jockey (on the horsewalk out) was a wince of pain as wind, rain and chill took hold. Bookmakers leaned against their pitches like trawlermen facing into the teeth of a nor'westerly . . .'

A public schoolboy at Tonbridge in Kent, where he used to cycle across to Peter Cazalet's stables and simply gaze at the house, hardly ever seeing a horse, Gillespie went straight into racecourse management after completing a politics degree at York University. (He chose the university because of its proximity to local racecourses, and the subject because it left him time to run the university's Turf Club.)

He has never been much of a punter, he says, rarely risking more than £10 on a horse, but from an early age his mother remembered him coming down in his dressing gown before bed to listen to the racing results. 'It was the names as much as anything really – as if they came from some sort of Never-Never land.' At school he used to listen to race commentaries during lessons on a radio with an earphone wire up his sleeve. He even recalls manoeuvring himself out of the action on the pitch during a hockey match one spring to hear the Gold Cup broadcast.

At school and university his other love had been the theatre. Edward's father was a chartered accountant who had many clients in H.M.Tennent's West End entertainment empire. Having enjoyed his time in student theatre the young Gillespie nearly chose to tread the boards instead but reckoned racing offered the better chance of continual employment. He applied for a job as a management trainee with United Racecourses under Air Commodore 'Brookie' Brookes and kept pressing for a position while taking temporary posts as a London tour guide and working for North Thames Gas. 'He finally took me on, saying that it was cheaper to employ me than keep writing back to me.'

His fellow trainee manager was John Williams, who went on to become one of the highest paid figures in football as chief executive of Blackburn Football Club. Williams was put to manage Sandown while Edward, at the tender age of twenty-one, was made manager of Kempton Park. 'It wasn't very difficult really. There were no advance sales then. It was just a matter of opening the gates.' Brookie Brookes, he says, being an RAF man, was a bit of an outsider who used to present him as a curio: 'Come and meet my graduate.' 'All the jobs in racing in those days went to ex-army men between the rank of major and brigadier who could afford to work in racing buttressed by an army pension.'

Then to be seen wearing light blue suits and flared trousers, the young Gillespie was given the general manager's job at Cheltenham on his second attempt at the age of twenty-seven. Some eyebrows were raised, and the most urgent enquiry made among the doubters was: 'Does he wear a hat?' Says Edward: 'You could see the relief draining through people when on the first occasion I turned up I did wear a hat. Mind you, I haven't worn one since.'

He got his chance, he believes, thanks to the ground-breaking work done by his predecessor Alan Morris, another young man who had come in from industry and broken up the traditional way of doing things. Cheltenham until then, like many other race-courses, had been very much under the influence of Messrs Pratt, the traditional civil service-style team who provided the administration for many tracks, and with whom Edward still had to work as racecourse secretaries for some years. 'It was like Mike Brearley coming in after Tony Greig running the England test team. Alan Morris, who moved on into the fast-developing world of video entertainment would never have worked as a long-term investment. There was a parting of the ways. But he had taken things by the scruff of the neck. I'd never have got the job without what he had done. In contrast to him I looked like a traditionalist, a safe pair of hands, I'd been brought up in an Establishment nursery. But at the same time they were looking for innovation, energy, change.'

Those Gillespie has supplied. He is a man of theatrical manner and relentless energy. On the coldest of days he will be the one man at Cheltenham without an overcoat as he fizzes between grandstand, office and weighing room sorting out friction over an owner whose tickets have not arrived, demanding the fire be lit in the Hall of Fame, discussing the going and the hostel facilities with visiting Irish trainers. 'Edward, write a biography?' said one colleague on hearing such a project had been mooted by a publisher. 'You would never get him to stand still long enough for that, let alone sit.'

Even without the hat, the public-school vowels reassure the traditionalists and before they quite know what they have done they find they have authorised another mini-revolution: new stands, a re-sited parade ring and winners' enclosure, a cross-country course, a four-day Festival . . .

Reflecting now in a modern office cluttered with books, admin impedimenta, books and racing cartoons, Edward recalls how small it all used to be: 'It was very simple. I looked at the balance sheet and realised that all it needed was volume. I had been given an extraordinarily good grounding at United Racecourses, and things weren't that much different. It was just such a small unit – there were probably seven of us where now there are twenty-five.'

The annual profit in his first year under Miles Gosling as chairman was around £1.2 million; now it is ten times that. Says Gillespie: 'I was very conscious of the scope. They stood back and gave me the rope to hang myself. It was seen as something of a poisoned chalice. It had the reputation of high interference, with one director saying "Paint it black" and another the next day saying "Paint it blue." I suppose they felt if it doesn't work out it won't cost us much to get rid of him. But it was a great board. I have always believed in partnership, first with Miles Gosling and with [long-time clerk of the course] Philip Arkwright, then with Sam Vestey and Simon Claisse.'

Obviously Cheltenham's profit figures are one reason why Edward Gillespie is still there as managing director. But running a racecourse like Cheltenham is about far more than that bottom line. From flares to flair, the story of the Festival has been one not just of preserving, but developing a long-revered event to enthuse a new and wider audience while keeping the traditional devotees happy. That he has done, sometimes taking the breath away with audacious coups such as the year the course needed drying out and he brought in helicopters with their rotor blades to do the task, putting Cheltenham literally on the front pages as well as the back.

Few old-style racing administrators would have relished, as Edward Gillespie has, exchange visits with those who run the Glastonbury Festival. Partly that derives from Gillespie's mantra of allowing everybody to relax, for the duchess and the lad in jeans to enjoy together a common passion when other tracks are eager to keep them even physically apart. But part of his success too is down to seeing the Festival as theatre, and for years after moving to the spa town Edward Gillespie was not only the racecourse supremo but an active participant with the Bishop's Cleeve Players as an actor, director and even props man in the theatre. He has been fifteen years on the board of the Everyman Theatre and was for many years on the boards of Cheltenham's literary, jazz and science festivals as well as the racing one.

'This,' he says, 'is a town of 100,000 people which behaves like a city. Anybody can make a big name for themselves if they've got the appetite.'

Under Edward Gillespie, who also sits on the board of Gloucestershire Tourism, racing has been good for Cheltenham and Cheltenham has been good for racing. And both have been ready to move with the times.

Chapter 12

The Speed Kings of the Champion Chase

*'You might win many championships but to ride a winner at
Cheltenham is a really special feeling.' (Ted Walsh, Irish
amateur champion who rode Hilly Way to win the Champion
Chase.)*

Evidence of the Cheltenham management's ability to sense
and respond to public tastes has been the race programme
itself. A prime example was the instigation in 1959 of what
rapidly became a third major event alongside the Gold Cup and
Champion Hurdle.

The third of the Festival's true championship races is just over
half a century old. It was in 1959 that Cheltenham's shrewd race
planners introduced the Champion Chase over two miles, which
replaced the little-lamented National Hunt Juvenile Chase for
four-year-olds. In 1980 the Cheltenham executive renamed it the
Queen Mother Champion Chase to mark the eightieth birthday
that year of the most revered patron of the Festival, Queen
Elizabeth the Queen Mother. Typically that proved to be both an
appropriate tribute to a genuinely popular figure on the racecourse and a shrewd piece of marketing. She would surely be
pleased that racing folk are now as likely to talk about the race as
'the Queen Mother' as they are to refer to it as 'the Champion
Chase'.

The feature event of the Festival's second day may lack some of the history of the Gold Cup and the Champion Hurdle, and it may often have smaller fields than either of those two races but nevertheless it is often the most thrilling spectacle of the meeting. Tony McCoy has been heard to call it the true 'professionals' race'. Very rarely is there a below-par winner. Nor is there a race at Cheltenham in which mistakes are more harshly punished. You cannot afford a moment's loss of momentum.

Jessica Harrington, who trained Ireland's great Moscow Flyer to win the race twice, says she loves the two-mile races at the Festival 'because you can't afford to make a mistake. If you make a mistake you are pushed to get back into the race. It doesn't matter where it is in the race, even if you make a mistake at the first you use up energy to get back in the race.'

The 'sprint chasers' compete at furious pace over the minimum distance of two miles, on the way tackling twelve fences more than four and a half feet high. We have seen epic contests like the tussles between Barnbrook Again and Waterloo Boy in 1990 and between Edredon Bleu and Direct Route in 2000, while heroes of the race have included jockey Pat Taaffe, who won it five times, and Irish trainer Tom Dreaper, who sent over six winners of the Champion Chase in the 1960s. That represented an incredible strike rate of sixty per cent with the ten horses he ran in the race. In recent years Jessica Harrington's Moscow Flyer was virtually unbeatable so long as he stood up. Prizes for consistency would have to go to Badsworth Boy and Viking Flagship.

The inaugural running of the race in 1959 did not lack for quality. It was won by Quita Que, who had twice run second in the Champion Hurdle and who was ridden by five-times Irish amateur champion Bunny Cox. In 1960 and 1961 it was won by Fortria, trained by Tom Dreaper and ridden by Pat Taaffe. Fortria was odds-on on both occasions but there was a sportier price of 100-6 for the 1962 winner, ridden by Dave Dick. Northern owner-trainer Archie Thomlinson only had three horses. One of these was was Piperton, whom he had bought for a knacker's price because he was so lame his owner was going to shoot him. Piperton beat the short-priced Scottish Memories by one and a half lengths, thanks largely to the favourite's jumping errors.

Pat Taaffe and Tom Dreaper combined to win with Ben Stack (in the Arkle colours of Anne, Duchess of Westminster) in 1964 and with Straight Fort in 1970. But their most spectacular success was with the great Flyingbolt in 1966. Many insist that Flyingbolt was second only to his stablemate Arkle in the all-time greats list, and the handicapper could only separate them in his prime by a couple of pounds.

Flyingbolt won the Champion Chase at odds of 5-1 on. Pat Taaffe held him up, cruised into the lead two out and won with total ease by a margin of fifteen lengths. The next day, demonstrating his versatility, Irish money made Flyingbolt favourite too for the Champion Hurdle. He led into the final flight, only to finish third in the end to the talented Salmon Spray, partly because Flyingbolt uncharacteristically took the fourth-last obstacle by the roots. To give a further indication of his quality, Flyingbolt won the Irish Grand National the next month carrying 12st 7lb, giving at least 40lb to all the other runners. Sadly, aged only seven, he contracted brucellosis later that year and was never the same force again.

Another ill-fated horse, the Peter Cazalet-trained Dunkirk, a lightning-quick jumper who died in a fall when vying with Arkle at Kempton, was the winner in 1965, and in 1967 and 1968 Drinny's Double, trained by Bob Turnell, took the title two years running under Frank 'Bonky' Nash.

Muir was another of Tom Dreaper's successes in 1969, and one of the truly memorable Champion Chases took place in 1971 when Sir Chester Manifold's exhilarating Australian chaser Crisp, once nicknamed 'the Black Kangaroo', took the title. Before he ever came to England to be placed under Fred Winter's charge, Crisp had won two Flat races, five hurdles and a couple of chases including the Melbourne Cup Chase and the Carolina Hunt Cup. He had

THE SPEED KINGS OF THE CHAMPION CHASE | 119

scarcely had time to acclimatise from his winter arrival when he ran in the Champion Chase and yet, ridden by Paul Kelleway, he won by twenty-five lengths on tacky ground.

Crisp is one of those racehorses remembered and respected as much for an unlucky defeat as for his victories. In the 1973 Grand National, carrying 12 stone to the 10st 5lb of Red Rum, he led by fifteen lengths over the final fence after a spectacular jumping display but then ran out of stamina, wandered around on the run-in and went down by a length to Ginger McCain's multiple National winner.

Royal Relief, trained from his wheelchair by Edward Courage, was a dual winner of the Champion Chase in 1972 and 1974. In between those victories, the growing international interest in the Festival was demonstrated by Inkslinger's success in 1973. An American chaser who came over to be trained in Ireland by Dan Moore after winning ten chases in his homeland, he won in the hands of Tommy Carberry. But this tough customer did not stop at that. He turned out again in the Cathcart Chase at the same meeting and won that too.

Ireland was having a good run. Lough Inagh won for Tom Dreaper's son Jim in 1975 before we saw two more dual Irish-trained winners in Skymas and Hilly Way. Skymas was the two-mile champion in 1976 and 1977, on both occasions ridden by Mouse Morris, who later trained Buck House to win in 1986. He used to run with his head down, says Mouse, grinning: 'I needed extra long reins.' No horse older than ten had won the race before; Skymas was aged eleven and twelve when he secured his victories. He was trained by Brian Lusk, who was for a few years a successful trainer operating from Northern Ireland, until the 1979 breaking of the link between the British and Irish currencies and the levying of fifteen per cent VAT on training fees north of the border made it uneconomic for him and a few colleagues in the North to continue.

Hilly Way was trained for his two victories by Peter McCreery. For the first he was ridden by Tommy Carmody. On the second occasion he won in the hands of Ted Walsh, who won over 600 races as an amateur and who is one of the Festival's affectionately adopted Irish pillars, quite apart from being the parent of those outstanding riders Ruby and Katy. He says modestly: 'It's a special place. It's one thing if you are a Tony McCoy or a Ruby Walsh, a Pat Taaffe or a Jonjo O'Neill but when you're a lesser-known man down the line like I was, to ride a winner at Cheltenham is a huge thing. It's part of your career. You might win many championships but to ride a winner at Cheltenham is a really special feeling.' Ted rode four winners at the Festival and among his training successes produced Commanche Court to win the 1997 Triumph Hurdle. Back in the sixties, though, two horses dominated public attention.

Chapter 13

Himself and the Big Horse:
Arkle and Mill House

*'I can still hardly believe that any horse living could have done
what Arkle did to Mill House.' (Mill House's trainer Fulke
Walwyn)*

Wise trainers do not hype their horses, and Fulke Thomas
Tyndall Walwyn was a very wise trainer indeed. When
he began preparing Mill House for the Gold Cup of 1963
he had already sent out the slightly fragile Mont Tremblant and
the gutsy little battler Mandarin to win the Gold Cup. But even to
a handler as experienced as the master of Saxon House it seemed
that Mill House, the animal he liked to refer to as 'the Big Horse'
was something special, the kind of horse who, with reasonable
luck, might run up a sequence in the Gold Cup to rival that of
Easter Hero and to stand comparison with the phenomenon of
five-times winner Golden Miller.

Even after Mill House's career we can say that 'with reasonable
luck' he might have done just that. But he did not have reasonable
luck. It was unfortunate for Mill House and heartbreaking for his
connections that the Big Horse's racing career coincided with that
of one of the greatest jumpers ever to have lived – Arkle.

It all began so well for Mill House. Good big 'uns tend to beat
good little 'uns and as the great big bay, nearly seventeen hands,

loped loftily around the parade ring and moved majestically to the start under Willie Robinson for that 1963 contest, it seemed his stride covered twice the ground of the others. He had the muscle to go with his frame. There was nothing ungainly about his size, nothing of the clumsiness of the overgrown.

In the race he confirmed his jumping prowess. It had been expected that Tom Dreaper's Fortria, a son of Fortina ridden by Pat Taaffe, would give him a race. But when Willie Robinson let Mill House surge to the front as they turned for home, English hearts lifted. Here was a big horse with the power to match. He strode down the hill, cleared the last imperiously and was applauded up the finish in front of the stands as he won by twelve lengths. A glittering future seemed assured.

A fine future it still was, but it was never quite bright morning again. On the first day of that 1963 meeting Tom Dreaper had sent out in the Broadway Chase – a traditional stepping stone for Gold Cup horses – an intelligent-looking, athletic six-year-old bay in the colours of Anne, Duchess of Westminster. He was called Arkle and he won on the bridle – that is, without the competition forcing his rider to get serious – by twenty lengths.

As they paraded for the Gold Cup in 1964 after a brief snow flurry, Mill House was the 13-8 on favourite. His leaner Irish rival with the inquisitive eyes was available at 7-4. For anything else you could get 20-1 and more. Even as good a horse as the former Gold Cup winner Pas Seul, now eleven, was being quoted at 50-1. It was effectively a two-horse duel, and the kind of duel the Festival crowd likes best, a match between an Irish hero and one from England.

The giant champion had given Arkle 5lb and beaten him by eight lengths in the Hennessy Gold Cup in November, though on that occasion Arkle had slipped badly after one fence. Now Willie Robinson, full of confidence, took Mill House straight into the lead, powering over his fences, ready to test Ireland's hope all the way. At first Arkle seemed to have a little trouble staying with him, but then he too settled into a rhythm, fencing economically. Mill House had set a good gallop, but as they went out on the second circuit English binoculars were lowered for nervous exchanges about why their fellow hadn't shaken him off yet.

At the ditch on the hill Mill House once again jumped it stylishly. But Arkle, tucked in behind him, was going ominously well, having no trouble at all in going the pace. Round the turn and down the hill they came, and as they jumped the second last and rounded the bend into the straight, Arkle moved upsides, challenging Mill House to show what he was made of. The writing was on the wall and it did not make happy reading for partisan English spectators. Willie Robinson went for his whip and dropped it, but it wouldn't have made any difference if he'd had one which imparted 20,000 volts. To ecstatic Irish cheers, Arkle and Pat Taaffe were off and away, over the last and up the finish five lengths clear. He had not just beaten Mill House, he had crushed him. Fulke Walwyn declared: 'I can still hardly believe that any horse living could have done what Arkle did to Mill House.'

At least for Mill House's rider Willie Robinson there was a consolation. He and Pat Taaffe had agreed that the winner would buy the loser a consolation present whenever the two horses met. So Taaffe paid for the airline tickets for the Robinsons' honeymoon.

Some say the Big Horse was never the same horse again after that first encounter with Arkle, although Willie Robinson used to insist that it was back and leg problems that restricted Mill House's future. What was certain was that Mill House never beat his Irish rival again.

Arkle, who was not kept in cotton wool for championship races but subjected to weight-carrying tests in big handicaps too, finished his season by winning the Irish National, giving 30lb to the second. But Mill House hinted that all was not lost by coming out in the Whitbread Gold Cup at Sandown and being beaten only three lengths by the useful chaser Dormant, to whom he was giving 32lb.

In 1965 Mill House took on Arkle once again, one of only three horses whose trainers were prepared to give it a go. The Big Horse had again been turned out looking superb by Fulke Walwyn but this time it was Arkle who was the 100-30 on favourite. On this occasion Arkle, who never made the slightest jumping mistake, almost played with his rival, who was struggling to keep pace. From the top of the hill Arkle began to move away, and as he jumped the second last well clear, Pat Taaffe let him go. Arkle accelerated still further, cleared the last with feet to spare in an exuberant leap and was twenty lengths clear of Mill House at the finish. As others marvelled at the engine inside the Irish phenomenon, Pat Taaffe simply pronounced that he was the best horse he had ever ridden.

In the 1965–66 season Arkle simply took the breath away, putting together a sequence of victories which is unlikely ever to be equalled. Those who have only heard tell from parents and grandparents of a wonder horse should study the record and, if possible, see the video. First time out at Sandown in November, Arkle won the Gallaher Gold Cup by twenty lengths, giving 26lb to the useful Rondetto and 16lb to Mill House, who was third. He did it in course-record time too. Three weeks later at Newbury he won the Hennessy Gold Cup by fifteen lengths, carrying two stone more than any of his rivals. On Boxing Day at Kempton Park he won the King George VI Chase by a distance from Dormant. He next raced in Ireland, giving three stone to Height of Fashion and winning the Leopardstown Chase. This was his final preparation for Cheltenham where the Gold Cup was, appropriately, to be run on St Patrick's Day.

The Irish crowd, cheered by the 1,000 sprigs of shamrock flown over courtesy of the Lord Mayor of Dublin and with one of them tucked in Arkle's browband, nearly got the shock of their lives in the Gold Cup. Arkle was going well when he began looking at the huge crowd and thumped into the eleventh fence with his chest. Others might have been brought down by such a mistake. But while Arkle's supporters gasped, Pat Taaffe never moved and the horse didn't stop. The exercise canter continued and he won on a tight rein from Dormant. This time the margin was thirty lengths. Afterwards Tom Dreaper said that the horse was 'a bit of a swank' who was playing to the crowd. 'But I couldn't think he would fall. He is as clever as any hunter and would always find a fifth or even a sixth leg.' Admitting to having been 'surprised', Pat Taaffe blamed himself for not giving the horse the usual kick coming into the eleventh.

Tragically that imperious display was the last the Festival crowds saw of Arkle. In the 1966–67 season he was only second to Dormant in the King George VI Chase. The Irish champion finished lame because during the race he had fractured the pedal bone in the hoof of his off-fore leg. He never came back from that injury and he ended with a record of twenty-four victories from thirty starts. In chases his record was twenty-two from twenty-six. His old rival Mill House, who might have been an outstanding champion himself at any other time, had the consolation of winning the Whitbread Gold Cup at Sandown Park in 1967.

Arkle was put down in May 1970 after suffering increasingly painful leg problems. At Cheltenham 'Himself' not only has a fine statue to commemorate him (like Golden Miller and Dawn Run) but both a Festival race and the most famous bar on the premises are named after him.

After his long lifetime in racing, Sir Peter O'Sullevan is in a better position to judge than any of us and I asked him what he had thought of Arkle's physical presence. He replied: 'I never fell for any sort of physical presence. I thought he was quite sparky and attractive in that he was inquisitive and had a bright look about him, but body-wise I thought he was pretty ordinary, frankly. But he was really something. The rules of racing had to be rewritten to accommodate his talents and that is quite something.'

The debates on who is the greatest – Arkle or Golden Miller – will go on. You can only beat what comes out against you, but it is fair to say that Arkle's victories were achieved against higher quality opposition than the Miller faced. There have however been many other famous Festival rivalries and many more great champions to keep such debates going. Often too there are come-back stories to warm the unashamedly sentimental heart of Festival racegoers.

Chapter 14

The Return of the Prodigal

*'As the crowd gave me three cheers I was thinking less of the
actual victory than of my gratitude to Alcoholics Anonymous
and the others who had helped me to knock the booze and to use
racing as a means of rehabilitation.' (Captain Christy's winning
jockey, Bobby Beasley)*

Part of the appeal of the Cheltenham Festival is its sheer
variety. Not only does the pendulum swing between success
for England and Ireland but between North and South.
Sometimes it is the hurdlers who seem to be enjoying a vintage
period, sometimes it is the speedy two-mile chasers running in the
Arkle Chase (for the juniors) or the Queen Mother Champion
Chase who catch the eye. Occasionally the highly competitive
handicaps will throw up a crowd-pleaser or a character who is
embraced by the racing world. If for some reason the horses
themselves fail to provide a drama or a spectacle then you can be
sure there will be a 'human interest' story involving riders, trainers
or owners to compensate. Sometimes you get them all together. In
the seventies and eighties the pendulum swung several times. But
the Gold Cup itself, the ultimate championship at the pinnacle of
the jumping Olympics, never seems to lose its allure although that
does not mean the results are always predictable.

In 1967 the injured Arkle was an absentee from Cheltenham for the first time in years and, as already recounted, the race went to Fred Rimell and Terry Biddlecombe with Woodland Venture. Arkle, who in fact never returned to racing, was still on the sidelines when the 1968 race was held. The second Cheltenham without him might have been expected to be a little low key, especially as the 1967–68 jumping season had been severely curtailed by Britain's worst ever outbreak of foot-and-mouth disease. (Because of livestock movement restrictions there had been no racing between 25 November and 5 January.) But the Festival was enlivened instead by the first of Persian War's Champion Hurdle victories and the Gold Cup itself provided continuity. Once again Arkle's trainer Tom Dreaper and his regular partner Pat Taaffe were involved with the winner – this time Arkle's 'deputy', Fort Leney.

With his superstar rival off the stage, Mill House managed to fluff his lines again as he had done the previous year, falling at the open ditch after the water. Fort Leney showed considerable courage under one of Pat Taaffe's ungainly but effective driving finishes, holding off the challenges of The Laird and Stalbridge Colonist by a neck and a length.

It was a triumph over adversity for the Fortina gelding. Back at the 1965 Festival he had strained a heart valve when narrowly beaten in the National Hunt Handicap Chase by Rondetto, to whom he was conceding lumps of weight, and had to take a year off to recover. Ever since, he had been checked over by a cardiologist after every contest. But as Pat Taaffe exultantly proclaimed on returning to the winner's enclosure: 'There's nothing wrong with this fellow's heart now.'

Cheltenham racegoers needed cheering up the next year too after one of the wettest winters in history, with many meetings flooded off. Indeed there were two inspections on the first morning before it was decided that racing could be risked on the first Festival day. The old stagers had gone; Arkle, Fort Leney and Mill House would not be coming back. Whoever was to succeed

Fort Leney as champion needed to be able to handle heavy ground – in the National Hunt Chase only four of the thirty-five starters finished. Tim Fitzgeorge Parker wrote: 'Few of the horses actually fell, most of the riders just dismounted prematurely. I have never seen so many 'voluntaries'.'

In old What A Myth, by now aged twelve, trainer Ryan Price and jockey Paul Kelleway had just the right kind of mudlark (that is, a horse who relishes racing on soft or heavy ground). The veteran chaser, his enthusiasm rekindled by two seasons' hunting with the Quorn and a couple of point-to-point victories, stuck on after the last to hold off the advancing Domacorn, on whom Terry Biddlecombe had lost his whip. Immediately after his victory the veteran was retired. Job done.

Ryan Price, a flamboyant, hardworking and uncompromising figure who combined a relish for a good gambling coup with a tender concern for looking after his old horses, was almost the stereotype of how the non-racing world envisages a racehorse trainer. His dark features and the trilby worn at a rakish angle played to the image. On looks, you would not have been surprised to see him behind a street stall flogging dodgy nylon stockings, and he was certainly no soft touch. Once, when a stable lad attempted to foment a strike in his yard, Captain Price called him forward, knocked him out with a single blow, and had him paid off and out of the yard within hours while the others went back to work.

It was not wise to argue with the ex-commando who swam to shore on the Normandy beaches after his landing craft was hit by German shells. When one of his owners complained that he had learned he was being charged £5 a week more for his horses than other owners in the yard Price Retorted: 'Quite right. That's because you're more bloody trouble than the other owners.'

Captain Ryan Price was five times champion National Hunt trainer before he turned his attention to Flat racing in 1969 and went on to win an Oaks and a St Leger. In long associations with stable jockeys Fred Winter and Josh Gifford, who both went on to be outstanding trainers themselves, he won the Champion Hurdle with Clair Soleil (1955), Fare Time (1959) and Eborneezer (1961) and sent out Kilmore to win the Grand National. After Rosyth's controversial victory in 1964 in the Schweppes Gold Trophy, the richest handicap hurdle in the calendar, he lost his licence for the rest of the season. After Hill House won the same race three years later and failed a dope test Ryan Price was again up before the stewards on suspicion of wrongdoing, but after a lengthy inquiry it was discovered that Hill House effectively manufactured his own 'dope' and he was exonerated.

In 1970, which turned out to be a bumper year for the Irish with six winners in the eighteen Festival races, there was an international flavour to the Gold Cup. The winner, trained in Ireland by Dan Moore, was L'Escargot, owned by America's polo-playing Ambassador to Ireland Raymond Guest, who also bagged Epsom Derby victories with Larkspur (1962) and the great Sir Ivor (1968). L'Escargot ran in the Gold Cup not on his trainer's advice but at his owner's insistence. In the race the favourite, Kinloch Brae, wearing the Arkle colours of Anne, Duchess of Westminster and unbeaten in four races leading up to Cheltenham, fell at the third last fence when going ominously well. L'Escargot's jockey Tommy Carberry admitted that he didn't know if he would have won had Kinloch Brae stood up.

Maybe he would not have done, and L'Escargot could have been lucky in 1971 too when the fancied Glencaraig Lady fell. But not only was Raymond Guest a lucky owner – eight horses fell in the Derby he won with Larkspur – but the strength and power L'Escargot showed in waterlogged conditions in 1971, when the race was started at a different point and they jumped an extra fence, stamped him as a worthy champion. Scoring by ten lengths he was only the fifth horse in the history of the race to retain his crown. Nobody did so again until Best Mate.

After his horse had won, Raymond Guest declared that he would like to win the Grand National too and that Dan Moore had told him L'Escargot was the one for Aintree in 1972. The trainer was right about the result, but it wasn't until 1975 that the altogether inappropriately named L'Escargot won at Aintree. He was third, second and then first in the Grand Nationals of 1973, 1974 and 1975 and thus became the only horse, along with Golden Miller, to have achieved the Gold Cup/Grand National double.

L'Escargot was close up in the 1972 Gold Cup until the second last where he was vying with Glencaraig Lady and The Dikler. But there he made a mistake and the other two were left to battle to the line with the fast-finishing Royal Toss, with Glencaraig Lady – a faller at the previous two Festivals – this time prevailing. She was the first mare to win since Kerstin in 1958 but sadly injured herself in doing so and was retired to the paddocks.

The Dikler's victory over Pendil in 1973 was discussed when we looked at Fulke Walwyn's career. Both horses were back for the 1974 Gold Cup, Pendil having twice thrashed The Dikler in intervening races. Centaurs they may be sometimes, but this was to be one of those years where the storyline was to come from the man in the saddle as much as the horse beneath him.

Bobby Beasley, from one of Ireland's great racing families, first figured large in the Cheltenham story when he won the 1959 Gold Cup on Roddy Owen. The next year the glamorous new star took the Champion Hurdle for Ireland on Another Flash and in 1961 he won the Grand National on the handsome Nicolaus Silver, the first grey to win the race in nine decades. Very few jockeys have achieved that formidable treble. The talented Beasley rode for Paddy Sleator, for Fred Rimell and for Fred Winter. Happy-go-lucky fellow riders like Terry Biddlecombe didn't always find the occasionally morose Irishman the easiest company, and a series of bad falls, weight issues and a drinking problem saw him quit the saddle. In 1974, however, Cheltenham racegoers cheered him to the echo for what was headlined by *The Times*, no less, as 'The Greatest Comeback Since Lazarus'.

Bobby Beasley had been Yesterday's Man with a vengeance. At

one stage his weight ballooned to over fifteen stone. But with the help of friends and of Alcoholics Anonymous he had fought his way back to mental and physical fitness. He had begun scratching for a few rides and a fellow trainer suggested to Pat Taaffe, in his early days training, that the horsemanship of the experienced jockey might be just what was needed to tame the tearaway Captain Christy. This was the talented but moody and intractable young hurdler he was handling for New Zealander Pat Samuel who raced jumpers in England and Ireland, the United States and Italy.

'Yesterday's Man' and Captain Christy proved a revelatory combination. Swiftly they won four races together, although they only managed third in the 1973 Champion Hurdle. Captain Christy had fretted much of his chance away travelling to the race and his jockey realised too late he had let others set too slow a pace. They did win the Scottish Champion Hurdle however, even if Captain Christy demolished so many obstacles on his way to the winning post that the others had little to jump behind him.

They came to the 1974 Gold Cup with a couple of spectacular falls behind them and a couple of equally spectacular wins in novice chases. With the Captain it seemed literally to be 'win or bust'. But the Samuels did not opt for a novice alternative, they went for the big one, the Gold Cup against the outstanding Pendil and the previous year's winner The Dikler, a horse almost twice the size of little Captain Christy. Coming down the hill, a sixth sense made Bobby Beasley pull out from behind the leader, High Ken, who promptly cartwheeled and brought down the luckless Pendil. With only one serious rival left, Captain Christy jumped the second last faultlessly. And then came near disaster. At the final fence Beasley asked him for a big one. His mount didn't come up. Instead he crashed into the fence with his chest. Somehow the horse found a leg the other side and somehow Beasley managed to stay in the saddle. Coolly, he then allowed Captain Christy a few strides to gather himself before setting off after The Dikler, who was never found wanting on the final hill. They passed him as if he were galloping through treacle, and went away to win by five lengths. The Irishmen in the crowd sang 'When Irish Eyes are Smiling' and, this being Cheltenham, the English crowd who had mostly lost their money on Pendil and The Dikler cheered in the near forty-year-old 'comeback kid' with the generosity that is the hallmark of the Festival. This time it was the prodigal son. Beasley was touched and grateful. But he added: 'As the crowd gave me three cheers I was thinking less of the actual victory than of my gratitude to Alcoholics Anonymous and the others who had helped me to knock the booze and to use racing as a means of rehabilitation.'

Bobby Beasley did not ride on for long. Captain Christy fell in the Irish National and came out again the next day to win the two-and-a-half-mile Power Gold Cup. Soon after that his partner upped sticks, moved to England and tried his hand unsuccessfully at training. He then took the ultimate step for a reformed alcoholic of running a pub. Friends say that he used to come downstairs of a morning, look at the spirit-serving optics behind the bar and say with a grim relish: 'You thought you were going to get me, you little bastards, but you didn't.' The same gritty spirit has often manifested itself in the equine characters who have dominated Cheltenham's premier hurdle race.

Chapter 15

The Champion Hurdle Picks up Pace

'A miserable, scraggy individual but a real fighter.'
(Aubrey Brabazon on three-times Champion Hurdle winner
Hatton's Grace)

The Champion Hurdle has been a feature of the Cheltenham card since 1927 but it began to achieve much greater prominence after the Second World War, starting with National Spirit's two successive victories and then Vincent O'Brien's trio with Hatton's Grace, a 'miserable, scraggy individual but a real fighter', according to his jockey Aubrey Brabazon. Those two dominated the Champion Hurdle for five years and their duels helped to establish it in racing's consciousness. Other keen rivalries were to follow later, like those between Lanzarote and Comedy of Errors and between Monksfield and Sea Pigeon, building that spirit of continuity which is an essential part of Cheltenham's narrative appeal as the stars turn up again and again to renew their challenges.

Curiously, as the panel on page 166 shows, the hurdlers' championship has thrown up many more sequence winners than there have been among the chasers contesting the Gold Cup.

Five horses have won the race three times each: Hatton's Grace (1949, 1950, 1951); Sir Ken (1952, 1953, 1954); Persian War (1968, 1969, 1970); See You Then (1985, 1986, 1987); and Istabraq (1998, 1999,

2000). Only four people have both ridden and trained a Champion Hurdle winner. Dessie Hughes, who trained Hardy Eustace to win in 2004 and 2005, shares that record with Fred Winter, Fred Rimell and Gerry Wilson.

Festival *aficionados* believe there was a golden age of hurdling from 1968 to 1981. During those fourteen years the title was won by just seven horses: Persian War, Bula, Comedy of Errors, Lanzarote, Night Nurse, Monksfield and Sea Pigeon, every one of them an outstanding champion. Of the seven, only Lanzarote failed to win the title more than once. All were Cheltenham favourites but many would give the ultimate accolade to Night Nurse. Sired by a sprinter, he not only went on to be a successful chaser too, like the mare Dawn Run, but he won his Cheltenham crowns against dual winners Comedy of Errors, Monksfield and Sea Pigeon.

A bold front-runner who was ridden for most of his career by Paddy Broderick, then latterly by his great admirer Jonjo O'Neill, Night Nurse not only won races because of his indomitable will but because of his speed and precision over the obstacles. In 1975–76 he was unbeaten in eight races including the English, Irish, Welsh and Scottish champion hurdles.

The Champion Hurdle originated, as we have seen, in 1927, and the first trainer to win it twice was Basil Briscoe. He did so in 1932 and 1933 with Insurance, whom he sold to Dorothy Paget in a package deal with Golden Miller. Other notable pre-war winners included Victor Norman, Frenchie Nicholson's only Champion Hurdle winner, the amateur-ridden Our Hope and African Sister, who was partnered to her victory in 1939 by one-time champion jumps jockey Keith Piggott, father of the great Lester. She was the first mare to run in the race and it was to be forty-five years before another of her gender won it.

When Festivals resumed in 1946 after the war, continuity was underlined as Dorothy Paget's Distel took the title. He was trained in Ireland by Maxie Arnott at Clonsilla, County Dublin, super-intended by Charlie 'Romeo' Rogers, one of the few males with whom Paget could bear to have dealings. Poor Distel ran in the race again next year but after performing disappointingly was found to be suffering from heart trouble and a brain tumour and was put down.

Victory in 1947 went to Vic Smyth's popular National Spirit, ridden by the about-to-retire Danny Morgan. He should probably have been beaten by the French entry Le Paillon, trained by Willie Head and ridden by his son Alec, who was to become the trainer supreme on the French turf as well as the father of jockey/trainer Freddie and trainer Criquette Head-Maarek. At only twenty-two, however, and with no experience of Cheltenham, Alec Head rode on the wide outside all the way round while Morgan stuck as close as paint to the inside rail and covered far less ground. Despite the different distances travelled the margin at the line was only half a length. Le Paillon showed his quality later that year by not only winning the French Champion Hurdle but the Prix de l'Arc de Triomphe as well.

National Spirit, this time with Ron Smyth in the saddle, was back at the Festival again in 1948 when he not only won a second Champion Hurdle but sliced five seconds off the record time in doing so. Nobody much noticed the gritty little bay Hatton's Grace, who finished in fifth place behind him. But that summer, owners Moya and Harry Keogh sent Hatton's Grace to join an up-and-coming Irish trainer in Churchtown called Vincent O'Brien, and that was to settle the destination of the hurdles title for the next three years. National Spirit ran eighty-five times in all and won nineteen hurdles and thirteen Flat races in the course of his career. National Spirit's second victory meant that his trainer Vic Smyth of the Epsom clan had produced his fourth winner of the race in six attempts, while for his jockey nephew Ron it was his third Champion Hurdle winner.

Hatton's Grace's record has already been discussed and he was to be succeeded by another multiple winner, this time for an English stable.

After a three-year reign Hatton's Grace, who was twelve by then, finished in the ruck in 1952 behind Sir Ken, with the new champion showing the greatest turn of speed after taking the last upsides with Noholme and Approval.

Sir Ken was trained by Willie Stephenson, who spotted him at Auteuil when on holiday in France, and snapped him up for £1,000. The shrewd handler clearly knew what he had got. On his British debut Sir Ken won the Lancashire Hurdle at Aintree on Grand National Day, backed down from 50-1 to 7-1. He was then bought by Manchester businessman Maurice Kingsley.

Sir Ken was not the nicest of characters – when out at grass that summer he fought and killed a paddock companion. But he was certainly consistent. Few of his contemporaries could match him and he won twenty of the twenty-nine races he ran over hurdles as well as four over fences. When he won his second championship it was his seventeenth consecutive victory, and this time the race was not run to suit. Sir Ken liked to come from behind but with the pace too slow, jockey Tim Molony was forced to go on from two furlongs out before holding Galatian by two lengths.

Sir Ken had perhaps lost a little of his zest when he went for his third title in 1954 as a 9-4 on favourite. He was a full three lengths behind Impney at the last. But then the champion showed he had courage too. Tim Molony drove him furiously into the last obstacle and he then won a ding-dong slogging match up the hill.

In 1955 it was Clair Soleil's turn and in 1956 the outsider Doorknocker triumphed. In 1959 Fred Winter won the hurdlers' championship for the first time on Fare Time and as Another Flash scored for Ireland in 1960, trained by Paddy Sleator, English race-goers took note on his first time around of the talented Bobby Beasley.

Eborneezer, named after a butler and owned by a Dr Burjor Pajgar from Croydon, whose wife had brought the horse up on a diet supplemented with whisky, eggs and milk, was another winning ride in the Champion Hurdle for Fred Winter in 1961. In

1962 trainer Fulke Walwyn won the race for the first time with the roan Anzio, who thrilled the crowds with a tremendous burst of speed after the last.

The next year, 1963, took things back a bit. For the first time since Perry Harding in 1938, the Champion Hurdle was won by an amateur rider, Mr Alan Lillingston, a renowned Irish breeder and rider to hounds, who triumphed on the one-eyed Winning Fair. Only one amateur has won the race since.

In 1964 Sir Winston Churchill had a runner in the Champion, Sun Hat, but the race went to Magic Court, trained in Cumberland by vet Tommy Robson. Magic Court, a wayward character in his early days when trained by Noel Murless, had the dubious distinction of having dumped Lester Piggott on the Flat. When he hit the front in a race he would stop and swerve. Robson gelded him and sorted out his muscular problems. After jumping the last at Cheltenham, Magic Court, ridden by Pat McCarron, swerved across to the rails in front of Another Flash and there was a stewards' objection. But when they looked at the head-on film it was clear there was no interference and he kept the race.

In 1965 big race specialist Fulke Walwyn scored again in the Champion, but this time it was a huge shock as Willie Robinson brought Kirriemuir home at 50-1. He may have been helped by the falls of Cheltenham specialist Salmon Spray and Nosey, and by the fact that Magic Court's jockey McCarron was under par, opting out of a later ride because he was in considerable pain with a shoulder injury. But another contributor to Kirriemuir's generous price was that Walwyn also turned out for the race the American champion Exhibit A, ridden by Dave Dick. Exhibit A led all the way until they were over the last, but Kirriemuir touched down with greater momentum and then held off fast-finishing challenges by Spartan General and Worcran. I felt he won on merit, but then I did back him for the first decent return of my betting life!

In 1966 everything was overshadowed by Arkle, but the career of that incomparable chaser tended to overshadow the fact that Tom

Dreaper had in his yard at the same time another outstanding jumper in Flyingbolt. As related earlier, that year the big chestnut won the two-mile Champion Chase in a canter without changing gear, and they ran him again in the Champion Hurdle. For once his jockey, the great Pat Taaffe, was held to be at fault for going the long way round and for not making enough use of Flyingbolt's staying power, but he did also lose ground when getting too close to one of the late obstacles. He still managed to finish in third place to Salmon Spray, ridden by the stylish Johnny Haine for Bob Turnell.

Such a performance in his second race at the meeting took nothing away from Flyingbolt's fine Festival record. Before that 1966 Champion Chase victory Flyingbolt had won the Gloucestershire Hurdle in 1964 and the Cotswold Chase in 1965. Peter O'Sullevan puts him firmly among the all-time greats of Festival racing.

The 1967 Champion Hurdle crown fell to Peter Easterby's Saucy Kit, ridden by Roy Edwards. He was one of the few ungelded horses ever to win at Cheltenham. Following Magic Court's victory three years before, it was only the third in the race's history for a North of England trainer, a curious imbalance given the number of fine trainers the North has produced. Saucy Kit's victory was in itself confirmation of the shrewd Easterby's skills − the horse had trodden on a stone and lamed himself for a fortnight in February. He had not had a race for ten weeks and it had been touch and go getting him ready. His trainer was to go on from there to register four more Champion Hurdle victories, a record. Though always known as 'Peter', Saucy Kit's trainer was actually christened Miles Henry, and the name M.H. Easterby will always be on racing's record boards. Although Nicky Henderson in 2010 finally equalled his record of training five Champion Hurdle winners, Peter Easterby, who also farmed thousands of acres, remains the only trainer in British history to have trained more than a thousand winners both on the Flat and over jumps. Of his winners over jumps, thirteen were Festival victors.

Cheltenham's joy is its resilience, the sheer range of the Festival programme. Perfectly on cue following the disappearance from the Cheltenham stage of Arkle, the spotlight stayed on a magical era for the Champion Hurdle, with a parade of four-legged characters who, if there had been an equivalent for horses of a TV soap opera, would have been a casting director's delight.

Chapter 16

Making Winning a Habit

*'It's a pity pigeons can't swim.' (Trainer Peter Easterby after
Sea Pigeon's narrow defeat in the mud)*

After the depredations of a foot-and-mouth outbreak which saw more than 400,000 cattle slaughtered and racing suspended from November 1967 until early January 1968, racing folk were keener than ever to get to the Festival that spring. With Arkle out of action and Mill House misfiring there was more attention than usual focussed on the hurdlers, and this year a real warrior came on the scene; Persian War was to become one of those horses 'adopted' by the Cheltenham crowds. They loved him for his honesty and courage. They loved him too for his ability to come back patched up from one injury after another to deliver his best at the track he clearly relished. Always forcing the pace, he won on every kind of going from firm to heavy.

Now trained by Colin Davies (he had previously been with Dick Hern, Tom Masson and Brian Swift), Persian War had won the *Daily Express* Triumph Hurdle the year before and had also taken the Schweppes Gold Trophy under 11st 13lb. Also in the Champion field were the two previous winners Salmon Spray and Saucy Kit. But the favourite was the in-form Chorus, who was known to relish the prevailing firm ground.

Taking over from his stable companion Straight Point, Persian

War, ridden by the stylish hurdles specialist Jimmy Uttley, led them down the hill to the second last where the challenging Saucy Kit landed awkwardly and so left Henry Alper's horse, the 4-1 co-second favourite to come home in his claret and blue West Ham colours a comfortable winner, pursued by Chorus.

In 1969 Persian War came to defend his crown with a question mark or two against him. He had fallen and injured himself on his seasonal debut, fracturing a femur and being unable to run for three months. He had also been beaten in a prep race at Wincanton after running a temperature. In the race, Drumikill with Barry Brogan aboard took up the running three flights out. Rounding the bend for home Persian War was still four lengths behind, already being hard driven, although by the last he was gaining ground. There Drumikill sprawled and Persian War was left with an easier task than expected to win by four lengths.

Some horses are true Cheltenham horses, seeming to relish the testing, undulating course and its fearsome finish. Some, usually the mettlesome ones who can cope with big fields and bustling crowds, will leave their previous form on simple park courses behind them when back on their happy hunting ground. Coming to the 1970 Festival, Persian War, whose life never seemed to be without complications, had not won a race since the previous Easter, although he had been placed in top company, finishing third in the new Irish Sweeps Hurdle.

His trainer Colin Davies, who used to ride the horse himself in all his work, had once again brought him to a peak at a time which mattered and had tied down Persian War's tongue to prevent the champion swallowing it as he had become prone to do – an affliction which leaves a horse short of air and effectively running on an empty tank. On this occasion Jimmy Uttley took the tough old campaigner into the lead at the fifth hurdle and they stayed in that position until the winning post, resisting the challenge of Josh Gifford on Major Rose.

Following his third victory, Persian War had an operation on the 'soft palate' condition that had been inducing his tongue-swallowing. In the course of that it was discovered he had a broken wolf tooth which must have been causing him pain. Differences between owner and trainer saw him removed at this stage to the Epsom yard of Arthur Pitt.

Could this gritty old customer triumph over all his vicissitudes in 1971 to win a record fourth Champion Hurdle? Some must have hoped so when he won the Irish Sweeps Hurdle at Christmas. But no one goes on forever; Persian War had run down the field in the Schweppes and been beaten ten lengths by Bula at Wincanton. He was behind both the unbeaten Bula and Major Rose in the betting. In the race he acquitted himself bravely and beat his old rival Major Rose once more. But Bula, produced at the last by Paul Kelleway to storm away up the hill, left Persian War four lengths behind. His reign was over. In all Persian War, a good-tempered horse with a decent turn of foot, won eighteen of his fifty-one hurdle races.

At the end of the 1971 season Henry Alper took Persian War away from Arthur Pitt's yard to Denis Rayson. Rayson refused the owner's demand that he should be put to fences and the old warrior was moved on again to Jack Gilson near the Cheltenham course. There, perhaps fortunately, he injured a leg and finally arrived at the retirement he deserved.

The then unbeaten Bula — the Champion Hurdle was his thirteenth consecutive victory — was one of a clutch of superstars whom Fred Winter had in his yard at that time. By the time he came back to defend his title in 1972 however, he had lost his unbeaten record and spent three months on the sidelines with a leg injury. In the race Paul Kelleway switched to the outside rather than follow Dondieu down the hill. It proved a wise move. Dondieu fell, bringing down Garnishee and hampering Coral Diver. Bula came to the last in company only with Boxer and was pushed away up the hill to win by eight lengths. Next year though there was tougher opposition, and two Champion Hurdles was the limit for Bula.

In looking at Fred and Mercy Rimell's careers earlier we have already discussed Comedy of Errors, who was to be the dominating figure over the smaller obstacles for the next three years. They liked smaller horses and he was the biggest they ever handled. In 1972 Comedy had been beaten by a neck in a division of the Gloucestershire Hurdle. Now in 1973 there was no mistake. Peter Easterby's Easby Abbey made the running and still led at the last, where he was joined by the held-up Captain Christy. But the Rimells' stable jockey Bill Smith had Comedy of Errors really travelling at that point and he swept past them like a motor launch past two dinghies.

Fred Rimell and Fred Winter were the best of friends – the two families stayed in the same hotel and worked their horses together when Lanzarote, another of Winter's stars, and Comedy went to Ireland for the 1974 Sweeps Hurdle, but they were also rivals. Defending his title the next year, Comedy of Errors was beaten by Lanzarote. His trainer blamed jockey Bill Smith, reckoning he had chosen the wrong route, while Smith believed the horse was off colour. Either way, when Comedy challenged at the last Richard Pitman had enough left on Lanzarote to go away again up the hill and win by three lengths.

Ironically neither horse tended to be at his best at left-handed Cheltenham. Both preferred right-handed courses. Comedy's best record was at Newcastle, Lanzarote's at Kempton. But Comedy of Errors looked a picture when he came back in 1975 and he raced as well as he looked.

Ridden by the new stable jockey Ken White on desperately waterlogged ground, Comedy of Errors cruised up to Lanzarote when he wanted, swung wide for better ground round the bend, and stormed up the stand's side rail to win convincingly. It was the first time a deposed Champion Hurdler had taken back his crown, but that was to be his last hurrah. By 1976 there was a new star in the making amid another resurgence for the North, and that remarkable trainer was Miles Henry Easterby, known to all as Peter.

Night Nurse was the latest top hurdler from the Easterby academy and he began his career by winning three races on the Flat. In 1976 at only five years old, he made all the running under Paddy Broderick to win the Champion Hurdle from Bird's Nest, a talented hurdler who did not always run up to his full ability because he suffered from a heart murmur and tended to feel his joints by the spring. Night Nurse was a brave horse who made the running, not because he was a tearaway, but because he was comfortable out in front, a natural jumper. He skimmed his hurdles and was quickly away from them.

Brilliant when he was in the mood, Bird's Nest was made favourite for the 1977 renewal on very heavy going. Bookmakers didn't reckon Night Nurse would handle it and he was pushed out from 5-2 to 15-2, encouraging his owner Reg Spencer to double his bet. He had the advantage of knowing that they had taken Night Nurse for a racecourse gallop on soft ground and he had handled it well. Also in the field were two more outstanding hurdlers whose careers were to be interwoven over the next few years and who were both, like Night Nurse, adored by the Festival crowd: Sea Pigeon and Monksfield.

Despite the appalling conditions, Ron Barry opted to make the pace as usual on Night Nurse, hoping that way to find the best ground. He was briefly headed midway through the race by Beacon Light then challenged in turn by Fulke Walwyn's Dramatist, Bird's Nest, Monksfield and Sea Pigeon. The race was really on as they came to the hurdle at the bottom of the hill. Monksfield hit it hard, while Night Nurse jumped cleanly and was off up the rise to the winning post to record an authoritative win by two lengths. Tommy Kinane rallied Monksfield but he didn't have the time to get to the leader. Dramatist was third and Sea Pigeon fourth.

Asked in recent years, at least until the arrival of Istabraq, who was the best hurdler ever, leading racing figures tended to name either Night Nurse or Sea Pigeon. But the less well-bred Monksfield, it should be remembered, managed both to dethrone the mighty Night Nurse, who liked to dominate from the front, and twice to defy the speedy Sea Pigeon, who liked to come from behind.

The tough little 'Monkey', trained in Ireland by Des McDonagh, had already performed in fifty-two races over four years by the time he came to the 1978 Champion Hurdle. That season Monksfield, who had a taste for Granny Smith apples and kept other stable inmates awake with his snoring, was two months off the course in the autumn with a leg infection. Maybe the unaccustomed rest helped bring him to a peak.

This time at the top of the hill Night Nurse was in trouble, not skating over his hurdles with the usual facility, and Tommy Kinane, aware of the need to draw the finish from speedsters like Sea Pigeon, committed for home from that point. Approaching the last, Frank Berry, who was deputising on Sea Pigeon for the injured Jonjo O'Neill, brought his mount up to challenge. It was too soon and Monksfield, who always responded when the gauntlet was thrown down, drew away again up the hill to win by two lengths, with Night Nurse back in third. At forty-four it made Kinane the oldest man ever to win a Champion Hurdle.

Monksfield was never out of the first two in his five Cheltenham appearances and the same pair dominated the next year's Champion Hurdle. This time Jonjo O'Neill was back on Sea Pigeon and Dessie Hughes had taken over on Monksfield. But Jonjo too, on his own admission, got it wrong. Jonjo attacked Monksfield on the final bend and jumped the last in the lead, confident that he was going to win. Both took the last obstacle perfectly, but half-way up the run-in Sea Pigeon began to 'empty' on the sticky going. The gutsy Monksfield, who never knew when he was beaten, clawed his way back. Sea Pigeon's stride shortened, and in clinging mud which had probably blunted Sea Pigeon's speed, Monksfield, his head lowered almost to his knees as he thrust forward, passed him fifty yards out to win by three quarters of a length. 'It's a pity pigeons can't swim,' observed Easterby.

Mick O'Toole described it as 'one of the greatest races I have seen at this course'.

It was a canny ride by Dessie Hughes. He reckoned Monksfield to be far better on good going. 'I decided that the only chance we had was on the best ground on the wide outside so I rode him on the outside and I made it so I chose my own path. I kept in on the bends and went back out wide down the hill.' As for Monksfield: 'He was very tough. You wouldn't be allowed to ride him today the way we used to in those days. You'd definitely hit him five or six behind the saddle before he'd even bother. Then he'd say, "OK, OK, OK." He was a real character, no doubt about it.'

Like Monksfield, who had thus beaten him into second place in the 1978 and 1979 Champion Hurdles, Sea Pigeon, trained in Yorkshire by Peter Easterby, won the adoration of the Cheltenham crowds over the years. If racegoers thrill to the front-runners who set sail for home and defy the others to catch them, they thrill even more to the 'hold-up' horse who swoops like a predator with a well-timed burst of speed at the death.

A son of the great Sea Bird, Sea Pigeon, known as 'Pidge' in the Great Habton yard, ran seventh in the Derby for Jeremy Tree and won a total of thirty-seven races on the Flat and over timber. If, as they say, champagne was flowing down the York stands when he won the Ebor Handicap in a photo-finish (after Jonjo had dropped his hands) Sea Pigeon's victory in the Champion Hurdle at his fourth attempt was a roof-threatening moment.

Jonjo, who admits he was at fault in the Ebor (for which he'd only got medical clearance to ride when he hoodwinked the course doctor into examining his uninjured foot, not the one with the crushed toes) blames himself too for losing the Champion in 1979, having paid too much attention to owner Pat Muldoon's admonition as he was legged up: 'Don't come too soon.'

In 1980 it was a different story, a story which he believes was affected by a change to the Champion Hurdle course which reduced it by 200 yards to exactly two miles. Sea Pigeon had had an interrupted preparation after an injury and was only ninety per cent fit. At the top of the hill, his jockey related, he was wheezing and gasping. So Jonjo switched him off, gave him time to get his second wind, and jumped the last this time a length down on Monksfield. They landed level and Sea Pigeon produced such a surge of power that they were clear half-way up the run-in, sooner than the jockey had intended. But he need not have worried. Jonjo said he had never felt such speed under the saddle in a jumper, and they went clear to win by seven lengths to the roars of an ecstatic crowd.

The Cheltenham crowd loved the classy, quirky Sea Pigeon and they loved Jonjo, whose cherubic grin and twinkling eyes were accompanied by a steely determination once in the saddle. Sadly, when Sea Pigeon came back to defend his crown in 1981 it was without his usual partner. Jonjo's leg had been shattered in thirty-six places in a fall at Bangor, and his efforts to get back in time to ride Sea Pigeon exacerbated the injury, requiring a further operation. This time it was John Francome, himself another Cheltenham legend, who provided a silk-smooth ride, delivering Sea Pigeon half-way up the run-in to pip Pollardstown and Daring Run. 'Pure class,' said Francome, who also declared that he had never ridden a jumper with such acceleration.

Sea Pigeon, who survived a major intestinal operation, lived on in his Yorkshire retirement to the ripe old age of thirty. He and Night Nurse won seventy races between them, Night Nurse once going ten races and twenty-one months without a defeat. The pair are buried side by side at the Easterby yard of Habton Grange with a plaque which reads: 'Legends in their Lifetime.' As they were.

Jonjo says now of the epic races between Monksfield and Sea Pigeon: 'In 1979 I definitely arrived too quick. He was a very good horse but you just didn't need to hit the front too soon on him. Once he hit the front he thought he'd won. When the race was on he was unbelievable. Him and Night Nurse were the two best horses I ever rode. They were magic. When Night Nurse jumped a fence – even when he took off from behind – when he landed he was like a sprinter coming out of the stalls. He was an unbelievable horse. He was like riding Concorde over fences. On Sea Pigeon normally you'd be cantering on him. He'd be absolutely cantering but he was a great "lepper" as well and if you put in a good leap at the second last you could get there too quick. I had to take a pull really, which is a hard thing to do at that stage, especially if it is Cheltenham.

'He didn't win the Champion Hurdle when they went up the hill twice, he didn't win until they cut out going round the stables. He never even looked like winning it until they went round the bottom . . . he probably didn't quite get the trip. Monksfield did. It's a front runner's track. Monksfield was a great little horse. When you beat him you had to go past him quick because he would battle every time. It was hard to collar him because he was so good.'

The year of 1982 may have seen a temporary end to the cluster of multiple Champion Hurdle winners, but the race didn't lack for drama. Instead it became the subject of an audacious old-fashioned betting coup as Colin Magnier became the first amateur to win the big race for nearly twenty years.

The English contenders Ekbalco, Pollardstown and Broadsword were all fancied but there was a massive punt on For Auction, trained in County Meath by Michael Cunningham. He ran out a convincing winner by seven lengths at 40–1 and the Irish celebrations went on late into the night.

In 1983, as already discussed, it was the turn of Gaye Brief, making Mercy Rimell the first woman to train a Champion Hurdle winner. Gaye Brief was ridden by Richard Linley and owned by Sheikh Ali Abu Khamsin, that year's champion owner. His victory and that of Sheikh Mohammed's Kribensis in 1990, trained by Flat supremo Michael Stoute, (who was not at that stage Sir Michael), had some National Hunt traditionalists worried that the whole jumping scene might be transformed by Arab money. But the Dubai ruling family's interest in the winter sport was not sustained and Sheikh Ali, who was in fact a Saudi, retreated to Riyadh after his business interests were hit by the first Gulf War. Mercy Rimell says simply: 'I trained for him for eight years and I liked him immensely.'

Dawn Run's 5-4 on victory was predictable after the withdrawal of Gaye Brief from the 1984 race. She had already beaten Mercy Rimell's hurdler, even if he was not fully ready, at Kempton earlier in the year. She vied for the early lead with Buck House, later a Champion Chase winner and Desert Orchid, later like her a Gold Cup winner, and despite making a bad mistake at the last when she was distracted by the ecstatic shrieks of the crowd, she ran a textbook race to win by three quarters of a length. That year the hard, tough mare won eight of her nine starts and in her career she won the English, Irish and French Champion Hurdles. She was to go on, as we know, to an even more scintillating success, becoming the only horse ever to win both the Champion Hurdle and the Gold Cup. But there were other extraordinary champions to follow her at the hurdling game.

Chapter 17

Keeping Cool about 'Percy'

'Mick forgot to declare the blinkers. No blinkers. Off the bridle the whole way, never on it, pushing and shoving for three miles.'
(Rider Dessie Hughes on Davy Lad's Gold Cup victory)

The 1974 Festival was remarkable for one of the greatest examples of professional restraint we will ever see in a commentator. Among the races the great race-caller Sir Peter O'Sullevan was covering for the BBC was the Triumph Hurdle, in which his own brave little hurdler Attivo, better known to him and the lads in the yard as 'Percy', was running. He never missed a beat nor let his personal feelings show as Attivo stormed up the hill to victory. But the day was not only a tribute to Peter's professionalism as a broadcaster, it was evidence of his shrewdness as an owner. Let Peter tell the story in his own words, beginning with Attivo's Cheltenham preview:

'I knew Frenchie Nicholson well and one of his main occupations was telling everybody what the ground would be like because he lived just behind the ditch on the far side, and nobody trusts clerks of the course. They've got a PR job to do looking after the course. They can't afford to be absolutely impartial.

'It was New Year's Day 1974. The weather had been very, very dodgy. Racing looked extremely doubtful. I had the opportunity of either running this little horse Attivo first time over hurdles in a novices' race in which [trainer] Cyril Mitchell said, "Barring an Act of God, you'll collect" or running in the Evesham Four-Year-Old Hurdle against some pretty useful novices including Park Lawn, whom I remembered calling prominently in the Irish Derby right to the home turn, and a mare of Frenchie's which I think had won three, Fighting Kate. I remember staying down there in a motel and everything was white. I called Frenchie. "Good or bad news?" "Good news. It's odds-on there'll be racing. The bad news is you've got no f****** chance. Kate will not get beat."

'We ran in the Evesham and Cyril Mitchell came up to the commentary box. A boy called Robert Hughes rode Attivo, claiming a 5lb allowance. He set off in front while the others played cat and mouse with each other. Come the top of the hill, Cyril said something. I took my headset off and he repeated: "They'll have a job catching him now." They all rolled down the hill and they never got near him. He won by a distance. Afterwards Mercy Rimell was disparaging about the race and Fred Rimell said, "I'm not sure you'll do that to us next time, mate." Anyway Attivo took no notice. He came into the winner's enclosure with a right swagger as if to say, "They can think what they like."

'The next race he ran was the Stroud Green Hurdle at Newbury, which he won by twenty lengths from Supreme Halo with [subsequent Champion Hurdle runner-up] Birds Nest in third. So then Cyril said: 'Do you want to go for the Yellow Pages [a February race falling between that meeting and the Cheltenham Festival]?' I said I'd rather he went fresh to the Triumph and Cyril said: "He won't need to do any more in the Yellow Pages than he does at home." It was worth five grand and Cyril said: "If you want to behave like a millionaire it's up to you." I said: "I've always told myself that if I was ever fortunate enough to have a horse with more than a squeak at Cheltenham I would at least turn up fresh." "All right," he said.'

As for the Triumph Hurdle itself, Peter says: 'Attivo could have got done. We stuck to the lad, the boy Robert, even though he couldn't claim his allowance because the race was worth too much. He only had one instruction. He was told: "Never take your finger out of the neckstrap, because he's got a launch mechanism like Cape Canaveral." Attivo used to really take off at his hurdles and land galloping, that was his great forte. Of course approaching the last there was nothing in sight and he virtually said, "OK, I'll take over now." Out comes Robert Hughes's finger and into the hurdle goes Attivo and comes to an absolute standstill. His rider goes rocketing into the air. Mercifully when he comes down Attivo is still there. If he hadn't been fresh he wouldn't have sprinted up the hill as he needed to to win.'

Listen to the broadcast and you would never have known that it was Peter's own horse it was happening to but as the runners came back to be unsaddled the crowds turned to the commentary box to applaud.

The 1975 Festival was in danger of looking more like Glastonbury than Cheltenham. With the course waterlogged, the first day's programme was cancelled and the Gold Cup went to the mud-loving Ten Up, trained by Jim Dreaper in the year that his father, who had won the blue riband with Prince Regent, Arkle and Fort Leney, had died. Like Arkle, he was owned by Anne, Duchess of Westminster but he needed rather more help than Arkle to win his races. Ten Up had a tendency to break blood vessels under the stress of racing and he ran in Ireland with the assistance of a coagulant drug which was permitted under the rules of Irish racing provided that the authorities were notified in advance of a race. In 1976 Jim Dreaper sought the permission of the Cheltenham stewards for Ten Up to be injected with his medication by a Jockey Club vet but was informed that this could not be permitted under English rules because it was a substance which could 'alter racing performance'. The horse was withdrawn from the Gold Cup and subsequently the Irish stewards began applying the rules in the same way as their English counterparts, limiting Ten Up's future opportunities.

The 1976 Gold Cup went to Royal Frolic, whose victory was discussed earlier in looking at Fred Rimell's career, and in 1977, another year when conditions were dire and the going heavy, it went to Davy Lad, trained in Ireland by Mick O'Toole and ridden by Dessie Hughes. Only seven of the thirteen who started finished the race, and it was marred by the sad death of that great hurdler Lanzarote who broke his leg in falling at the ninth fence.

Dessie Hughes reckons he earned his money that day, recalling 'Mick forgot to declare the blinkers. No blinkers. Off the bridle the whole way, never on it, pushing and shoving for three miles. They went very fast: Tied Cottage was fifteen lengths in front going past the stands first time and I'm stone last. I persevered and persevered and persevered. At the top of the hill they were twenty lengths in front of me, but they weren't going anywhere and he was getting his second wind and starting to stay and stay. He got down to the second last, I sailed through that and turned in. He got between Tied Cottage and another horse at the last – he threw a tremendous "lep" at it and it was all over. He'd done nothing for two miles, absolutely nothing, but when he got past the last horse and then caught another he began to race. He was always a very lazy horse.'

In 1978 racegoers had to wait until 12 April to see who succeeded Davy Lad as blue-riband winner after snow fell on Gold Cup day, forcing a postponement. Several horses who would have run in March did not make the April contest, including Gay Spartan, Davy Lad, who had injured a foot, and the previous year's favourite Bannow Rambler. But Royal Frolic was back in the line-up and Fred Winter, still awaiting his first Gold Cup winner as a trainer, was delighted by the delay. The prospect of much better ground suited his Midnight Court, the winner of all six of his chases so far that season. Jockey John Francome let Fulke Walwyn's Fort Devon and Royal Frolic cut each other's throats at the head of affairs, shot through on the inside at the third last fence and when Royal Frolic fell at the last in second place he had no serious rival in powering

The Cheltenham scene adored by so many; in this case the runners in the 2000 Royal and Sun Alliance Novices Hurdle won by Monsignor. © *Cranhamphoto.com*

Above: George Duller, the hurdles supremo of the pre-war years was also a racing driver, here seen at Brooklands in 193 *Courtesy of Popperfoto/Getty Images*

Left: Owner Dorothy Paget wit Golden Miller, five times the winner of the Cheltenham Gold Cup. *Courtesy of Mirrorpix*

bove: England's Mill House (with the cross belts) and Ireland's hero Arkle at the second last
the Gold Cup of 1964. *Courtesy of Bernard Parkin*

Below: Persian War with jockey
Jimmy Uttley and trainer Colin
Davies (behind) after winning
the first of his three Champion
Hurdles in 1968. *Bernard Parkin*

Above: Fred Rimell and Comedy of Errors after winning the 1975 Champion Hurdle. *Bernard Parkin*

Top right: Fulke Walwyn, trainer of four Cheltenham Gold Cup winners. *Bernard Parkin*

Centre right: The great jockey tutor Frenchie Nicholson in 1966. *Bernard Parkin*

Bottom right: Vincent O'Brien, the man who launched the Irish assault on Cheltenham. *Courtesy of Fox Photos/Getty Images*

Below: Fred Winter: a Gold Cup winning trainer at last with Midnight Court in 1978. *Bernard Parkin*

Above: Trainer Michael Dickinson (second from right) celebrates Bregawn's Gold Cup victory in 1983 with jockey Graham Bradley. He trained the next four home as well.
Bernard Parkin

Left: Martin Pipe in 2005 with yet another trophy.
Bernard Parkin

Below: The most popular duo in jump racing: Henrietta Knight and her husband, former jockey Terry Biddlecombe.
Bernard Parkin

Above: Sea Pigeon (Jonjo O'Neill) leads Monksfield (Dessie Hughes) in the 1979 Champion Hurdle. *Bernard Parkin*

Below: Dawn Run leads Buck House and Desert Orchid in the 1984 Champion Hurdle. *Bernard Parkin*

Right: See You Then at the 1986 Champion Hurdle. *Bernard Parkin*

Left: See You Then with trainer Nicky Henderson 1986. *Bernard Parkin*

Below: Desert Orchid leads the field at the half-way stage in the 1989 Gold Cup. *Bernard Parkin*

Above: Fred Winter in action as a jockey, here on Fulke Walwyn's Kirriemuir. *Bernard Parkin*

Left: Two Cheltenham heroes: John Francome on board Fred Winter's Bula. *Bernard Parkin*

Below: Terry Biddlecombe on Amarind a Cheltenham, the last ride of an illustriou career. *Bernard Parkin*

Above left: The Great Comeback: Irish jockey Bobby Beasley on Captain Christy before the 1974 Gold Cup. *Bernard Parkin*

Above right: Former champion jockey Peter Scudamore, a great judge of pace. *Bernard Parkin*

Left: Jonjo O'Neill: a favourite with the Cheltenham crowds both as jockey and trainer. *Bernard Parkin*

Below: One of so many awards: Tony McCoy's achievement in breaking Gordon Richards' record for the most winners ridden in a season is acknowledged at Cheltenham. *Bernard Parkin*

Above: A famous upset. The 100-1 Norton's Coin (nearest camera) at the last fence with Toby Tobias in the 1990 Gold Cup. *Bernard Parkin*

Below: The tussles that thrill: Waterloo Boy and Barnbrook Again fight it out in the Queen Mother Champion Chase of 1990. © *Cranhamphoto.com*

Right: The face of triumph: Charlie Swan aboard Istabraq after their Champion Hurdle victory in 1998.
Bernard Parkin

Below: The Cheltenham victory he waited for: One Man takes the Queen Mother Champion Chase in 1998.
Bernard Parkin

Above: The most famous follower of all: Queen Elizabeth the Queen Mother at Cheltenham 1997. *Courtesy of Tim Graham/Getty Images*

Below: The Queen meets Desert Orchid in 2003. *Bernard Parkin*

Left: Lord Vestey, the long-time Cheltenham chairman, at Arkle's 50th birthday celebrations in 2007. *Bernard Parkin*

Right: The unmistakable voice of racing: Peter O'Sullevan with microphone in hand. *Bernard Parkin*

Left: John McCririck: a highly individual member of the Channel Four team. *Bernard Parkin*

Below: Channel Four's Alastair Down, part of the Cheltenham passion. *Bernard Parkin*

Above: Willie Mullins at Cheltenham in 2004. Punters always watch for his selection in the bumper. *Courtesy of Julian Herbert/Getty Images*

Below: Victorious again: Jim Culloty on Best Mate after his third Gold Cup win in 2004. *Courtesy of Julian Herbert/Getty Images*

Right: Ruby Walsh shows his delight as Kauto Star takes the Gold Cup in 2009. *Courtesy of David Davies/ Press Association Images*

Below: Trainer Paul Nicholls with his stable stars Kauto Star and Denman. *Bernard Parkin*

Above: Cheltenham's impresario, managing director Edward Gillespie. *Courtesy of Julian Herbert/Allsport/Getty Images*

Right: The man who gets them off on time: Simon Claisse, Clerk of the Course and Director of Racing. *Bernard Parkin*

Below: The jockeys' view of proceedings: Runners in the 2005 Fulke Walwyn Kim Muir Challenge Cup Chase take a pre-race look back at the stands. © *Cranhamphoto.com*

up the hill to win by seven lengths. It was an emotional moment for a trainer who had been unable to win the race with such good horses as Pendil, Bula and Lanzarote, and the crowd showed their appreciation.

Once again in 1979 the going was terrible and the weather atrocious. The Gold Cup began in a snowstorm and Ireland's Tied Cottage, who had been second in the race back in 1977, made the running. Only one horse came to the second last ready to make a race of it with him and his jockey Tommy Carberry and that was Peter Easterby's Alverton, on whom Jonjo O'Neill had timed his effort to the second. They took the last together but as all of Ireland gasped, Tied Cottage pitched on landing, slipped and fell. Jonjo was left in solitary state to gallop up the hill and win by twenty-five lengths.

Arguments still rage about whether Tied Cottage would have won if he had stood up. The tragedy was that there could be no return match to settle the question. Six weeks after the Gold Cup, Alverton, who had started favourite for the race, fell at Becher's second time round in the Grand National and broke his neck.

Says Jonjo of Alverton's Gold Cup: 'He'd been broken down. Peter Easterby did a fantastic job keeping him sound. It was heavy that day and we were well strung out. Tied Cottage was in front as he usually was.' And then the urgency comes into his voice as he replays the race again in his mind: 'We were catching him and catching him. Catching him and catching him . . . I kept telling Tommy that I'd have beaten him anyway but he was unlucky to fall . . . They were two very tired horses. I was sorry for Tied Cottage but at the same time I must admit that I was very pleased to see him go and be left with the race at my mercy.'

At least for Dan Moore, Tommy Carberry and the now twelve-year-old Tied Cottage there was another chance in 1980 and the horse took it well. Once again with the going heavy Tied Cottage made the running. He was never headed and came home an eight-length winner from Master Smudge. That was how it looked on race day. But sadly for his connections a routine dope test then showed that Tied Cottage's urine contained small traces of an illegal substance, theobromine. Dan Moore and his staff were not held to blame – the horse's corn feed had been accidentally contaminated by cocoa beans, although only in such minute quantities it could not have affected his running. However the authorities had no option but to disqualify the horse who had been first past the post on a technicality, and to award the race to Master Smudge, who had plugged on into second place on the day, overtaking the fifteen-year-old Mac Vidi after the last fence. What made the post-race events even more of a tragedy was that Tied Cottage's owner, Anthony Robinson, who had himself ridden the horse to victory in the previous year's Irish Grand National when terminally ill, was to die within a few months. So did trainer Dan Moore, who had been too ill to come to Cheltenham.

Only What A Myth (1969) and Silver Fame (1951) had been first past the post in the Gold Cup at the age of twelve. Tied Cottage actually ran twice more in the big race. As a thirteen-year-old he fell at the third in 1981 and at fourteen he led the 1982 Gold Cup field until the third last fence, although fading to finish ninth.

Alverton's trainer, Peter Easterby, could almost have pitched a tent in the winner's enclosure in 1981. He took the Champion Hurdle with Sea Pigeon and was back there again when Little Owl won the Gold Cup. Northern yards dominated that year with Michael Dickinson's Silver Buck starting as the 7-2 favourite after winning twelve out of thirteen chase starts including two King George VI Chases. The joint second favourites, former Champion Hurdler Night Nurse and Little Owl, both came from Peter Easterby's Great Habton stables.

Coming down the hill for the final charge the three fancied horses were heading the field with Silver Buck seemingly going the best. The ground though did not suit him, and it was Little Owl, ridden by the amateur Jim Wilson, who injected speed and drew away with Night Nurse battling on after him. In fourth place was the gallant Spartan Missile who was bred, owned, trained and ridden by Mr John Thorne. We may by now have been fully in the era of the professionals but this was a glorious celebration of the amateur talent that has always been an integral part of Cheltenham's character. John Thorne and his mount were to go on to add further lustre by finishing second in that year's Grand National to Aldaniti. Little Owl himself was a 'gift horse', having been left to Jim Wilson and his brother Robert by their aunt Mrs Bobbie Grundy; his rider raised his whip to heaven in a thank you as he rode back into the winner's enclosure.

It was very much Jim Wilson's Festival because he was associated too with another extraordinary victory, piloting the handicapper Willie Wumpkins to victory for the third successive year in the hotly contested Coral Golden Hurdle Final. Class horses which are good enough can score repeat victories in the level-weight 'championship' races. Winning a Festival handicap for three years running is extraordinary because you are not just battling the other horses, you are fighting against a handicapper who is trying to make it harder for you to win again. But Willie Wumpkins's story is another part of what Cheltenham is all about, and why the Festival events remain a sport as well as a business. The horse had been bought by a Cotswold farmer's wife, Jane Pilkington, for £1,800 in 1972. Trained initially in Ireland by her nephew, Adrian Maxwell, he won the Aldsworth Hurdle at the Festival. But then he developed a leaky heart valve which caused him to make a noise like an express train, and Irish vets recommended he be put down.

His owner was having none of that. She brought him home to England, took out a permit to train in the 1975–76 season and rode Willie herself every day. Steadily she brought him back to health, making use of neighbours' gallops and of Jim Wilson's equine swimming pool. Since the horse was a poor traveller she and her husband gave him a Shetland pony as a companion, and they ate their picnics outside his box on race days so he didn't feel lonely. So well did Willie thrive on this equine 'tlc' that he won the Coral

Hurdle in 1979, in 1980 and again at the age of thirteen in 1981. There have been few more honest and sentimental cheers for a horse at any Cheltenham Festival.

Chapter 18

Good Years for the North

'Thank you very much, Ma'am, but would you mind if I did the
horse's legs first?' (Jenny Pitman's response to a royal box
invitation after winning the Gold Cup)

Northern yards continued to do well in 1982. That year
Silver Buck found underfoot conditions more to his
liking and ran out a comfortable two-length winner of
the Gold Cup from Bregawn. Both were trained by the remarkable
Michael Dickinson, who thus had a 1-2 in the blue-riband race in
only his second year after taking over from his father Tony as a
trainer. Michael Dickinson, who had benefited from a riding
education beside the course with Frenchie Nicholson, as well as
from spells at Coolmore watching the O'Brien training operation
with Flat horses, had already enjoyed Festival success as a jockey.
But this Gold Cup 1-2 was to prove no more than an *hors d'oeuvre* to
his extraordinary success (described elsewhere) in training the first
five home in the 1983 Gold Cup.

In 1984 the redoubtable Jenny Pitman wrote her name in the
Festival records. The success of Burrough Hill Lad made her the
first female trainer of a Gold Cup winner, just a year after she had
become the first woman trainer to win a Grand National with
Corbiere. That same year, 1983, Mercy Rimell, as discussed earlier,
had become the first woman to train a Champion Hurdle winner,

and Caroline Beasley, on Eliogarty in the Christies Foxhunters' Chase, became the first woman to ride a Festival winner.

In 1984 two of Dickinson's Famous Five, Bregawn and Wayward Lad, were trying again, and Fred Winter had three candidates in the race including the Cheltenham specialist Brown Chamberlin. Less of a threat was the 500-1 outsider Foxbury, ridden by the first female rider to participate in a Gold Cup, Mrs Linda Sheedy.

Brown Chamberlin, ridden by John Francome, made the pace and when the race began in earnest he was closely attended only by Burrough Hill Lad, ridden by Phil Tuck, and by Ireland's hope Drumlargan. At the second last it was clear that Brown Chamberlin was tiring. As Team Pitman had anticipated, he drifted right and Burrough Hill Lad nipped through on the inside, coming up the hill best to win by three lengths. Invited to the warmth of the royal box afterwards by the Queen Mother, Jenny Pitman puzzled those present by keeping her coat on. She had to. Setting off for the races she had picked a sweater with a large ironing hole in the front of it. She didn't notice until she took her coat off after the race to wash and bandage Burrough Hill Lad's legs before heading for the royal box, having shown the right priorities by asking if she might do that before enjoying her champagne.

The year of 1985 was a poor Festival for the Irish, with only two winners. But the good run by Northern stables continued. Sadly Burrough Hill Lad, who had easily won the Hennessy Gold Cup in the meantime, was not in the Cheltenham Gold Cup field to defend his crown. A horse with a low head carriage in running, he had managed to cut himself behind the knee with his own teeth! Fancied runners included David Elsworth's Combs Ditch, Captain Tim Forster's Drumadowney, and Righthand Man, now trained by Michael Dickinson's mother Monica. But the North's strongest hope this time was Forgive 'n' Forget, with whom Jimmy Fitzgerald had landed a huge gamble in the Coral Golden Hurdle Final at the 1983 Festival. With Mark Dwyer aboard he took control jumping the last, and held on despite a fast finish from Graham

Bradley on Righthand Man. What we did not know until after the race was that Forgive 'n' Forget had run with only three racing plates and one ordinary shoe because of a corn that had developed the week before.

Bradley had to be content with second place in the next year's Gold Cup too, the race described at the start of this book in which the mare Dawn Run became the first Champion Hurdler to go on and win a Gold Cup.

In 1987 the crowd and the Gold Cup participants had to be patient as the start was delayed for some eighty minutes by the snow that had begun falling during the preceding Foxhunters' Chase. It was weather for gritty northerners again and the softened ground suited The Thinker, a horse trained in County Durham by the veteran Arthur Stephenson and ridden by Ridley Lamb. His fellow Northerner Forgive 'n' Forget, who had been winning consistently, was favourite, and also in the field was the Grand National winner West Tip. Two fences out, six horses were still in with a chance and as the twelve-year-old veteran Wayward Lad jumped to the front at the last it looked as though it might finally be his year. It was not to be. Four horses passed him on the climb to the post and it was The Thinker who came out the best of them. His 66-year-old trainer was not there to collect his prize: he had opted to supervise his runners at Hexham that day instead.

One of the curious things about Cheltenham's history is how long it has taken some outstandingly good trainers and jockeys to record their first Festival winner. Such an idea has to be pure fancy, but it is as if their eagerness, their desperation even, transmits itself to their horses, who tighten up, freeze and under-achieve. Then, the moment they have achieved that first victory the floodgates seem to open and they carry on in 'business as usual' style to record many more Festival wins. Jockey Peter Scudamore was afflicted by the bogey, and so were trainers Josh Gifford, David 'the Duke' Nicholson and Noel Meade. The 1988 Festival was a case in point. Former champion jockey Josh Gifford, an accomplished and successful trainer too, had gone seventeen years without a Festival winner. But not only did he shake off the hoodoo by winning the Kim Muir Chase with Golden Minstrel on the first day. He then sent out Vodkatini and Clay Hill to be first and second in the Grand Annual Chase and completed a hat-trick by capturing the Coral Hurdle with Pragada.

David Nicholson had a similar experience. Having started training in 1968 with a string of Festival victories as a jockey behind him it took him until 1986 to train a Festival winner when the 40-1 outsider Solar Cloud, on whom Peter Scudamore had totally ignored his riding instructions, won the Triumph Hurdle. It was a first for Scudamore too, who had endured seventy-four Festival rides without a win. No sooner had the pair broken their Festival ducks than they won the Ritz Club Chase as well with Charter Party. It was the same horse who gave the local boy David Nicholson his first Cheltenham Gold Cup in 1988, appropriately for his patron Colin Smith who built the magnificent Jackdaw's Castle training complex now occupied by Jonjo O'Neill.

Peter Scudamore had won the Champion Hurdle on Celtic Shot and Richard Dunwoody was now riding for David Nicholson. Charter Party, who had been Hobdayed to tackle a wind problem and operated on for a soft palate, was never a lucky horse. The previous year he had suffered from a blood disease. But he had still managed to win nearly one in three of the thirty-nine races he had contested. He had fallen in the Gold Cup of 1987 but this time made no mistake and won convincingly from Cavvies Clown. There was tragedy however back on the hill. Former winner Forgive 'n' Forget, who had been travelling well, had shattered a leg and had to be put down. He ran six times at the Festival, on four occasions in the Gold Cup, and his ashes were buried near the royal box.

Chapter 19

The Horse They Called 'See You When?'

'He was a wonderful horse outside but inside the box he was a brute. He would eat people.' (Nicky Henderson on his three-time Champion Hurdle winner See You Then)

Perhaps the finest training feat among the series of multiple Champion Hurdle winners was that of Nicky Henderson in preparing See You Then to win three consecutive titles from 1985–87. Apart from being a brute in his box who would take chunks out of lad, trainer or vet given the slightest opportunity, See You Then had legs like china and could only be raced at rare intervals. He was in consequence less a public icon than a mystery horse.

Some National Hunt horses are celebrated for their sheer durability. That was not so with See You Then, a son of the Derby winner Royal Palace. The quality was there – he ran fifteen times over hurdles and won on ten occasions – but the problem was keeping him sound. After he won his first title in 1985, See You Then only ran six more races but they included two more Champion Hurdle victories.

See You Then started on the Flat with Con Collins and after he was bought by the Italian-based Stype Wood Stud he joined Nicky Henderson for the Triumph Hurdle in 1984, finishing second to Edward O 'Grady's Northern Game.

In the 1985 Champion Hurdle, the year the favourite Browne's Gazette whipped round at the start under jockey Dermot Browne, who was later to earn notoriety in racing circles and be 'warned off' after being named in a doping scandal as 'the Needle Man', See You Then was a 16-1 shot. He stormed home seven lengths clear under Steve Smith-Eccles.

He won by the same distance in 1986 from former champion Gaye Brief after the two had crossed the last hurdle together. In 1987 See You Then was barely fit – trainer and jockey acknowledge that he 'blew up' on the run-in – but he was simply in a different class to the other runners and he won by one and a half lengths after America's champion jump jockey Jerry Fishback, on a rare visit to Cheltenham, misjudged the last obstacle on Flatterer.

Following that third victory, See You Then was retired after injuring a back leg at Wincanton, only to come back amazingly and run in another Champion Hurdle at the age of ten following a two-year interval. Sadly he finished down the field and that was his final appearance.

Steve Smith-Eccles – famous for being asleep in the back seat and shocking the life out of a joyrider on awaking when his car was stolen at a Grand National meeting – only got the ride on See You Then for his first Champion Hurdle at ten minutes' notice. John Francome had been down to ride him but suffered a scary fall in the previous race which left him hanging upside down from a twisted iron.

Smith-Eccles believes that See You Then's second success in a year when much racing was frosted off was achieved only because his trainer drove a tractor at intervals through the night to keep the all-weather strip at his stables usable when many trainers were unable to work their horses. The jockey said of Nicky Henderson's feat: 'Winning two Champion Hurdles with such a horse would have been an outstanding training achievement. To win three was a horse-racing miracle.'

Says Nicky Henderson: 'For us he was the start of the whole

thing, really. Steve and I had been together for some time but J. Francome was going to ride See You Then. He had a bad fall on a horse of Fred Winter's called The Reject and couldn't ride. Steve was sat in the weighing room doing nothing and so he got the ride. He'd never sat on the horse.

'We'd bought See You Then in Ireland to go to Italy and the man behind that was my vet Frank Mahon. We put a Yorkshire boot [protective strapping] on him one day because we thought he was knocking a leg. It took us four days to get it off him. He was a wonderful horse outside but inside the box he was a brute. He would eat people. Glyn Foster looked after him all his life and got bitten and kicked to ribbons over the years. [Head lad] Corky Browne and I couldn't go in the box without Glyn. Nor could Frank Mahon.

'See You Then went to Italy but came back to England with a problem for Frank Mahon to sort out because he was vet to the Italian owners as well. At Windsor House we had a swimming pool and he swam and he swam and he swam. We decided to keep going each year but on less and less runs every time. We went to all sorts of places to work him. We used to take him down to the beach. Everyone was wondering where he was. He was nicknamed 'See You When?'

'We got one Flat race into him one year. Then we just ran him once in the last year. It was on the Saturday, I think, he went to Haydock and it was obviously going to be a tense night waiting to see what was going to happen to his legs. I woke up in the early hours and thought, "I'm going to go into that box and take those bandages off and see what those legs are like", knowing full well that I couldn't really go into the box without Glyn and that since it was a Sunday morning he probably wasn't going to be coming in until about 7.30 or 8.00.

'I got up and went to his box and, oh my God, the door was open. I thought, "What on earth?" and there was Frank Mahon sat on the manger. I said, "What are you doing?" and he said, "I couldn't sleep. I thought I'd come and take those bandages off and see how he was." "So what are you doing up there?" He said, "He won't let me out." "But how are his legs?" "I don't know because he won't let me near him to take the bandages off." Frank was penned up at one end of the box, See You Then, who used to buck and kick, wouldn't let me in at the other end of the box and we both had to stay there until Glyn finally came in to work. Anyway he got away with that race and he got away with his Champion Hurdle.'

Multiple winners of the Champion Hurdle

1932, 1933	*Insurance (2)*
1947, 1948	*National Spirit (2)*
1949, 1950, 1951	*Hatton's Grace (3)*
1952, 1953, 1954	*Sir Ken (3)*
1968, 1969, 1970	*Persian War (3)*
1971, 1972	*Bula (2)*
1973, 1975	*Comedy of Errors (2)*
1976, 1977	*Night Nurse (2)*
1978, 1979	*Monksfield (2)*
1980, 1981	*Sea Pigeon (2)*
1985, 1986, 1987	*See You Then (3)*
1998, 1999, 2000	*Istabraq (3)*

Chapter 20

Turning a Race into a Family Tradition

'It would be amazing enough if it had been the first fence, but to jump the last like he did was ridiculous. He went around for three years doing that sort of thing' (Trainer Nicky Henderson on Champion Chase winner Remittance Man)

Like the Champion Hurdle, the Queen Mother Champion Chase tends to produce cohorts of supporters for regular participants, a factor which enlivens both the atmosphere and the betting market. It has also often proved to be a race attracting close finishes and bizarre stories. In 1980, for example, there was controversy when the race was later awarded to Fred Rimell's Another Dolly. Mick O'Toole's Chinrullah had been first past the post on the day but was disqualified for failing a post-race urine test, thanks to a batch of contaminated feed for which the trainer was blameless.

In 1982 a remarkable family involvement with the race began with the victory of Rathgorman, trained by the perfectionist former jockey Michael Dickinson. Rathgorman was followed as the two-mile champion for the next three years by Badsworth Boy, who was trained on the first two occasions by Michael Dickinson and for the last of them by his mother Monica. On the first occasion Badsworth Boy was clear of his field three fences out, still on the bridle, and he won for the next two years in similar style, each time ten lengths clear of his field.

After Mouse Morris's Buck House in 1986, there was another dual winner, Pearlyman in 1987 and 1988. Owned and bred by Bill Jenks and trained by John Edwards, Pearlyman was ridden on the first occasion by Peter Scudamore, then by Tom Morgan, and his first 'Queen Mother' was a classic. As the 13-8 favourite, Pearlyman had two serious market rivals. One was the charismatic grey Desert Orchid at 9-4 and the other was the Mackeson Gold Cup winner Very Promising, who had been second to Buck House the year before and started at 3-1.

The bold-jumping Desert Orchid, who had never won in four outings at left-handed Cheltenham, led at half-way with Very Promising in fourth and Pearlyman, the two-mile specialist, waiting in eighth place. A big leap took him from eighth to fifth place but Scudamore, not wanting to play his hand too soon, eased him back again. Desert Orchid, Charcoal Wally and Very Promising led Pearlyman over the second last but he was gaining ground and at the last Scudamore drove him between Desert Orchid and Very Promising. Richard Dunwoody, however, conjured a leap at the last from Very Promising which put him back in front. Very Promising was a neck up and had the greater momentum but as Scudamore began asking serious questions of his mount Pearlyman began to close, inch by inch. The stands were in uproar as the pair were vociferously urged home by their partisans.

Very Promising's half-a-length margin became a neck, then a head. Finally, as the line approached, it was Pearlyman's nose which inched ahead and at the post he was half a length up on the gallant Very Promising, with Desert Orchid, who had wandered off a true line, three lengths back.

The next season Edwards's new stable jockey Tom Morgan took over on Pearlyman, able to provide a continuity the champion jockey could not. Very Promising, who had twice beaten Pearlyman since the previous Queen Mother but only when in receipt of weight, lined up against him once more, as did Desert Orchid.

Interesting new opponents included Josh Gifford's Midnight Count and Arthur Moore's Weather the Storm. Again Pearlyman was favourite, again Desert Orchid made the early running and again his jockey put Pearlyman to sleep at the back of the field. Running downhill to the last it seemed to be an open race with Panto Prince challenging Desert Orchid and Weather the Storm and Long Engagement close up. But Tom Morgan and Richard Dunwoody on Very Promising had been awaiting their moment. This time Morgan took the cruising Pearlyman past the leaders entering the straight and jumped the last two lengths clear of Desert Orchid.

Very Promising, hard-driven by Dunwoody, kept up his effort but this time there was no doubt. Pearlyman drew away as a champion should and Desert Orchid, who was to go on to win that season's Whitbread Gold Cup and the next year's Cheltenham Gold Cup, re-passed Very Promising for second.

If he had been disappointed by Desert Orchid's efforts at two-mile chasing, trainer David Elsworth had the perfect substitute ready for his flamboyant grey. He won the next two Queen Mothers with Barnbrook Again. When Barnbrook Again had won the Champion Chase for the first time in 1989 Waterloo Boy had signalled that he could be a force to be reckoned with in future by winning that year's Arkle Chase contested by the younger steeplechasers. Their clash in the 1990 Champion Chase was therefore eagerly awaited. Both had vociferous fan clubs and committed punters urging them on. Scorching down the hill, the pair of them saw off Sabin du Loir and hurtled into the final fence with Waterloo Boy, ridden by Richard Dunwoody, perhaps a neck ahead at that point. All up the run-in, with both jockeys demanding everything of their mounts and then some, there was never more than half a length between the pair as the shouting rose to a crescendo.

Jockeys recall that the pale-faced Hywel Davies, who was riding Barnbrook Again for David Elsworth, used to say that he hated

Cheltenham. That may have been because he, like so many, had a long wait for a Festival winner. But the day before he had broken his duck on Katabatic and he was not going to give an inch to the relentless, determined Dunwoody. Stride for stride they battled all up the hill, with Barnbrook Again hanging to his right. At the line it was Barnbrook Again again by half a length. There was a stewards' inquiry, at which Dunwoody argued his mount had been taken off a true line. But he later conceded in his autobiography *Obsessed* that the best horse had won, adding of his Welsh rival: 'As for Hywel, whatever chance you had of outriding him in a finish, you had none of out-talking him in the stewards' room.'

Both received whip bans for their efforts but few who saw the race will forget it. Typically, when I remarked to Richard what a great race that had been, his comment many years later was still, 'I can't say it was for me.' For jockeys of his determination good second places are never good enough.

Dunwoody has been the model for so many who have come since. In turn, his idol had been long-time champion Peter Scudamore. 'It was Scu who stood out for me. He was my role model. Watching him operate in the weighing room at Cheltenham, the weighing room at Worcester. You were trying to pick things up from him all the time. Years of matching his intensity made me mentally hard.'

The year after Barnbrook Again and Waterloo Boy it was the turn of veteran jockey Simon McNeill. He gained his first Festival win on Andy Turnell's Katabatic and in 1992 Nicky Henderson won the Queen Mother for the first time with Remittance Man, one of five riding successes at that Festival for the stylish Jamie Osborne.

Remittance Man still has a soft spot in Nicky Henderson's heart. The great Cheltenham trainer says: 'He was a favourite and he was a freak – a complete freak. I bought him at the Derby sales in Ireland and got him back and he was mad, a box-walker. If I'd had any sense I would have sent him home but I rather liked the horse and kept him. He won his bumper at Cheltenham first time out and we put him away. It took two years and I couldn't win a hurdle race with him, at two miles or three miles, any distance you like, although as it turned out he got beaten by some pretty good horses. He was a terrible worrier, he used to go round and round his box, so we put a sheep in with him. We had another yard at Bourne House which I was renting off Barry Hills. We put him in the old coaching stalls with his sheep and tied him up with a ball and chain through the wall so that he couldn't walk. First was 'Alan Lamb' and then we had 'Ridley Lamb' and 'Nobby Lamb' – the sheep came from Dad's flock. But Nobby went home for the summer and joined his mates and another sheep was sent next year. Remittance Man flung it. He picked it up and chucked it out of the door. We put it back in. There was a lot of fur flying and then out it came again. I thought, "we can't do this to the poor sheep" so I had to go back to Dad's flock and look for the right sheep. "Where is he?" "He's one of those four hundred."

'Eventually we sent in a horse and 399 of the sheep went one way and one came out and that was Nobby. From then on we used to put a blue blob on his backside – the sheep – when he went home for his summer holidays! There's a Philip Blacker bronze of Remittance Man, complete with his sheep.

'When we finally switched him to fences he was narrow, short and wiry. He didn't show a lot at home [on the training grounds] but he was the most spectacular jumper you ever saw. There's a picture of him jumping the last in the Arkle, I think it was, with Richard Dunwoody on him which is the most spectacular picture. It would be amazing enough if it had been the first fence, but to jump the last like he did was ridiculous. He went around for three years doing that sort of thing.'

The 1992 contest including Remittance Man, who had won the Arkle Chase at the Festival the year before, was another absolute thriller between the pick of the country's two-milers. Waterloo Boy jumped into the lead three out and he and Remittance Man, who had jumped superbly, stealing lengths in the air from his rivals, scorched over the last together. Up the hill Remittance

Man's pace saw off the challenge of Waterloo Boy, and then had to hold off too the fast-finishing Katabatic.

On that occasion Jamie Osborne, who rode five winners at the meeting, was on Remittance Man, and Richard Dunwoody, his regular partner, was again on Waterloo Boy. Waterloo Boy himself was one of the best two-mile chasers for years, but though he had won an Arkle Chase at the 1989 Festival he never won a Champion Chase, instead finishing runner-up twice, and third on that occasion. Remittance Man never lost a Cheltenham race which he completed.

There was just as hot a contest, another of those races to remember, in 1994. The top-flight contestants included the winners of the race for the three previous years – Katabatic, Remittance Man and Deep Sensation – plus the 1993 Arkle winner Travado and the tough Viking Flagship. It was anyone's race until three out when a huge groan from the stands marked the fall of Remittance Man, the only time he ever did capsize. From that point Viking Flagship, Travado and Deep Sensation virtually matched strides. Locked together up the hill, the three fought out a magnificent finish with the 4-1 Viking Flagship, trained by David Nicholson, just nosing ahead under Adrian Maguire. His rider said that turning for home Viking Flagship had appeared to be the first one beaten but he just kept fighting on.

Viking Flagship, owned by Graham Roach and trained by David Nicholson, who found he needed more work than virtually any other horse he had ever handled, came back to defend his crown in 1995. This time he was ridden by Charlie Swan in the absence of Maguire, who had just lost his mother, and he won again from Deep Sensation, this time by a comfortable margin. Swan was on board once more when 'the Flagship' finished second to Klairon Davis in the 1996 Queen Mother. When the horse had to be put down after breaking a leg at only thirteen, Swan said he was one of the most courageous he ever rode.

Another crack two-miler with whom the Flagship battled,

particularly in an epic three-way contest with Deep Sensation at Aintree in 1995, was Martha's Son. Viking Flagship contested his fourth Queen Mother when Martha's Son won the race for Tim Forster in 1997 but was retired soon after that, the winner in all of twenty-four races.

Through these exciting years for the Champion Chase there was, however, a small cloud looming. The participants in the Champion Hurdle were beginning to stir worries in National Hunt circles. Those who had always seen jump racing as a sport were becoming worried that the more business-minded tycoons who dominated Flat racing might be planning to muscle in.

Chapter 21

The Threat from the Flat

'The winner who came back from the dead.' (Tabloid headline about Champion Hurdle winner Beech Road)

It was to be another decade after See You Then before we saw another multiple winner of the Champion Hurdle in the shape of the great Istabraq. Once again it was the story of a great hurdler trained by an O'Brien, this time young Aidan O'Brien, who then turned his back on jumping and went on to stellar success on the Flat. But there was no shortage of excitement in the intervening years and for a year or two it appeared to be a case of jump trainer Toby Balding against the Newmarket Flat racing establishment.

Two months before the 1989 Champion Hurdle, everyone had feared the worst for Beech Road, a gelding trained by Balding. He had taken a crashing fall at the last fence in a Cheltenham novice chase on 2 January and, ominously, the green screens had been erected around his seemingly inert body. But after ten minutes the horse got to his feet. He then recovered sufficiently for his trainer to be advising all and sundry to back him each way for the 1989 Champion Hurdle, in which he faced the previous year's winner Celtic Shot, ridden again by Peter Scudamore, and Celtic Chief, who had finished third in 1988. Up against them too was the grey Kribensis from the distinguished Flat yard of Michael Stoute.

The sentimental money was on the second favourite Celtic Chief, the final runner in the race for the retiring Mercy Rimell, but he did not quite deliver the storybook ending. At a Festival bedevilled by snow, sleet and grimly heavy going, Beech Road stayed on best to prove a clear winner under Richard Guest at 50-1 with Celtic Chief second and Celtic Shot third. Beech Road was held up waiting at the back of the field. This is a tactic often employed with horses who may have trouble lasting the distance or who are inclined to down tools once they have hit the front, reckoning that they have done their job at that point. He came with a storming run at the end under his talented jockey Richard Guest. Guest, who actually 'took a tug' at the top of the hill on Beech Road (that is, he deliberately pulled back his mount to stop him making an effort too soon) was famous for his use of such tactics. But those riding 'waiting races' often find their motives misinterpreted and their integrity impugned. On more than one occasion Guest was unfairly accused of not trying. His response, when called in once by the Perth stewards on such a suspicion, was to throw his licence through the door and tell them what they could do with it. Restricting a jockey's style and tactics, argued Guest, was like trying to tell an artist which brush he must paint with. He rather proved his point by winning the Grand National on Red Marauder. As for Beech Road, the tabloids called him 'The winner who came back from the dead.'

The next year, 1990, it looked as though the blue-bloods from the Flat were taking over National Hunt racing. The Champion Hurdle was now worth more than £50,000 to the winner and not only was Kribensis back again from Newmarket but he was joined in the field by the Cesarewitch winner Nomadic Way, trained for Robert Sangster by another Flat maestro Barry Hills. Those two dominated events, with Scudamore on Nomadic Way driving clear round the last bend. On the better ground Kribensis found his speed and the resolution he had appeared to lack the previous year, and Richard Dunwoody drove him past the Sangster horse to victory in a new record time. After the race, noting Sheikh Mohammed's ownership of Kribensis, Cheltenham executives had an impromptu huddle to discuss whether he might be tempted into sponsorship of some jump racing. But so buoyant was the sponsorship market that when they looked they could not find a slot in the programme which they could have offered to entice funds from Dubai.

In 1991 Toby Balding struck back for the traditionalists with Morley Street, ridden by Jimmy Frost, coming home a length and a half clear of Nomadic Way, who was to lower his sights at the next Festival and win the Stayers' Hurdle. Then in 1992 it was Newmarket to the fore again as James Fanshawe, the former assistant to Michael Stoute who had worked previously in jumping yards and done much to prepare Kribensis, now sent out the winner Royal Gait as a trainer in his own right. Like Kribensis, Royal Gait was owned by Sheikh Mohammed. Royal Gait, once disqualified after winning the Ascot Gold Cup, had to survive a stewards' inquiry before keeping the race, having been involved in scrimmages after six tired horses had jumped the last with a chance.

As we awaited the arrival of the next hurdling giant, there were two 1990s successes in the race for a man who was to rise to third place in the all-time list for Festival races won, and whose career is discussed elsewhere, the Somerset training revolutionary Martin Pipe. In 1993 he took the race with Granville Again, ridden by Peter Scudamore, and in 1997 Peter Deal's six-year-old Make A Stand led all the way to score in a new record time under Tony 'A.P.' McCoy. In a tribute to Martin Pipe's training methods, Make A Stand's handicap rating had improved about three stone in the course of the season as he rattled up nine victories.

Oh So Risky, second to Royal Gait, filled the same position in 1994 when the race was won by the mare Flakey Dove for Richard Price who trained at Eaton Hall, near Leominster. It was no fluke; Richard's uncle Gordon had won sixteen races with Red Dove and the Prices knew their horses. But it was welcome confirmation that there was still room for the small battalions in the Cheltenham Hall of Fame. At 6.15 on the morning of the Champion Hurdle Richard Price had been lambing ewes.

The small men still came from over the water too. For two years, in 1995 and 1996, a touch of class was provided by Alderbrook, who ran first and second in the big race. But far more was written and said at the time about a horse who managed only one third place in the Champion Hurdles of those two years, Ireland's darling Danoli.

Danoli, owned by local bone-setter Danny O'Neill and his wife Olive, the name a combination of Danny's and their daughter Olivia's christian names, was trained by small farmer Tom Foley who landed an almighty Irish gamble with the gelding in the 1994 Sun Alliance Novices Hurdle and then beat the hurdling stars of the day in the Martell Hurdle at Aintree. Danoli had won all of his three bumpers (races on the Flat for National Hunt horses) in the 1992–3 season and three of his five hurdles before that big race double so he came to the 1995 Champion Hurdle as 4-1 joint favourite with Large Action. Nobody knew quite what to make of Kim Bailey's entrant Alderbrook, an entire horse by the great stayer Ardross who had won Group 2 and Group 3 races on the Flat. He would certainly have been favourite had there been no obstacles, and it was Alderbrook who came out the best, accelerating smoothly under Norman Williamson after the last to cruise clear of Large Action with Danoli, who hit the final obstacle and bruised his knee, only in third.

After that impressive performance Alderbrook was an odds-on favourite to triumph the next year too. With Norman Williamson injured, trainer Kim Bailey booked the talented but wayward Graham Bradley to ride but then sacked him after he failed to turn up in time for a training gallop. Bradley, who had over-indulged the night before at fellow jockey Dean Gallagher's birthday party, overslept when a power cut disabled his alarm call but the trainer was unimpressed with the explanation. Richard Dunwoody got the plum ride instead.

As for Danoli, the extraordinary thing was that he was able to participate at all in the 1996 race. After the previous year's Champion he went on to Liverpool and won the Aintree Hurdle again. But he finished that race, showing the utmost courage, with a broken fetlock joint. It was touch and go whether he would race again, and vets had to insert three screws into his leg. Amazingly, nine months later he was racing again, and after Tom Foley had put him through an intensive rehabilitation programme he sent the whole of Ireland 'Danoli-crazy' by winning his Cheltenham prep race.

In the event Collier Bay took control of the 1996 race rounding the home turn and went on to win by two and a half lengths from Alderbrook, whose trainer and owner felt he had been left too much to do. Jockey Richard Dunwoody disagreed. The winner's jockey Graham Bradley, ever the comedian, appeared to be pointing at the non-existent watch on his wrist as he rode triumphantly back into the winner's enclosure. The Yorkshire-born jockey claims it was a Leeds United short-arm salute, but few in racing would have known what that was. Danoli ran a respectable race to finish fourth but his career was far from over.

The horse who ran second to Make A Stand in 1997 was the 33-1 outsider Theatreworld. He proved to be an admirably consistent animal, occupying the same place for the next two years. But he had no serious chance of improving on that position because from 1998 onwards he was competing against the phenomenon known as Istabraq, who raced in the green and gold hoops of J.P. McManus (originally the colours of East Limerick's South Liberties Gaelic Athletic Association of which he was once chairman). Another whom his rivals found it hard to beat was the West Country trainer Martin Pipe. The statesmen who matter in history, it is said, are those who manage to 'change the political weather' and affect the thinking of parties other than their own. In the 1980s and 1990s, Martin Pipe forced the whole training profession to rethink its processes and either follow him or go under.

Chapter 22

A Phenomenon Called Martin Pipe

'The first time I had fifty winners they were all hurdlers.
I couldn't afford to buy a chaser.' (Martin Pipe)

When he took out his first training licence in 1977, Martin Pipe was not an overnight sensation. He had never worked in anybody else's yard and he learned his business by trial and error, starting with the cheapest of horses at the lowliest tracks. For ten years he averaged no more than a dozen winners a year. But the results by the end of his 29-year career were phenomenal. He trained the winners of 4,182 races, 3,926 of those over jumps. He was champion National Hunt trainer fifteen times and appointment as his stable jockey virtually guaranteed the chosen rider a jockey's championship too. He took Peter Scudamore, Richard Dunwoody and, many times, Tony McCoy to the title. He rewrote the record books: the fastest 100 winners in a season; the fastest 200 winners; the most prize-money won; the most winners trained in a lifetime – after just 25 years. His record total of 243 winners in the 1999/2000 season will probably never be beaten, and he won the Grand National with Minnehoma.

Although he never trained the winner of the Gold Cup, Martin Pipe twice trained the winner of the Champion Hurdle. He saddled four winners at the Festival in both 1997 and 1998, the highest by any trainer for fifty years, and that was before it became a four-day event. Nicky Henderson is the only man living who has trained more Cheltenham Festival winners than Martin Pipe's thirty-four. It is no exaggeration to say that Pipe revolutionised jump racing and in the process he finally turned it from a sport into a business.

Until Pipe came along training had been a sometimes leisurely affair for many, with horses being brought to the racecourse two or three times well short of full race fitness. With his interval training up steep slopes and a ruthless eye for the opportunities offered by race conditions, Pipe sent his horses to contest the right races hard and leathery fit. Peter Scudamore would make the running on them as often as not and leave fields strung out behind him.

Punters owe Pipe a vote of gratitude because, since his day, most horses from other yards too have been sent to the races ready to run. French bloodstock agents too should bless him – Pipe was one of the first to spot the possibilities of importing early-maturing and early-schooled young horses from France who could exploit the significant pull four- and five-year-old novice chasers enjoyed in the weights. He was the first to have his own laboratory on site to analyse blood samples rapidly and monitor the health of his horses. Until he began no trainer had been quite so meticulously organised or so ruthlessly efficient in his planning.

Martin Pipe first registered on the Festival scene with Baron Blakeney, who took the Triumph Hurdle at 66-1 in 1981. In fact it was his first winner at the course, let alone the Festival. With typical self-deprecation he says: 'We really fancied it. If it had been trained by a proper trainer like Fred Winter it would have been about 14-1. It had won its last couple of races and had reasonable form. Baron Blakeney was about sixth or seventh on ratings but because it was trained by an idiot, an unknown, it was such a big price. We told everybody to back it. All the owners' kids had £10 each way on it and all won nearly £1,000.

'Paul Leach rode it, beating a horse of David Nicholson's ridden by Peter Scudamore. We always had a picture of Baron Blakeney

beating Broadsword in the hall and so when he came to work here
Scu had to walk past it every day as soon as he came in the house.
He didn't appreciate it.'

Self-taught he may be, but the lessons were still painful. 'We
used to buy only cheap horses, the cheapest we could buy. The first
horse we bought was £300. I got it home from Ascot sales and
didn't realise until then it only had three legs. It had a bowed
tendon. That was how much I knew. From that came all my
involvement in veterinary matters, I loved it so much. We had to
get the vets to treat the tendon and give the horse a year off. Once
you start paying through your pocket it makes you learn so much
quicker. The horse was called Bobo's Boy and we got it to win a
point-to-point about eighteen months later. It was a very valuable
lesson.

'I wanted to win sellers. I managed to with cheap horses. I
thought that if I could win sellers, since there's one every day,
I could get fifty winners a year, wouldn't that be fun? I wanted to
start at the bottom. The first time I had fifty winners they were all
hurdlers. I couldn't afford to buy a chaser.'

Working in his father's bookmaking business wasn't such a bad
preparation for training, says Martin. Indeed it was a very good
one, teaching him method and a respect for figures and for information. He learned to handle paperwork and organise systems.

'Dad had forty or fifty betting shops in the West Country. All
gave us what we called daily returns. All the facts, coming through
the post every day. Things were much slower in those days. But we
knew – James Street, Taunton: 300 bets, £100 there in cash . . . We
knew how much money there was everywhere, though of course
we had to do spot checks.

'You were handling money and you couldn't make mistakes. If
you paid over too much money you didn't get a second chance,
you didn't get the money back, it was lost. So you have to try and
be spot on with your figures. If you work out your bets wrong
you've lost your money, it teaches you to pay attention to detail.

'So we now have a sheet with all the horses on, all the work they do. All our jockeys have to give written reports on their rides. We have a written report every day on every horse in the stables, so we know. The head lad does one, all the assistants do. So David [Martin's popular son and successor] can look on the sheets and see this one has a cut on his knee, it's been treated with ointment, it's OK or he can't run for four days . . .

'It's just having all the facts that are available. Facts and figures, that's what life's all about. You must have your finger on the pulse and know everything. All their temperatures are taken every day. By 7.30 every morning David knows the temperature of the horse, whether he's eaten up, everything, and he says, 'Ah that one will have to have an easy day', or whatever.'

His father's experience as an owner also explains the Pipe approach. 'Dad had horses in training with other people and he used to have, say, £100 on when they said the horse was fancied. The horse would get beat and they'd come back and the trainer would say, "Ah, I thought he'd get beat, he didn't eat up last night." There would be all these excuses after the race: "They didn't go fast enough for him." So why didn't we make the running? "Ah, you can't do that." Or, "He jumped badly." All the excuses. They're still about today probably. When I started training I started to try and iron out these excuses.

'"The pace wasn't fast enough." Why didn't we make the pace, then? Well, you can only do that if you jump well. So you've got to teach your horse to jump well. When I first started training my horse would jump one hurdle. "That's it. He's good. He's jumped it well, take him to the races." But of course racing's different and they didn't jump so you had to do it properly. You have to school them loads and loads of times.'

He was worried at first that too much work would crock his horses and they would be unable to race. 'But that's a risk you've got to take. You've got to have practice at what you're doing. Jumping is all about jumping. If you don't jump you don't win.

That's why Make A Stand was a Champion Hurdler. I remember seeing it loads and loads of times: Group horses coming out to run over hurdles and they couldn't jump, and got beaten.'

His second Festival winner at Cheltenham, a full eight years after the first, and in the Supreme Novices Hurdle, was an obvious example of Pipe practising what he preached: 'Sondrio went to be a stallion in America and was gelded just before he came to me. He hadn't raced for some considerable time and he was a gross horse, he was very fat. He was a lovely horse, a giant of a horse. He had won nearly $450,000 in America. We ran him at Hereford. I remember apologising to the owner and saying, "He looks in foal [he was of course a gelding]. I've given him as much as I can but he's a big gross horse who needs bags of work." Of course he won, didn't he, and was aimed at the Festival. Two weeks before that he ran at Ascot. He was a certainty. He couldn't possibly get beat. Scu rode him, and he *was* beaten. He never jumped a hurdle and did get beat. Scu didn't want to ride him at Cheltenham, he'd been offered another ride in the race and so Jonathan Lower, who was our second jockey at the time, came in and we schooled him every day, two or three times a day trying to get him to jump. He was a big strong horse and he probably didn't respect the hurdles and could go straight through them but you can't do that in championship races. So Jonathan was schooling him morning noon and night and he rode him.

'Scu rode this other horse and fell early on and he was lying on the ground listening to the commentary. Jonathan made all, and as he was going past the post and it was announced that Sondrio was the winner Scu was beating his whip on the ground in frustration. The ambulanceman ran across and said, "You're obviously in great pain." And he was saying, "Go away, go away, leave me alone."'

For a man with thirty-four Festival winners there is a host of memories. Of Olympian winning the Imperial at Sandown and going on to win the Coral Cup and picking up a hefty bonus. Of

Cyborgo winning the World Hurdle (then the Stayers' hurdle) on his first run of the season. Of Omerta, ridden by a certain Mr A. Maguire, winning the Fulke Walwyn/Kim Muir Chase. Of Lady Clarke, Stanley Clarke's wife, fainting after Rolling Ball won the RSA Chase . . . 'Unsinkable Boxer was one. We dreamt all season of him winning at Cheltenham and it came off and he won very easily. I told A.P.: "It doesn't matter how you ride him, he can't get beat." '

His first Champion Hurdle winner was Granville Again in 1993. 'He was very laid back. I owed that one to Michael Dickinson. He had a lot of problems and Michael Dickinson came across and helped me with them. I am very friendly still with Michael. He gave me advice on what to do with him and how to train him and that has helped me train many more winners.' It is appropriate that the two should be friends. Both are totally imbued with the work ethic and with a voracious thirst for knowledge. If he isn't watching the horse-racing monitor screens Martin Pipe will have his head in some obscure veterinary volume.

The second Champion Hurdle winner was Make A Stand, whom he plucked from Henry Candy in a seller at Leicester. '[Well-known owner] Peter Deal lost him in the claimer and gave me a telling-off the next day. I said, "Sorry about that – you can have him back for the same price, no problem, as long as you keep him with me." There were a couple of others in with him, including John Inverdale, but he never came back in.

'I said it would run in Mr Deal's colours. We sent out a letter to all our owners offering a half share for £4,000, and my wife told me off, saying no one else would buy the other half. Lo and behold we couldn't sell it and we retained the half share. I am very glad we did because over the next year the horse won £250,000.

'Make A Stand was a real athlete. It took him a while to get going, he wasn't a natural early on, but once he had the hang of it he could really jump. A.P. got on very well with him but loads of jockeys won on him. Jockeys who got on him just had to understand the pace, to allow him to dictate and just conserve his energy. Nigel Twiston-Davies or somebody said, "Don't let that Pipe horse go out too far in front", but the other jockeys just couldn't stay with him. He was really exuberant, he really enjoyed it. He really enjoyed his racing. In the Champion Hurdle we were really anxious but it was great that he went on and kept going up the hill.'

After suffering a number of health problems, Martin Pipe handed over to his son David in 2005, but an ankle operation has very much improved his mobility (a man without 'side', he used to keep a child's bicycle at Cheltenham to help him get around). He is still very much in evidence at Pond House, and full of relish at what they do. 'It's just such a buzz all the year round trying to get them going. As time went on I had two or three you could dream of winning at the Festival. You've got to keep them sound and healthy and well, and get them there, run them in the right races, make sure that the ground's OK wherever you run them, and get them to the pinnacle of their fitness to compete, whether it's the Triumph Hurdle or the Gold Cup or whatever race it is. To get them to win is a great dream and a great training performance by all the trainers.'

He loves to see the young horses being taught their job. 'There's nothing better than watching youngsters, three-year-olds, going round in a loose school. They're only playing, enjoying themselves, but you see them jumping, you see them having to think for themselves – "There's a jump coming up here, I've got to shorten or to lengthen" – and they learn. Conditional jockeys would see them in the loose school and think, "I want to ride this one, this one is super, he just goes there and pings it" – all you've got to do is to point him at the jump and he'll jump it, so the horse is full of confidence.'

And if he likes to see horses being taught to think for themselves, the same goes for jockeys at Pond House. It is, says Martin Pipe, a much more professional era: 'Everything is much more professional now in every field, in every walk of life. With television, with videos, we can now see all the replays and see what went wrong. A.P. didn't like it at first when we had all the slow motion replays although he does it all the time. You can see the mistakes you make. I made loads of mistakes in entering horses in the wrong races. You have to learn by your mistakes. We have tutors now and mechanical horses. We've always had one of those. We don't allow our jockeys or the lads to carry whips on the gallops so they can go and practice on the mechanical horses and learn how to use their whips there and be instructed how to use it correctly, how to change their whip hands.'

One puzzle is that after his success over jumps Martin Pipe wasn't tempted, like Vincent O'Brien, another profession reformer, or his friend Michael Dickinson, to switch to the Flat. He did train Royal Ascot winners, especially in the Ascot Stakes for stayers which he won six times. He says that he never refused a horse – 'I would have loved it if somebody sent me fifty two-year-olds' – but he simply wasn't offered enough Flat horses. And in the end, 'I was born in the West Country. I love jumping and that was it.'

His quest for more knowledge is still there. He still says he would like to go along and see how another yard does it. But there is pride too in what they have done at Pond House: 'The system we've evolved seems to work for us', and pride too in the success of a son who has already trained his first Grand National winner and who has also proved himself a chip off the old block.

'In 1998 the Cheltenham team came down and said: "Is there anything you want to discuss about races and conditions?" and David said, "You ought to open the Cathcart Chase to five-year-olds." [It used to be for six-year-olds plus.] "Yes, we could do that," they said. In Cyfor Malta we had the horse and he was the first five-year-old to win the Cathcart. As we were coming in, one of the executive said, "I had my tenner on. I thought you Pipes would win this race!"'

Martin Pipe started as a little guy and ended as the most

successful jumping trainer ever. Cheltenham loves winners, but it has a special place in its heart for little guys who make it to the big time.

Chapter 23

A 100-1 Shot and a Gold Cup for France

'I'd have won a lot of money if The Fellow had won his first Gold Cup. I'd have won quite a lot of money if he'd won at his second attempt, but by the third I was virtually a bystander, just a commentator.' (Sir Peter O'Sullevan on his friend Francois Doumen's Gold Cup success)

The story of the 1990 Gold Cup and of its 100-1 winner, the longest-priced in the history of the race, is one of the best-loved tales in Cheltenham history. It is not just a potent reminder that the little guys can always dream of winning the big prizes, it was confirmation that they sometimes do. Sirrell Griffiths, who owned and trained Norton's Coin on his farm at Nantgaredig near Carmarthen, had milked seventy cows at four o'clock in the morning before setting off to the races in a cattle truck because he didn't own a horsebox.

Norton's Coin ran in the Gold Cup as the result of an accident. Griffiths had really been aiming the horse at either the Cathcart Challenge Cup or the Mildmay of Flete Handicap but he was ineligible for the first and had missed the entry date for the second. Even so he should still not have been at the extravagant price he was. It happened partly because nobody knew much about the horse or his trainer and partly because the public were besotted with Desert Orchid, the brave, bold-jumping grey who had won the previous year's Gold Cup (see chapter 20). They backed him down to odds-on favourite to become the first since L'Escargot in 1971 to retain his crown because they loved his flamboyant style. They forgot that he had won only once on six visits to Cheltenham and was now possibly past his peak at eleven years old.

As for Norton's Coin, admittedly two of his previous runs had been poor, but one race, over two miles at Ascot, was patently too short for him and in the other he had been up against Desert Orchid in the King George VI Chase at Kempton, a sharp, level, right-handed track which, unlike Cheltenham, played to 'Dessie's' strengths. Norton's Coin was well-bred and had won four races to the value of £23,000. He had run decently at Cheltenham in January to finish second over two and a half miles. He had been second in the Cathcart at the previous Festival and he had an effective pilot in the shape of Graham McCourt.

In the race Kevin Mooney set a fast pace on Fulke Walwyn's Ten of Spades. Down the hill, as they approached the second last, he was passed by Jenny Pitman's Toby Tobias, ridden by Jenny's son Mark, and by Desert Orchid, ridden by Richard Dunwoody. Just coming into the action behind them was Norton's Coin. Suddenly there were sharp intakes of breath amid the 57,000-strong capacity crowd. Their grey hero was patently running out of steam; Dessie was not going to win. Toby Tobias led over the last two fences but suddenly, as late as he dared leave it, there was Graham McCourt challenging on the 100-1 shot just fifty yards from the post. The force was with him and Norton's Coin swept past Toby Tobias to win by three quarters of a length, with the packed stands almost silent with shock. Perhaps the fact that Toby Tobias had kicked him before the start added to Norton's Coin's determination to prove a point. On good to firm going he broke Dawn Run's course record time by four seconds.

Having torn up their betting tickets the crowds then applauded Norton's Coin and his trainer and jockey into the crucible of the winner's enclosure, recognising the romance of the achievement by a permit-holder with just two other horses, most of whose neighbours had had a ride on the nine-year-old. One of the first to congratulate them was Dessie's trainer David Elsworth. The first prize of £67,000 was enough to be going on with but Sirrell Griffiths revealed in the aftermath: 'A local bookie knocked on my door last night and asked if I wanted to have a bet of £25,000 to £200 each way, but I refused.' When the trainer and his wife Joyce drove home from Cheltenham they wondered if anybody would be there. In fact the whole village turned out. The local pub, The Railway, had a banner out saying, 'Welcome back Norton's'. The mini-bus from the pub had returned from Cheltenham bearing punters with £17,000 between them, and the Griffiths had to send out for ten bottles of whisky to lubricate the celebrations.

The celebrations of a sporting success went well beyond the boundaries of Nantgaredig, however. Earlier in the week the success of Sheikh Mohammed's classy ex-Flat racer Kribensis in the Champion Hurdle had seen a doleful wagging of heads among many National Hunt enthusiasts. They feared that the arrival of horses like Kribensis and Robert Sangster's Nomadic Way, handled by top Flat trainers like Michael Stoute and Barry Hills, was going to lead to an influx of big money and a transformation of their passion too from a sport to a business. The success of Norton's Coin and of a small-scale permit holder like Sirrell Griffiths was for many a reassertion too of the values and instincts of National Hunt racing with its roots so firmly embedded in farming and the countryside. And while we have over the decades since seen rather more ex-Flat horses coming in to the jumping game it has not been taken over, as so many feared, by a different coterie of more money-minded people. If nothing else, the fact that so many jumping horses are geldings and that there is nothing like the same multi-million dollar breeding industry with stallions shuttled between the northern and southern hemispheres every six months, has seen to that.

After the defeat of her Toby Tobias by Norton's Coin, it did not take Jenny Pitman long to get back into the Gold Cup winners' enclosure with Garrison Savannah, and she did so in a year in which the Gold Cup field contained real strength in depth. The fourteen horses lining up in 1991 included five past, present or future winners of the big race, plus a former winner of the Champion Hurdle and a future winner of the Grand National. Desert Orchid was trying yet again at the age of twelve on the track he had never favoured but the favourite was the 1988 Champion Hurdle winner Celtic Shot, trained by former Fred Winter assistant Charlie Brooks. There was money too for Welsh National winner Cool Ground and for two entrants trained in the north by Gordon Richards. From France there was The Fellow, trained by the suave Francois Doumen, while Jenny Pitman's near neighbour in Lambourn, Nick Gaselee, had sent the giant Party Politics. On the second circuit Desert Orchid asserted in the lead and Celtic Shot began to take more interest in proceedings while Richards's Carrick Hill Lad moved up along with The Fellow, ridden by the Polish-born Adam Kondrat, a man with little Cheltenham experience. At the third last Desert Orchid had had enough, so too had Celtic Shot, and Carrick Hill Lad broke down. Garrison Savannah, who had had only one run that season thanks to a shoulder injury, led over the last two but then began to tire. Was Mark Pitman going to be caught like his father Richard had been on Pendil and he himself had been on Toby Tobias the year before? The two were locked in combat through the final hundred yards, and at the post Garrison Savannah was given the verdict by a short head.

It was a sweet success for Mark Pitman, though one which soured within hours as he broke his pelvis in the final race of the day. That left him with a struggle to get fit in time for the Grand National in which Garrison Savannah – before he ran at Cheltenham – had been allotted only 11st 1lb. With the iron determination that jump jockeys so often demonstrate in recovering from their injuries – and preventing their weighing-room friends from inheriting their rides – Mark made it back into the saddle in time and rode a perfect race on the horse known affectionately in the Weathercock House yard as 'Gary'. They led over the last, raising hopes that this could be the first horse since Golden Miller to win a Gold Cup and the National in the same year. But, alas, it had rained that morning and the ground was a little softer than Gary would have liked. He jumped the last better than his pursuers, Seagram and Auntie Dot, and went six lengths up but then history began to repeat itself. Just as Mark's father Richard had heard the hoof-beats of Red Rum behind his tiring mount Crisp so Mark was pursued to the Elbow by Seagram and passed in the last hundred yards. Once again the Pitman family had to be content with a gallant second.

The Gold Cup of 1992, though a smaller one with only eight horses, was just as talent-filled and just as exciting as the year before. Toby Tobias was back for Jenny Pitman, so was The Fellow, the hope of France, who had won the King George in record time. But the new star on the block was Carvill's Hill, a classical stamp of chaser previously trained by Jim Dreaper and now handled by the Somerset phenomenon Martin Pipe. Carvill's Hill, the even-money favourite, had been winning his races by dominating from the front. Peter Scudamore set off to do the same again, but from the start he was dogged at every stride by Golden Freeze, a 150-1 outsider from the Pitman yard and, possibly unsettled by having such close attention, he thumped the first fence. Further errors followed as Golden Freeze continued to fight him for the lead, and by the time they were out on the second circuit it looked unlikely that Carvill's Hill would figure in the finish. The three who were in contention racing down the hill were The Fellow, Docklands Express (ridden by Mark Perrett) and Cool Ground, trained by Toby Balding and ridden by the latest discovery of that remarkable jockey talent-spotter, Adrian Maguire. The Fellow just led over the last but was swiftly passed by Docklands Express, who then rapidly ran out of juice and began to wander. That let The Fellow back into the race and he was challenged by Cool Ground, who got up to win by a short head. His adversaries would have sympathised with The Fellow's jockey Adam Kondrat; The Fellow was owned by the Marquesa de Moratalla, who does not allow the whip to be used on her horses. Docklands Express was third, and Carvill's Hill, who turned out to have chest and tendon injuries, was last of the five finishers.

Cool Ground was the only Gold Cup winner ridden by Adrian Maguire, one of the best jockeys never to be champion and a rider who seemed to be jinxed where Cheltenham was concerned. Twice in his prime he missed the Festival through injury, once because his mother had died in the run-up to the Festival. A compact horseman of great personal charm once he conquered his initial shyness, Maguire thrilled jumping folk with his epic battle with Richard Dunwoody for the jump jockeys' championship in the 1993–94 season. Maguire, who had succeeded Dunwoody as stable jockey to David Nicholson, drove home 194 winners that season and yet still lost the championship by three to his great rival.

Jodami, trained by Peter Beaumont and ridden by Mark Dwyer, took the 1993 Gold Cup for the North. The Fellow had been made the 5-4 favourite but although he beat the previous winners Garrison Savannah and Cool Ground he did not jump as well as usual and could manage only fourth. It is almost unknown for a horse to fail in three attempts at the Gold Cup and to come back and win it on his fourth but that was what The Fellow managed to do in 1994. Red Rower in 1945 and Mandarin in 1962 had managed to win the Gold Cup on their third attempt but only The Dikler had won the big race at the fourth time of asking.

In a year when the Irish were excited by Danoli's victory in the Sun Alliance Novices' Hurdle on the Wednesday, Jodami was back to defend his title in the Gold Cup, faced by Garrison Savannah, Docklands Express and the Cheltenham specialist Bradbury Star. Pitched in against them were the front runner Young Hustler and Martin Pipe's Minnehoma, both of them former winners of the

Sun Alliance Chase. But there again too was The Fellow, twice narrowly defeated and now wearing blinkers as an aid to concentration. Four fences out, a dozen horses still had a chance. By the second last it was down to Young Hustler, Jodami, Bradbury Star and The Fellow. Bradbury Star weakened and then there were three. Young Hustler was only hanging on in there and at the last The Fellow got away from Jodami and kept his margin going up the hill. At last he had done it: France had its first Gold Cup winner, even if on this occasion he had compromised his allegiances by wearing a sprig of shamrock.

No French trainer has ever been more appreciated by British crowds than Francois Doumen, and the applause was generous for him and for the frequently criticised jockey Adam Kondrat. The man who lost out was Sir Peter O'Sullevan, a good friend both of Doumen and the horse's owner, the Marquesa de Moratalla. Says Peter, 'That was one of my greatest joys ultimately to call him the winner when he'd got beaten whiskers twice. Kondrat had been the victim of the kind of unrestrained criticism that was reserved for visiting jockeys.

'He was the best Cheltenham bet I ever had. He didn't win but I did have very long odds, certainly the first time, and when I say long odds I mean 66-1, 50-1, that sort of thing. I'd have won a lot of money if The Fellow had won his first Gold Cup. I'd have won *quite* a lot of money if he'd won at his second attempt but by the third I was virtually a bystander, just a commentator.'

It is an intriguing question, examined later, as to why French trainers in general haven't done better at the Festival given the obvious ability of Francois Doumen and others. Doumen not only won a Gold Cup with The Fellow but took a couple of World Hurdles (the old Stayers' Hurdle) too in 2002 and 2003 with Baracouda. In 2000 he also won the Triumph Hurdle with Snow Drop, ridden by his son Thierry. The basic reason for the paucity of French-trained winners is that the French have mostly sold on their best Festival prospects to British owners and trainers.

The French contribution to the Gold Cup has been a significant one. But it has more often been a case in recent years of French-bred horses being trained in Britain to win the top prizes for English owners in quest of a Gold Cup. It is the enduring appeal of that prize which has helped to make the Cheltenham Festival what it is and Gold Cup memories are the ones which dominate Festival history.

Chapter 24

Three Famous Gold Cups

'I have never sat on a horse that showed such courage. By hook or by crook he was going to win.' (Jockey Simon Sherwood on Desert Orchid)

From the time of 'Himself' onwards, Gold Cups have been about the search for the next Arkle, with Best Mate so far coming closest to achieving the Holy Grail. But racing is about emotions as well as results, about character as well as quality.

We opened this book with one of the most emotional Gold Cup victories of them all, that of Dawn Run in 1986, but there have been many other Gold Cup heroes, many other amazing performances down the years which wrestle for inclusion in any anthology. Every race fan stocks his own Pantheon, but here are three other Gold Cups which will never be forgotten, followed by the story of how one Lambourn trainer plotted and achieved his two victories in the race.

Michael Dickinson's Famous Five in 1983

Trainers occasionally score a 1-2 in a race. Some have even been known to send out the first three in one or two races. But in 1983 Yorkshire-based Michael Dickinson did the unthinkable — he saddled the first five horses home in the most competitive event in the jump-racing calendar.

Dickinson, who nowadays concentrates his efforts on developing racetrack surfaces but who went on from his extraordinary jump-racing career to train Breeders' Cup winners on the Flat in America, was a perfectionist. Listing his hobby as 'work' he had honed his riding skills with Frenchie Nicholson and studied training methods with Vincent O'Brien at Coolmore. When he took over the trainer's licence from his father Tony his super-fit horses soon dominated the jumping scene and he was twice champion trainer in his thirties.

In 1983, having scored a 1-2 in the Gold Cup the previous year with Silver Buck and Bregawn, he supplied five of the eleven-strong field. The bookmakers were giving odds of 33-1 against the cerebral 33-year-old Dickinson training the first three home and 150-1 against him getting all his five home before the others crossed the line. Dickinson himself, a worrier aware that he was becoming a target for everybody, lost a stone between Christmas and the Festival from an already lean frame.

Of the five Dickinson entrants, Bregawn was ridden by Graham Bradley, one of racing's more controversial figures but a marvellously cool and skilful horseman. On Wayward Lad was the future star Jonjo O'Neill. Silver Buck was partnered by Robert Earnshaw, Ashley House by Dermot Browne, a racing figure who was later to lose his way, and aboard Captain John was David Goulding.

The three jockeys from the Dickinson yard (Bradley, Earnshaw and Browne) were taken for a walk around the course with three-day-event champion Ginny Leng as Dickinson's meticulous plans were unfolded. But by the time the big race began the trainer was not at his most hopeful. On the first day Delius, favourite for the Supreme Novices' Hurdle, had come home lame and his two in the Kim Muir Chase, as first and second favourites, fell and finished sixth.

Ideally, said Dickinson, Browne was to make the running on Ashley House and Bregawn was to be held up. But Ashley House failed to make the running and after the sixth, deciding that they were going too slowly, Bradley decided that he would make the pace. At the top of the hill, with their trainer back in the stands allegedly shouting 'Come on my lot', Captain John and Silver Buck both came to apply pressure but Bregawn lengthened again to turn the screw on the others.

In his autobiography, appropriately entitled *The Wayward Lad*, Brad, normally a stylish rider rather than a tough one, declares: 'I had to ask Bregawn for everything and was very hard on him. These days it would certainly be called excessive use of the whip, but there was only one Gold Cup. Bregawn emptied his pockets for me and battled like a tiger up the hill.'

He sensed something coming on his inside but Captain John, all out and swaying like a drunk with tiredness, was five lengths behind. Wayward Lad was another length and a half back in third. At this point people began to think about the record books and look for the other Dickinson runners. Silver Buck, though also very tired having had a setback in training, was fourth and then there was the last of the quintet, Ashley House, toiling twenty-five lengths further back but clearly in fifth place. The first five home in the toughest non-handicap in the jump-racing calendar had all come from a single yard. It was an extraordinary feat by Michael Dickinson, on a par with Frankie Dettori's seven winners in a day on one Ascot card and it is an achievement that we can safely predict will never be equalled. But at least one trainer reckoned it a waste. Former Clerk of the Course Philip Arkwright recalls fellow trainer Toby Balding, perhaps being somewhat tongue-in-cheek, calling Dickinson's achievement a 'disgrace', on the grounds that he could have won four other races with the placed horses!

Bregawn sadly was never the same horse again. Brad reckons he 'blew his mind' with the effort he made that day and never wanted to go through the pain barrier again.

Desert Orchid's Gold Cup in 1989

There can be no serious controversy about including Dessie's triumph. When readers of the *Racing Post* and a panel of experts were asked to vote on the Hundred Greatest Races this one finished top of the list. Not only, the paper pointed out, because it was won by a hugely popular horse but because it was a great contest too.

The conditions on 16 March 1989 were foul. It was a day of heavy rain, sleet and snow. Only after a midday inspection was the ground ruled fit to race. Many worried that the spectacular grey Desert Orchid, who never seemed to like the Cheltenham track anyway, would be pulled out. Trainer David Elsworth was made of sterner stuff. He declared him to run, saying, 'The ground is horrible and conditions are all against him, but he is the best horse.' 'Elzee' even increased his bet as Desert Orchid drifted to 3-1.

Meanwhile as punters looked for a horse to beat Desert Orchid in the conditions the mud-loving Yahoo shortened from 50-1 to 25-1. Says his jockey, Tom Morgan: 'When the rains came we thought we had a small chance and were hoping to get placed.'

Team Dessie went for boldness in the race too, rider Simon 'Sharkey' Sherwood taking him out into the lead, his easy jumping helping to conserve his energy. On the second circuit he was joined by Elsworth's other runner Cavvie's Clown, second the previous year, and Fulke Walwyn's talented Ten Plus, who passed Desert Orchid at the fourteenth of the twenty-two obstacles. At the top of the hill Tom Morgan thought that Ten Plus, ridden by Kevin Mooney, was the one he had to beat. Tragically at three out, Ten Plus fell, fatally injured, and it was there the complexion of the race may have changed. Says Tom Morgan: 'My horse was trying to track Ten Plus, and Sharkey managed to give his fellow a breather there and fill his lungs. On the bottom bend I thought I had him beat, Desert Orchid was drifting right as he was inclined to do and Sherwood came over to me for a bit of company.'

When Tom Morgan drove Yahoo up the inside nearing the

second last he looked uncatchable. But Desert Orchid was ready for battle and set out after him. It is not only in humans that the spirit can triumph over burning lungs and leaden legs, somehow injecting the energy for one more supreme physical effort. Yahoo too was approaching the end of his tolerance.

At the last Desert Orchid had closed a little. Yahoo got in a bit close and landed a little flat footed, though without losing much momentum. Though they had surged clear of the rest, physically both horses and their mud-spattered riders were all but spent, and now it really was mind over matter. Two minds. Somehow Desert Orchid and a jockey who admits he was 'knackered' summoned up what was, in the dire conditions, the equivalent of a burst. Simon Sherwood said afterwards: 'I have never sat on a horse that showed such courage. By hook or by crook he was going to win.'

By contrast, with Desert Orchid coming back left to eyeball him, Tom Morgan felt his mount 'beginning to give up on me' after 150 yards. What clinched it, he thinks, was the roar of the crowd for the grey favourite. Tom Morgan, who was there for Dawn Run's epic victory, said that was the only other time he has ever heard a sound like it. 'It was like hitting a wall' and it seemed to boost Desert Orchid. Says the good-humoured Morgan wryly, 'I don't think too many were shouting for me.'

In the end Desert Orchid won by one and a half lengths. He and his gallant pursuer were eight lengths clear of Charter Party, the previous year's winner. Horse and jockey were applauded every step to the winner's enclosure and there was plenty of applause for Tom Morgan and John Edwards's gallant loser too.

John Francome, himself the supreme artist at Cheltenham, rated Simon Sherwood's performance in that race as good as he had seen from a National Hunt jockey. Sherwood had a remarkable understanding with Desert Orchid. He lost only one of the ten races he rode on him and entitled his autobiography *Nine out of Ten*. Ironically the horse who won when Dessie fell in the tenth of them was Yahoo.

Richard Dunwoody, who rode him after Sherwood retired, agreed that Kempton suited him best. 'A flat three miles suited him a lot better. The hardest bit of riding him was getting him down to the start. In the race he'd jump off and go his gallop. Jumping-wise it was usually a matter of leaving it to him. He'd make one or two careless mistakes the odd time but generally he was very good. At Kempton you would take the fourth last, give him a blow. He would fill the tanks and then you wouldn't have to move on him for the rest of the race. He was the most competitive horse that I rode. You felt his neck and it was hard as nails. He was such an athlete.'

Desert Orchid, the winner of four King George VI Chases, a Whitbread Gold Cup and of twenty-seven of his fifty races over fences, was the most popular jumper for decades. His exhilarating jumping and front-running gave him equine charisma, and though he retired in 1992 his racecourse parade reappearances were cheered to the echo. Often the old gentleman seemed to want to stay on for the race as well.

Best Mate's Third Gold Cup in 2004

Technique is vital but the best jump racing requires bravery too, in the saddle and underneath it. Best Mate, who won three Gold Cups in 2002, 2003 and 2004, had already demonstrated his high cruising speed, his natural fencing ability and his sheer class in the first two victories. On his third appearance in the Gold Cup, which tragically turned out to be his last, it was to be his courage and the nerve of his rider Jim Culloty which was tested to the ultimate. Best Mate's third Gold Cup, the first time in thirty-eight years the feat had been achieved, showed that he was a battler too. 'We knew he had the class and the ability,' said jockey Jim Culloty. 'Now we know he's got the bottle too.'

The omens were not good. The other three defending Festival champions that year, Moscow Flyer (Champion Chase), Baracouda (Stayers' Hurdle) and Rooster Booster (Champion

Hurdle), had all been beaten, and although Best Mate could not read he would have sensed the tension in those about him. As his 'drained' trainer Henrietta Knight said afterwards: 'Everyone wanted him to win. He has been taken over by the country and I just couldn't bear the thought of letting anybody down.'

The course having suffered a late drenching, Culloty and Terry Biddlecombe, Henrietta's husband and assistant, had decided the best ground was down the inside. But going round the inside at Cheltenham you are gambling on getting a clear run.

As the French raider First Gold made the pace, Best Mate had been flicking over his fences in his usual neat way, maintaining a nice rhythm. But others were determined he was not going to be allowed to have things his own way. At the last ditch he was tightened up by Sir Rembrandt (Andrew Thornton) on his outside with Harbour Pilot (Paul Carberry) deliberately hemming him in at the front.

It was nothing outside the rules of racing. Knowing he was the one to beat, Jim Culloty didn't resent the tactics. He admits he would have attempted some boxing-in had he been in their place: 'You wouldn't get many rides in this game if you were a perfect "after you, sir" gentleman.' Best Mate may have been unimpressed but he never became flustered and was ready to force his way out of the scrimmage. At the second last, Culloty pulled him out and they jumped it with élan. But going for safety rather than the spectacular at the last they were a little slow, a touch flat-footed. Best Mate's usual fluency was not there and Sir Rembrandt was battling.

It was no time for kindness and Jim Culloty was as hard on his old partner as he had ever been driving up the hill. Best Mate had the courage to respond up the lung-bursting slope and in the end they prevailed, though only by half a length. For Henrietta, Terry and all of England. As owner Jim Lewis said, his class animal had shown he could be a street-fighter too. And the memory of that last Gold Cup will keep us all warm in our beds for a few years to come.

Chapter 25

How to Win a Gold Cup

'It did nothing for me. I didn't get a single extra horse in the yard.' (Trainer Noel Chance on the aftermath of training his first Gold Cup winner)

It sounds so simple, training a Gold Cup winner; in theory you just buy a quality horse, get it fit, turn it out at its best on the day and collect the money. But there is so much more to it than that. A trainer needs to construct the right programme over two or three seasons. He must find the key to the animal's quirks and nurse it through the setbacks and injuries so often incurred in jump racing. He must find the right jockey for the horse. He must prepare a horse both mentally and physically to peak at the right time. It requires infinite patience, constant adaptability and a decent share of luck.

Many trainers in top stables end their careers without ever training a Gold Cup winner. Noel Chance, with a small yard in Lambourn, has achieved the feat twice. Here as an illustration of the ups and downs of jump racing, is the story of his two winners, Mr Mulligan (1997) and Looks Like Trouble (2000), mostly in his own words.

'Michael Worcester recruited me in Ireland in 1995 to be his private trainer. In our kitchen on The Curragh he said: "I think I've got a horse that will win the Gold Cup." I thought: "Oh yes, you and half the owners in Ireland." We started that May in Lambourn and this big, gangly creature that was Mr Mulligan came into the yard. Kim Bailey had had him. He did a few bits of work – his first work was always the best – and then went progressively downhill. We ran him at Uttoxeter with Richard Johnson, who was then the amateur "Mr R. Johnson" riding. Michael Worcester said his horse had got to make the running. We had nothing to lose so I said, "Off you go. Make the running, but don't make it too searching a test" and he won his novice hurdle by half the track. I still wasn't convinced that he was a brilliant horse because he wasn't showing me much at home. Next we went to Wetherby in a four-horse race. He beat them even further so I thought, "Maybe Mr Worcester is right" and we decided to go chasing with him. He made his debut at Bangor. Richard wasn't available to ride him and Mark Dwyer did. It was Hennessy Day at Newbury and we were lucky to get a jockey of such a calibre up there. Mr Mulligan made a couple of little mistakes but he sluiced in and we began to get more excited. We were going to run him in the Feltham [a top novices' chase at Kempton] but that was frosted off and we went to Wetherby. Again, with Mr Richard Johnson riding, he made all the running and jumped from fence to fence, beating a good horse of the Duke's [David Nicholson]. Suddenly we were getting a bit excited and we put him in the Reynoldstown at Ascot. Again he won by about ten lengths, jumping from fence to fence. The further they went the more he liked it. It was one of the best Reynoldstowns in twenty-five years. He beat Jenny Pitman's Nathen Lad, and Josh Gifford's Major Summit. Lord Gyllene, a subsequent Grand National winner, was out with the washing behind him. So then he headed for the Sun Alliance [novice chase] at the Festival. He was the great English hope even though he was trained by me, an Irishman. But the race wasn't run to suit. There was a false start. He liked to dominate and he wasn't able to dominate. Nathen Lad turned the tables on him and we finished second.

'We were a bit disappointed but it wasn't the end of the world.

Off he went to summer quarters and when we brought him back next year he ran first in the Rehearsal Chase at Chepstow. Everything else came out and he was left with top weight. It was horrible ground and he didn't fire. He finished fourth. A little disappointed, we wondered if he hadn't trained on. He was still quite lethargic and then, about four weeks before the King George [the big Chase at Kempton on Boxing Day] he was being shoed. The farrier had Mr Mulligan's hind leg between his two legs and suddenly his coronary band erupted. He had a serious stone bruise. He was such a brave horse. He had never gone lame but he had been lethargic. But because he was always lethargic in his work the alarm bells weren't ringing. As soon as that pus was taken out of his foot he was a different horse.

'On the day of the big Kempton race the Duke [his main employer] sent Richard Johnson to Wetherby so [champion jockey] Tony McCoy rode. I told him, "We're under-cooked here, he's had a setback, so don't go too quick." But McCoy said to me, "The only chance we've got of beating the grey horse [Gordon Richards's spectacular jumper One Man, who barely lasted three miles] is to stretch him."

'Anyway, Tony stretched him. Turning into the straight I thought, "We might win this" but then One Man went past and I thought we were destined for second – and the twenty-five grand that went with it. But then he turned over and fell at the final fence. Tony came back and he said, "My fault. You know how the grey horse stops so I had to fire him at the last. But he'll never beat Mr Mulligan again and I'll ride him in the Gold Cup." So that was all right and we thought he was OK and brought him home.'

Not only that, on the strength of McCoy's comments both owner and trained backed Mr Mulligan there and then for the Gold Cup at 20-1. And the unluckiest guy around seemed to be Richard Johnson who had lost the ride on a potential Gold Cup winner.

But Mr Mulligan wasn't OK. Says Noel: 'He'd stripped some

ligaments in his back and he was very sore and sorry for himself, and he had a huge haematoma on his quarters. He had a month off and didn't come back into work until the first week in February. I remember saying, "If I miss another day with this horse not only will we not win the Gold Cup, we won't even run." Fortunately he didn't miss a day, but we had to hurry him along a little bit, which didn't suit him.'

Meanwhile Tony McCoy, having on his own admission decked the horse at Kempton, was trying to get out of his promise to ride Mr Mulligan in the Gold Cup, fearing that the horse would never be fit to do himself justice. McCoy's worst fears were realised when Noel Chance got him to ride Mr Mulligan in a racecourse gallop at Newbury, testing him alongside Sunley Secure, a novice hurdler.

Noel takes up the story again: 'I remember saying to the girl who rode him: "Whatever you do, do not finish in front of Mr Mulligan because there will be an audience here. When Tony shouts to you, you hang back." Of course Tony was shouting to her but they finished together and Mr Mulligan had worked awful. There was no one to be seen but suddenly the media descended from the woodwork. I said to McCoy: "What do you think?" He said, "Dreadful." I said, "But tell them all we're delighted, that he always works like that" and through gritted teeth McCoy told everyone he was delighted.' Noel did the same, with such apparent conviction that McCoy decided that there was one trainer he would never, ever play poker with.

After that, says Noel, 'We galloped Mr Mulligan a couple of times. We've got a gallop called the Home Gallop on Mandown on which they start heading back towards home. Timmy Murphy rode him and as soon as he turned the corner towards home he flew. It was the only time I saw him really work well.'

Tony McCoy came down and schooled Mr Mulligan over nine fences and the race-day part of the story is well known. Knowing Mr Mulligan was brave and would stay, and putting the memory of the disastrous Newbury workout behind him, McCoy made plenty of use of the 20-1 shot. They burned off the challenges of Dublin Flyer and One Man and after McCoy had fired his big-striding mount into the last two fences nothing else could get near him. As they stormed up the hill it was the veteran Barton Bank who followed them a full nine lengths in arrears.'

Was it a life-changing moment for the trainer? Not really. Says Noel, 'It did nothing for me. I didn't get a single extra horse in the yard. Partly because he was a 20-1 shot and his form was less than inspiring coming into the Gold Cup. People have short memories and forgot he'd been a good novice too. Also I was perceived as a private trainer – it's the nature of the breed in racing that people want to feel they are the masters of their own destiny. Although to be fair, Michael Worcester wasn't like that they would have felt that his horses would have got preference.'

It seemed too that one Gold Cup was enough for Worcester. Not long after the success he instructed Noel to sell all his horses. 'He rang up from France one day and said, "It's all over. Sell everything." I think he got into racing on a whim and he got out of racing on a whim.' As for Mr Mulligan, there was not much of a racing future for him either. He ran once more at Wincanton over just two and a half miles and was beaten by a specialist at that distance. Then he "got a leg" (developed tendon trouble) and his owner took him home to a quieter life in a field. Sadly there a kick from a hunter shattered his leg and he had to be put down. Noel says: 'Mr Mulligan was as brave as they come. But he was not a horse whom you could give to someone to ride. He was a bit of a Victor Meldrew. In fact he was a bit of an Alf Garnett, an unpleasant sod. He would rather put his backside to you than nuzzle you with his nose.'

When Michael Worcester decided to sell up there were a couple of promising horses in Noel's yard, Laredo and Looks Like Trouble. 'Do you even want me to sell Looks Like Trouble,' asked the trainer. 'Especially Looks Like Trouble.' At that stage Looks Like Trouble had never won a race, but his trainer felt there was potential there. 'I hadn't overfaced him. He'd run at Folkestone and finished third to a couple of good things, and then we'd been down to Exeter and he'd been beaten a country mile on horrible ground in a long distance hurdle and Worcester was really browned off with him.'

Noel sought to persuade local owner Tim Collins, like him a regular at the Queen's Arms in East Garston, to buy Looks Like Trouble for £30,000 and he agreed to do so if he won a big contract he was in for. He got it and bought the horse.

'When he said, "What are your plans for this horse?" I said, "The Feltham at Christmas." And he agreed. We kicked off with him in a novice chase at Warwick. Mick Fitzgerald rode him and got unseated and then things went from bad to worse with his jumping. Seamus Durack rode him a couple of times and he walked through fences at places like Newbury. He was slipping down the scale and he was getting very well handicapped, which is embarrassing for a horse you're aiming at the Feltham. It wasn't that he wasn't brave, he just lacked a little expertise. He'd take on any fence in England, but we didn't want him doing that so I sent him to the showjumper Andrew Hoy at Gatcombe for two weeks. I rang after seven days and he said, "It's not good. He's knocking everything down." "O.K., I'll take him back." "No," he said, "leave him for the fourteen days," and on the fourteenth he said, "I think we've cracked it, come and have a look." Well, the horse was jumping a pole about just eighteen inches high and I thought, "if that's cracking it then I'm a Dutchman. I could jump that pole myself." We brought him back – he was always all right jumping at home – and I said although I've been quite easy on him we'll have to run him to see if he can jump and then make a decision whether he goes back to hurdling.

'We sent him to Doncaster where he was about a 10-1 shot thanks to the presence in the race of Princeful, who had won the Stayers' race at Cheltenham the previous year. Well, Looks Like Trouble was in the lead with Princeful behind and I looked back and saw Woody [jockey Richard Dunwoody] changing his hands and knew he wouldn't beat us. Next fence he fell and Looks Like Trouble went on and won half the track. On account of his previous runs he was well handicapped so then we ran him in a novice handicap at Sandown and he won half the track again. After that we made an eleventh-hour decision to go to Cheltenham for the Sun Alliance [Novices' Chase]. He and Nick Dundee, the great Irish hope, went clear and allegedly Paul Carberry told Norman Williamson, riding ours, that he was cooked. Nick Dundee didn't jump and turned over at the third last and Looks Like Trouble went on to win. Obviously we were delighted at winning the Sun Alliance and I was a bit indignant when commentators said we'd been lucky. I thought we'd have won anyway. He wasn't just a plodder, he stayed well. But even before that win we'd had doubts about his tendons and taken advice about whether to put him away for the season. The advice was "proceed with caution" and by doing that we'd won a Sun Alliance.

'We did a good job on his legs after that and brought him back the following year in the Charlie Hall at Wetherby, where his inexperience showed. He was very novicey. He couldn't jump at speed and finished a creditable third, beaten by two battle-hardened handicappers. We realised we needed to do more with him, to run him more, and did so in an intermediate race at Sandown. After three or four fences he was a different horse, he'd learned so much from his race in the Charlie Hall. He won that and was made favourite for the King George.'

Then came the kind of drama which makes racing headlines for the wrong reasons. In the King George, Looks Like Trouble's jockey Norman Williamson, by then his regular partner, pulled up Looks Like Trouble because he wasn't going well and felt there was something wrong with the horse. To this day Noel says he doesn't know the explanation – whether there was something physically wrong or whether the horse didn't like the ground that day. But anyway the owner fell out with Norman Williamson and took the ride off him. Looks Like Trouble ran next in the Pillar Chase at Cheltenham in January and was a different horse, leading all the way for an impressive victory and becoming second favourite for the Gold Cup.

'The shit hit the fan between the owner and the jockey. Norman was sacked and we had no jockey. But it's funny how what goes around, comes around. Richard Johnson [now Noel's son-in-law and the jockey who had unluckily lost the ride to McCoy on Mr Mulligan in 1997] was due to ride a horse for Alan King in the Gold Cup. I called agent Dave Roberts and he said Dickie would ride it if he could get off the other one. Luckily they decided to run the other horse in a different race and he came free to ride Looks Like Trouble.'

In a dramatic race marred by the fall of the tiring young star Gloria Victis, Looks Like Trouble came home a clear winner from Ireland's big hope Florida Pearl, with the favourite and previous winner See More Business in fourth place. Noel's encouragement to Tim Collins to buy the horse had proved wise advice and this time round the trainer did get a benefit from his success, as much from Looks Like Trouble's Cheltenham victory the previous year as from the big race. 'He did me a lot of good. Our string went up to forty-five, nearly fifty horses and suddenly I couldn't buy a bad horse. Everything I bought won me at least a bumper.'

Chapter 26

See More Business
Starts the Nicholls Era

*'For that minute you own the place. For that minute it's yours.
It doesn't matter how many years have gone, it feels like yesterday.
They'll never be able to take that little moment of magic away from
me.' (Former jockey Mick Fitzgerald on winning the Gold Cup)*

In 1994 Channel 4 took over coverage of the Cheltenham
Festival from the BBC and the continued high quality and
inventiveness of the television coverage, as with any sport, has
been vital to the Festival's development. Television as a medium,
particularly the development of the video for instant playback, has
also had much to do with the growing professionalism of jump
racing. Go into Martin Pipe's drawing room cum office at Pond
House, Nicolashayne and he will be watching a bank of screens
showing racing from all over, including the French tracks, looking
out for suitable prospects to buy and for the quality of the riding.
Even Tony McCoy grumbled a little at first when asked to watch
playbacks, but over the past decade and a half jockeys have been
spending more and more time watching re-runs of their races,
constantly analysing their style and their tactics in the search for
improvement. If you want to be sure of seeing the latest episode of
Spooks or *Coronation Street* on time, don't marry a jockey.

If modern techniques, talented professionals and brighter

pictures have improved television coverage over the years so Cheltenham has sought to match its facilities to the quality of the sport on offer and to cope with the greater numbers wanting to attend. The early 1980s saw the development of the tented village down the slope from the parade ring which effectively increased capacity by some 10,000. Says long-time Cheltenham chairman Sam Vestey 'The tented village makes an enormous difference. A lot of people who go racing there don't come out of it. People happily stay in there and we don't really want them out of it. It means an extra 8–10,0000 can be accommodated.'

In 1984 a new extension to the grandstand had opened. There were thirteen new boxes each with a balcony and a lunch table for twelve. The cost at that stage was £4,500 a year and almost imme-diately there was a seventeen-year waiting list for their occupation.

When Master Oats won the 1995 Gold Cup for Kim Bailey, then training in Lambourn, it was part of a double for him and for rider Norman Williamson not achieved since 1950. The pair had already taken the Champion Hurdle that week with the speedy Alderbrook. Master Oats, who had fallen when coasting in the previous year's Grand National, had won the Pillar Properties Chase at Cheltenham in the Festival run-up and had taken the Welsh Grand National too, that year run at Newbury. He was a worthy favourite, but he was faced by two French hopes running for Francois Doumen, and by former Gold Cup winner Jodami. Few would have given much for his chances after a series of jumping mistakes on the first circuit, but the wily Williamson switched him to the outside to give him a better view of his fences and Master Oats flew the rest on soft ground that suited him. He left Ireland's Merry Gale for dead round the final turn and at the line was fifteen lengths clear of the mare Dubacilla.

With horses like Dorans Pride and Klairon Davis winning at the 1995 Festival there was plenty to cheer the Irish. But for years they had scarcely had a look-in in the Gold Cup. There had been a nine-year gap between Davy Lad's victory in 1977 and Dawn Run's in

1986 and since then not a single Irish runner had come home in the first three. But in 1996 Fergie Sutherland's Imperial Call, ridden by Connor O'Dwyer, won impressively, powering up the hill four lengths clear of Rough Quest, the horse who was to win that year's Grand National, and the Hennessy winner Couldn't Be Better.

England's hopes had been high with One Man, an attractive grey who seized public imagination with that combination of supreme talent and occasional fallibility which seems to appeal so much to the British psyche — much more heart-warming than the racing machines. One Man had twice won the King George VI Chase at Kempton and his trainer Gordon W. Richards (the W had been inserted by a fussy clerk of the scales in his riding days to avoid confusion with the great Flat racing jockey Sir Gordon Richards) declared on the morning of the 1997 race: 'If I am ever going to win a Gold Cup it is today. Everything is in One Man's favour.' Two fences out it had looked as though he was right. But then, like a human marathon runner who 'hits the wall' and finds his legs morphing to rubber beneath him, One Man suddenly reached his limit. He clambered over the last fence and had slowed virtually to a walk by the time he reached the winning post. Although he was to have his day dropped back to two miles in the Queen Mother Champion Chase the next year, he simply did not stay the full three miles, two furlongs and one hundred and ten yards of the Gold Cup.

In Fergie Sutherland the Irish had a hero with plenty to be said about him. Having lost a leg while serving in Korea in the 1950s, he was reputed to travel with three false legs: one for riding, one for shooting and one for dancing. Certainly he never let the loss of a limb restrict him. Pinned under a horse one day after a racing fall he had extricated himself by unstrapping the false leg, causing the St John's Ambulance lady in attendance, who had not quite caught on to the situation, to pass out.

Fergie Sutherland was in fact an honorary Irishman, an Old Etonian who had previously trained Flat horses at Newmarket. He wasn't always one for the *craic*; he had spent the two previous days in Cheltenham watching the races on TV in his hotel, saying, 'I don't want to go spivving about, bumping into people every five yards.' But he was nevertheless a fine raconteur, so much so that the Queen Mother, who was so much enjoying chatting to him and the two friends he'd brought up to the royal box with him after the Gold Cup, was still there at 5.30 being urged by anxious aides to depart.

For those who thought that the hell-raising days had ended with Biddlecombe and Barry, Imperial Call's jockey Conor O'Dwyer added an interesting postscript. He says he couldn't beg, borrow or steal a bottle of champagne when Imperial Call won but that when he scored again on War of Attrition 'we were practically swimming in it. I'd say we were there until about eleven o'clock and we went into town after that.'

The Irish were full of hope for 1997, being represented not just by Imperial Call but by Dorans Pride and Danoli. But it was an English-based Irishman, Noel Chance, as we have already described, who won the race that year, with Tony McCoy leading from the start of the second circuit and going on to score what is surprisingly his only Gold Cup success so far. The incomparable McCoy took the Champion Hurdle too that year, only the fifth jockey in history to achieve that coveted double.

In 1998 it was the long-legged Andrew Thornton who drove Cool Dawn to an all-the-way victory for trainer Robert Alner and his diminutive owner Dido Harding, herself a capable horse-woman who had ridden the horse to his early successes and who only reluctantly ceded the ride to a professional.

Cool Dawn's path to success was eased by an early drama in the race which nearly led to a major racecourse incident. The then up-and-coming trainer Paul Nicholls had high hopes for one of his outstanding chasers, See More Business. He was, he admits, desperate for that success, having thus far, like other top trainers, endured a drought when it came to saddling Festival winners. But suddenly as they approached the seventh fence, See More Business was out of the race, through no fault of his own. Approaching the fence jockey Tony McCoy had felt his mount Cyborgo falter and break down. He pulled out to the right to spare the stricken horse jumping the fence. But as he did so he interfered with his stable companion Indian Tracker and the two of them took See More Business with them off the course and out of the race.

On Paul Nicholls, as he admits himself, the red mist of fury descended. It was made all the worse because that season Tony McCoy had left Nicholls to ride as stable jockey for Cyborgo's trainer Martin Pipe. And it had been McCoy's decision to ride Cyborgo instead of a Nicholls-trained horse in an earlier engagement that had precipitated the final breakdown between Nicholls and McCoy. There was an awful lot of pent-up resentment riding out there with the Gold Cup horses and when he heard it was Cyborgo who had taken out his horse, Nicholls lost it. When he passed Martin Pipe as the horses came back and Pipe offered no word of commiseration, Nicholls admits, he had to be stopped by friends from picking up Pipe by his lapels and inflicting violence. See More Business, who didn't understand what had happened, was 'in a right strop' too for several days, says his trainer. The less demonstrative Martin Pipe makes the point that he too was pretty upset about what had happened to the broken-down Cyborgo.

Don't get mad, get even, they say, and Paul Nicholls effectively did just that by winning the last Gold Cup of the century. Adding sweetness, he did so with his old favourite See More Business, ridden by Mick Fitzgerald, one of the best Cheltenham jockeys of recent times. In 1998 'Seemore' as they called him in the yard, had been an 11-2 shot. This time, after some less impressive performances, he was available at 16-1, with his stable companion Double Thriller at 9-1. Favourite was Ireland's Florida Pearl at 5-2 and the other fancied entry was Venetia Williams's Teeton Mill at 7-2. Seemore had not had a good season and had been fitted with blinkers to improve his concentration. On the training gallops they had made a spectacular difference but John Keighley, his co-owner with the yard's sponsor Paul Barber, had been highly reluctant to see him fitted with what some call the 'rogue's badge'.

Cyfor Malta and Imperial Call were missing with injuries and Teeton Mill sadly injured himself so severely in the course of the race that he never ran again. Florida Pearl could not stay with Seemore and the ten-year-old Go Ballistic as they went clear before the last two fences, and up the run-in it was See More Business who prevailed by a length from his one remaining rival.

There has been no more eloquent man in the saddle over recent decades than Mick Fitzgerald, and you gain a real insight into race riding as he tells the story of the race: 'See More Business had made jumping mistakes in the past but he jumped beautifully at Cheltenham that day. You almost pinch yourself when you're in a race like that and you think, "I've actually got a chance of winning." When I jumped the fourth last – it's quite a tricky fence – I landed over it and suddenly I had a lot of horse underneath me. You think, "This could be it."

'I had several horses with me. Florida Pearl was there and Simply Dashing and Go Ballistic. Florida Pearl was a short-priced favourite and I remember looking at Woody [Richard Dunwoody] and thinking, "He's not actually running away." It looked to me like Woody would have liked to be sitting stiller and have a little more up his sleeve. When Florida Pearl landed over the second last I saw Woody give him a little squeeze. Nothing happened, and it was almost like a rush of blood to the head. I thought, "We've got him." Go Ballistic was in front of me and I had ridden him the two races he had won. I thought, "I will be very disappointed if I can't get past him. He's an OK horse but he shouldn't be good enough to hold See More Business going up the hill." At both the last two fences I didn't really see a stride but luckily for me he answered my call. I will never forget it when I went past that line. That moment belonged to me. It's a great feeling. For that minute you own the place. For that minute it's yours. It doesn't matter how many years have gone, it feels like yesterday. They'll never be able to take that little moment of magic away from me.'

It was also a magic moment for Paul Nicholls, a major force in jump racing ever since, who agrees: 'That was the turning point for me. Things changed overnight. John Hales joined me, then Andy Stewart. They thought: "Hey, this guy can train." I used to go home each time wondering what it would take to have a Cheltenham winner. Then Flagship Uberalles that year won the Arkle, Call Equiname won the Champion Chase and See More Business won the Gold Cup.'

Sitting in his office at Ditcheat looking out at the champions standing in their boxes in 'Millionaires' Row' he reflected: 'I had been so keen for a Cheltenham winner and then suddenly I got three at one go. It had always been my landlord Paul Barber's ambition to have a Gold Cup winner. He had set this up with me and it was job done. You can never beat the first one.'

I reminded him of how long it had taken the likes of Josh Gifford, Noel Meade and David Nicholson, and he responded: 'We were all keen, probably too keen and in too much of a hurry. We used to run horses at Cheltenham and then look back later and think, 'Why did we do that?' In reality it was only nine years after I had a licence but it felt like fifty years and they were probably all the same. You're in too much of a hurry and you have it in your mind they're good enough for Cheltenham but in reality they're not.'

Now firmly established as the four-time champion trainer with a stable full of stars, Paul Nicholls has risen fast. As a jockey constantly fighting his weight it took him ten years to ride his 130 winners, mostly for David Barons, although they included two Hennessy Gold Cups and an Irish National. Then a broken leg in 1989 which saw his weight balloon to thirteen stone forced Nicholls to switch to training horses instead of riding them. Fiercely ambitious, he started with just ten horses but steadily expanded his business, first to become with Martin Pipe and Philip

Hobbs part of a dominant triumvirate of West Country trainers, and then to go out on his own as the clear champion, his consistent results attracting some of the biggest cheque books in the owners' world. His link with Irish champion jockey Ruby Walsh has paid enormous dividends for both.

Not yet fifty, he has already trained four Cheltenham Gold Cup winners and broken prize-money records. At Wincanton in January 2006 he made history by being the first trainer to saddle six winners on the same racecard. He is already fifth on the all-time list for training Festival winners and seems destined to re-write the record books.

Famous for his precipice-like all weather gallop at Manor Farm Stables, Ditcheat, where his horses undergo the interval training that sends them out onto the racecourse super-fit, Paul Nicholls is an advertisement for the sport with his cheerful accessibility to the media. His thoughtful post-race dissections are genuinely illuminating. And his candour is remarkable. He admits that he lost horses, forcing them on too fast when he was title-chasing in the past. Now, he insists, he has mellowed and matured. 'You can't risk a horse because of personal glory.' Asked if he and a few others are becoming too dominant, with the richest owners concentrating their forces, he shrugs and says, 'The best teams tend to attract the best players', pointing out that he was only a small trainer when he first achieved success with See More Business. And is Cheltenham itself too dominant? 'Cheltenham is the Olympics of our sport. It is the best of the best. If you can train those big race winners you are doing something right. The Grand National is a great race to win, we'd all love to win it, but it's a bit of a lottery, the form book is out of the window. It's a different race, a different logic. Some horses take to it, some don't. I wouldn't even think about it at this point [we were talking in September] but I do think about Cheltenham, what we can win the Fred Winter with, what we can win this with . . .'

What makes Nicholls so good? Former jockey Mick Fitzgerald,

stable rider for so long to Nicky Henderson, also rode many good winners including See More Business for Nicholls. He says: 'I knew Paul Nicholls when he only had three horses and I never had any doubt in my mind he was going to be champion trainer. He's just got that vision. He knows what he wants and he's going to get it. He's gone out of his way to get the right owners, to get them to buy a horse he wants to train and that's part of the answer. PR isn't it. Anyone who works in the press will tell you that Paul is very open, he's very honest with his take on all his horses. He doesn't put horses in races they can't win. Placing horses in races they can win is part of the art of being a good trainer. Paul's been very good at that. So has Nicky. He's also a very good people person. But he'll say to owners, "Where would you like your horse to run?" whereas Paul will say to them, "This is where your horse is running." '

What is good, says Mick Fitzgerald, is that Nicky Henderson, the only current trainer with more Festival victories than Paul Nicholls, is also now in a position to buy the horses to run at the top tracks. 'He's got the horses now to compete with the kind of owners Paul has.' This is a point that was vividly underlined on 15 January 2011 when Nicky Henderson had a day to remember with his young star Long Run upsetting Kauto Star's hopes of winning a fifth King George, his Champion Hurdler Binocular purring to victory in the Christmas Hurdle, and Nadiya De La Vega winning the Novices' Chase. The Lambourn trainer took two more races on the nine-race card and might have had one more but for A Media Luz falling in the lead at the second last hurdle.

So if the big two have got such ammunition, along with Howard Johnson, backed by Graham Wylie's cheque book in the North and David Pipe with David Johnson's buying power behind him, is there any hope for the middle-ground trainers? That, says Mick Fitzgerald is where the game has changed in our more professional age.

'It's up to all trainers to push themselves forward and to attract those horses. Business is hard in every sphere now, the competition is hard. You have to go out there and get the people who are going to buy those horses and that's your job as a trainer. It's not as simple as training horses any more. You've got to get the owners into the yard who are going to put the better horses with you. That the trainer's job these days – you've got to be good with people as well as with horses.'

See More Business pulled up in seven or eight strides after his Gold Cup and walked back to the stands with his head bowed. He was drained. He had given his last ounce. The resilient champion was back in next year's Gold Cup but he did not win again. Victory went instead to Noel Chance's comparatively small Lambourn yard with Looks Like Trouble, whose preparation for the big race was detailed earlier. He joined an élite group – Arkle, Ten Up, Garrison Savannah and the lucky inheritor Master Smudge – in moving on from victory in the Festival's Royal & Sun Alliance Chase to winning the Gold Cup.

It was at the third last that the drama began to unfold, with Ireland's hope Rince Ri unshipping Ruby Walsh and See More Business dropping away. At the next, Gloria Victis, the athletic novice who had promised to be a future star, fell and broke a leg, reducing Martin Pipe and supposed hard-man jockey Tony McCoy to tears. Ireland yet again had to settle for second best as Florida Pearl plugged on behind Looks Like Trouble on whom Richard Johnson, a jockey who would have collected half a dozen championships had he not been riding alongside Tony McCoy, seized his moment. At that point Noel Chance had saddled three festival winners from just seven runners.

In 2001 of course there was no Festival, thanks to the dreadful scourge of foot-and-mouth disease, and when normality returned we were ready for a new hero in the shape of England's best for decades, Best Mate, the triple winner through 2002–4.

Chapter 27

Hen, Terry and England's Hero, Best Mate

'People say, "Buy me another Best Mate." If only it were that easy.' (Trainer Henrietta Knight)

I f Ireland had her favourites at the Festival – Prince Regent, Cottage Rake, Arkle, Danoli, Dorans Pride, Moscow Flyer and Florida Pearl, horses who tugged at racegoers' hearts as well as helping to fill their wallets, so too has England in the shape of Golden Miller, Mill House, Desert Orchid and One Man. But if there was one single horse who became the public property of English racegoers it was surely Best Mate, the winner of three Gold Cups from 2002 to 2004.

It helped perhaps that Best Mate was owned by a flamboyant showman in the person of Jim Lewis, who would lead a team of supporters into the parade ring all wearing the claret and blue colours of his beloved Aston Villa Football Club. But it helped even more that Best Mate's career was overseen by a contrasting pair who encapsulate the colour, the quirkiness and the enduring 'animals-first' honesty of character that gives National Hunt racing such a wide appeal. Henrietta Knight and Terry Biddlecombe, otherwise known as Hen and Terry or, with affection, as 'the Odd Couple' are for jumping folk the best double act in town since Morecambe and Wise. The combination of Henrietta Knight, the well-connected exdeb, ex schoolmistress and ex-Olympic three-day-event selector with Terry Biddlecombe, the battered, earthy, three-times champion jockey who lost some early rounds with the bottle and then came through to a new life, has proved a potent one.

The West Lockinge Farm trainer and her husband/assistant, who married late and who patently adore each other through the haze of banter, won three Gold Cups with Best Mate and scored other Festival successes with the likes of Edredon Bleu, Karshi and Lord Noelie.

Horses have been Henrietta Knight's life, all of which has been spent at West Lockinge. As a child at Didcot Grammar School she remembers dashing back to be in time to watch the 4.30 race on TV. On one occasion that enabled her to see a victory for her uncle's horse Ravenscroft, ridden by Fred Winter and trained by Fulke Walwyn.

Henrietta, whose apparent mild dottiness conceals a formidable strength and ambition, is an excellent judge of a horse. Terry, who rode as well as he celebrated, can read a race like few others, and plans the tactics for their jockeys. The now teetotal pair, who rise at 5.30 and feed the horses together before the staff come in, somehow fuse class and country, style and courage, toughness and fragility in a famously happy stable-yard cluttered with chickens, geese and ducks.

Henrietta has her superstitions, refusing to put up pictures of horses while they are still running or refusing to let the hay man deliver in key racing weeks. 'Hay you pay, straw you draw', goes the old saying. Famously, she used not to be able to bear the strain of watching her horses race, at least not in important contests, hiding away in a press tent, behind a bush or in the Ladies. She explains: 'I just cannot bear to see them beaten and their reputations fall.' Perhaps that is because she learned much of her racing lore from the late Captain Tim Forster, so much the pessimist that he told a Grand National-winning jockey who asked for instructions before the race: 'Keep remounting.'

Says Henrietta: 'I learned all my trade through Tim Forster and the types he liked were the ones that just kept staying on and on in heavy ground. The more they did the more he loved it. I used to ride a lot of his horses. He taught me a lot. The old captain's horses were a much different stamp to those we see today, the French horses with more quality and more Flat breeding in them.'

Like Forster, she goes for real chasing types, not skinny equine lurchers off the Flat which might survive a year or two's hurdling. But climate change and better drainage has shifted priorities. 'We go for a certain stamp. The ones we buy are the horses that have good actions. It's no good looking for Cheltenham horses that are going to be mudlarks because you won't get them. Mostly you get a Gold Cup run now on much better ground than in the old days. Less wet springs. The weather's changed.

'We bought many horses through Tom Costello in Ireland. We used to go to Tom Costello's because we would always see them jumping. So much better than going to a sale. At a sale you can only see them walking or trotting. At Tom's we would always see them out in their action and their movement and their jumping ability. At one time most of our young horses came from him. We had an open day one summer and I said in an interview with Richard Pitman, "We've got about twenty-five youngsters from Tom Costello in the yard. There are such lovely animals among these young horses there must be a Gold Cup winner among them."'

So there was. He was then unraced but was called Best Mate, a handsome dark bay with perfect balance and a bubbling personality whom Terry had spotted when he pulled up in an Irish point-to-point. Costello wouldn't sell him until he had won a race. By the time his racing days ended, Best Mate, by Un Desperado out of Katday, had completed in twenty-two races, winning fourteen of them and finishing second in seven (five of those were Group 1 races, the others Group 2). He won the Cheltenham Gold Cup for three years running and a King George. Only in his final race at

Exeter, when he pulled up and died after a heart attack, did he fail to finish in the first two, and he never fell at a hurdle or a fence.

Best Mate would have been fancied to win the Arkle Chase at Cheltenham in 2001 but the foot-and-mouth outbreak saw the cancellation of the meeting. When racing resumed in 2002, Best Mate was the baby of an unusually large field of eighteen. Having been beaten by Florida Pearl in that year's King George, he started as the 7-1 third favourite. The previous year's winner, Looks Like Trouble, was at 9-2, and Nicky Henderson's Bacchanal was at 6-1.

See More Business was back again, running in his fourth Gold Cup and seeming to enjoy it. Bacchanal never got into the race and Florida Pearl was back-pedalling when the leaders sorted themselves out in the latter stages of the race. It was the Irish outsider Commanche Court, trained by Ted Walsh and ridden by his son Ruby, who first came to dispute the lead with Seemore. There too as a trio approached the last two fences was the improving Best Mate, and the young horse quickened impressively on the inside rail. He drew away from Commanche Court up the run-in to win by one and three quarter lengths, with the twelve-year-old See More Business in third. Jim Culloty, who had given the horse a dream ride, went on to complete a rare double, winning that year's Grand National on Bindaree.

The next year, 2003, it was even easier. Best Mate was a stronger horse and this time he came to Cheltenham having won the King George VI Chase at Kempton on Boxing Day, beating Sir Robert Ogden's Marlborough. The young pretender this time was Beef Or Salmon, trained in Ireland by Michael Hourigan and only a seven-year-old, as Best Mate had been the year before. Sadly Cheltenham was never to be his happy hunting ground and he fell at only the third fence. The day only got worse for Michael Hourigan who lost his old hero Dorans Pride when he broke a leg in the Foxhunters' Chase.

See More Business, now thirteen, was back again in the Gold Cup field. He and Behrajan made the early running. Commanche

Court and Marlborough were soon out of it and at the top of the hill it was Valley Henry who made a move, along with Best Mate's stable companion Chives. But Best Mate had been playing with them. To the cheers of the crowd, Jim Culloty sent him on at the second last and up the hill he surged clear of Truckers Tavern to win by ten lengths. In a more competitive age it was the first time since L'Escargot in 1971 that a champion had successfully defended his crown.

Best Mate's third and final Gold Cup victory, the one in which he proved himself a rough-house fighter as well as an athlete, was described earlier. It confirmed Henrietta Knight's horse as a national hero. The sheer strain of handling a horse who becomes a national icon, particularly one whose constitution will only stand so much racing when the media are demanding to see more of their hero, is often forgotten.

Says Henrietta: 'Every month you had to plan what you were doing. You couldn't let the horse out of your mind or out of your sight. We went on holidays for short times but there was always somebody minding and watching. He spent a certain number of hours in a field and people would be looking over the fence. We had to make sure he was close to the house so no one could do anything to him. People would just turn up in the driveway saying, 'Can we see Best Mate?' Even when he wasn't racing we'd get letters all the time addressed to him. I'm sure it's been the same with Denman and Kauto Star, both good horses. But I don't think they captured the imagination of the public quite so much as Best Mate, partly because there were two of them on the go at the same time. He was unique.'

For trainers who stay in business after handling a hero there is another strain. In Henrietta's case, 'People say: "Buy me another Best Mate." If only it were that easy.'

Breeding fashions and economic circumstances play their part in bloodstock markets. Owners from the modern business scene rather than from the more rurally grounded landed aristocracy expect swifter results; few now have the patience to persevere with the old-style 'store' horses who are best left unraced for a couple of years to develop the strength to match their frames. Less severe winter weather and better turf management has meant a brighter future for lighter-framed, quicker-maturing chasers who can show their speed on good ground rather than battle their way though quagmires. With bloodstock agents like David Minton and Anthony Bromley making the pace, such chasers have been coming in ever-greater numbers, not just from Ireland but also from France, where horses are taught to jump at a much earlier stage of their careers.

The name of Taaffe was back on the Festival honours board in 2005. Again that year the Gold Cup was won by a comparative youngster, the seven-year-old Kicking King. The horse was trained by Tom Taaffe, whose father Pat not only rode Arkle to his Gold Cup victories in the sixties but had trained Captain Christy to win the race in 1974. But Kicking King nearly didn't run in a Gold Cup which was missing several principal players. Best Mate had been withdrawn after bursting a blood vessel at exercise and another fancied entrant, Farmer Jack, died on the gallops the week before the race. Kicking King was withdrawn by his trainer, who believed him to be ill but then reinstated after he made a rapid recovery. The horse's owner, Conor Clarkson, was in Spain when his trainer called to tell him they were out of the race and he was so shocked he pulled over his car and did not get going again for a couple of hours.

In the race, Kicking King, ridden by Barry Geraghty, certainly didn't behave like an invalid. Grey Abbey and then Sir Rembrandt, the runner-up in 2004, made the running. Kicking King hit the front three fences out and went on to win by five lengths from Take The Stand and Sir Rembrandt. Said Barry Geraghty, 'I was running away all the time, jumping brilliantly over the last three.'

It was the first Irish win since Imperial Gold in 1996 but though Kicking King, who suffered a tendon injury, missed the next year's race and never ran again in a Gold Cup, Ireland supplied the first three home in 2006 when the race was run on St Patrick's Day. The winner was War of Attrition, trained by Mouse Morris, owned by Ryanair chief Michael O'Leary and ridden by veteran jockey Conor O'Dwyer, just three weeks off his fortieth birthday. He owed his victory to his high cruising speed and some impeccable fencing. 'The way he jumped the last two was incredible,' said his jockey. Only twice in fifty years had the winner returned a faster time and many of those with hopes were burned off by the testing gallop set by the early leaders. In second place by two and a half lengths was Hedgehunter, the winner of the previous year's Grand National, and another seven lengths back was Forget The Past.

Owner Michael O'Leary pointed out that remarkably few Irish trainers had trained a Gold Cup winner, and said: 'I would have been more worried at a point-to-point than I was today. I think we were under more pressure last year in the Arkle when he was the Irish banker.'

War of Attrition too was injured and did not come back to defend his crown. Instead 2007 saw the Gold Cup debut of a new wonder horse, the athletic and handsome French-bred Kauto Star, owned by golf course developer Clive Smith and trained by Paul Nicholls. Kauto Star's rivalry over the next few years with Denman was to dominate the jumping scene, reviving memories of the contests between Arkle and Mill House, though producing more varied results than those and being given a special impetus by the fact that the two horses occupied adjoining boxes in Paul's Somerset yard. But before that era there was another Irish hurdling star to enjoy.

Chapter 28

Ireland Enjoys the Istabraq Era

*'Istabraq will destroy them.' (The accurate prediction of the
normally reticent Aidan O'Brien about his star hurdler)*

Istabraq was a phenomenon who won eighteen of his first
twenty contests over hurdles. The first of those at the
Cheltenham Festival was the 1997 Royal & Sun Alliance
Novices' Hurdle in which rider Charlie Swan was under phenomenal pressure. All the favourites had gone down the previous
day and all of Ireland's hopes had failed, including Finnegan's
Hollow, who had been cruising when Swan fell with him three
out. Owner J.P. McManus was known to have had a huge bet on
Istabraq and most of Ireland was on the horse with him. But in the
parade ring and at the start Istabraq had boiled over, becoming
agitated and covered in sweat. Many a horse has thrown away his
chance by expending nervous energy in this way and Charlie Swan
reckoned he could no longer afford to stick to his plan of staying
up with the pacemakers. Making the running with a horse so
charged up could have been a disaster – he would have been likely
to burn himself out early on. He therefore anchored his mount at
the back of the field, only to discover that by the top of the
Cheltenham hill all his rivals were toiling. Despite colliding with
another horse jumping the second last and being half winded and
nearly falling, Istabraq still managed to get to the line that year

before Mighty Moss. Even so, before the first of his Champion Hurdles in 1998, Charlie Swan was startled to hear his trainer, the normally shy, soft-spoken Aidan O'Brien, declare: 'Istabraq will destroy them.'

Swan reckoned that Istabraq, having won over two and a half miles, might be short of a true Champion Hurdler's speed, and resolved to ride him for stamina, forcing the pace. But he need not have worried. By the time they got to the top of the hill and began the descent, Istabraq's high cruising speed had demolished his rivals. He simply destroyed them with his sustained pace and came home twelve lengths clear. Jockey Chris Maude, asked by an owner the next year if his horse had a chance of beating Istabraq, replied, 'Only if he kicks him at the start.'

The most respected of all racing assessors, Timeform, gave Night Nurse a rating of 182 in 1976–77. The only other horse ever to make 180 in Timeform was Istabraq in the 1999–2000 season. Was Istabraq the best of all? The inter-generational comparison game, fun though it is, is something of a blind alley. But what we do know is that Istabraq soared above his contemporaries. With Istabraq we did not get the 'duel factor' with regular rivals. There was simply no one around capable of duelling with him. His winning margins over his three Champion Hurdle victories amounted to nearly twenty lengths. And he was trained by another Irish genius with horses – Aidan O'Brien. Ireland's champion amateur rider, O'Brien began training as assistant to his wife Anne-Marie Crowley but once he took out his own licence he set a new record for stakes won in his very first year. In 1994–95 he sent out an incredible 138 winners.

Although he too trains at Coolmore, Aidan O'Brien is not related to Vincent O'Brien, who died in 2009. But although the slightly Harry Potterish figure, still looking a decade younger than he is, does not share that great man's relish for a wager, he does share his uncanny ability to get into the mind of a horse and his infinite capacity for detail. Both were deployed in fitting a programme around the highly strung and easily upset Istabraq that kept him happy without letting him get too far above himself, as he was otherwise inclined to do when approaching race-fitness.

Istabraq himself had not always hinted at what was to come. On the Flat, in the hands of the canny John Gosden, he had registered only two wins from eleven starts for Hamdan al Maktoum before being sent up to the Newmarket sales. Tragically his buyer there for 38,000 guineas, John Durkan, died of leukaemia before he could begin his training career and new owner J.P. McManus sent him to O'Brien. Soon J.P. was saying: 'Whenever he runs, whatever Istabraq is doing, I'm there. I'll never take my holidays to miss anything he is doing.' His jockey Charlie Swan, now a successful trainer himself and a man who turned down the chance to be Martin Pipe's number one jockey, an instant passport to the British championship, said that but for Istabraq he might have quit the saddle.

As for the horse himself, he could hold his own at home with any of O'Brien's Flat stars over a mile and a half and McManus must have laughed when he got 3-1 about the £30,000 he placed with Victor Chandler for the Champion. Istabraq toyed with his field and the twelve-length margin by which he won was the biggest since 1932.

When he came back to the Festival the next year Istabraq's trainer said he was heavier, stronger and quicker, and a record first-day crowd of 46,470 turned out to see him defend his crown at 9-4 on. Some thought French Holly might have given him a race but at the second last Istabraq asserted and won as he liked, three and a half lengths clear of poor old Theatreworld. The previous year O'Brien had the stable staff money each way on Theatreworld at 40-1. This time they had to be content with the return from 25-1.

In theory the 2000 contest should have been a lot tougher for Istabraq. Among those lining up against him was Hors de la Loi III who had won the Supreme Novices' Hurdle the year before in a time three seconds faster than Istabraq's in the Champion. There was too a scare the day before racing. At the course, Istabraq had bled from one nostril. If it was an internal haemorrhage that could be serious, but it could equally be just a knock on the nose. So close to a race he could not be sedated and 'scoped' (i.e. the mucus from his lungs examined with a probe) and, because it was the Champion Hurdle with a third consecutive title involved, Team O'Brien chose to run. In the event there was no problem. Make A Stand, back in action, tried to repeat his all-the-way win from three years before but faded after the fifth. Nicky Henderson's runners Katarino and Blue Royal then took it up. But by the turn for the straight every whip except Charlie Swan's was in action. On ground that was merely good, Istabraq won by four lengths from Hors La Loi in a new record time. O'Brien commented that Istabraq probably hadn't been at his best but was so superior to other horses that that had not mattered. The tragedy is that the foot-and-mouth epidemic in Britain, which produced far more serious repercussions for many farmers, wiped out the Festival of 2001 and so gave Istabraq no chance that year of becoming a four-time champion.

He was back for the Festival of 2002 but by then rumours were flying that all was not well with the champion. It did not stop many hundreds of Irish fans wearing rosettes in McManus's green and gold colours demanding 'Gimme Four' and backing the champion down to favourite once again. But soon after they set off Charlie Swan could clearly sense something was amiss. Before the second hurdle he pulled up Istabraq and the extraordinary thing was that the crowd applauded. They actually applauded the pulling up of the favourite before the second obstacle. It was a tribute to the horse himself and it was a tribute to the sporting crowd that Cheltenham produces. Many of those applauding would have lost their money, but like Charlie Swan they had sensed there was something wrong and they did not want anybody to run risks with a great horse that had given so much pleasure to so many racegoers. And so came to an end one of the most remarkable Festival careers, although in 2011 Istabraq still holds the record for the fastest-ever Champion Hurdle at 3 minutes 48.1 seconds in the year 2000.

With Istabraq out of it, the way was clear for the talented and classy Hors La Loi, owned by Paul Green and ridden by Dean Gallagher, to provide a second Champion Hurdle victory for James Fanshawe, the lanky Newmarket Flat trainer who advertises himself with the skeleton symbol. How many more Festival winners might he have trained with a different focus?

Rooster Booster, the gutsy grey scrapper trained by Philip Hobbs who became Champion Hurdler in 2003, was a horse who had spent most of his life not in blue-riband events but humping weights in handicaps. In 2002, after a series of narrow defeats, he had won the County Hurdle for his owner Terry Warner, who has a penchant for grey horses. In 2003 he came to the Festival with four wins from four races. With Hors La Loi refusing to start, Rooster led for much of the way in the Champion and scorched up the hill to crown his career with the big one he merited, winning by eleven lengths.

Fanshawe and Hobbs, providing a brief interlude between Istabraq's domination of the event and the successes of a series of characterful timber-toppers from over the water from 2004 to 2008, were the only English trainers to get on the Champion Hurdle score-sheet over a period of nine years. The combative Irishman, it is said, enquires, 'Is this a private fight or can anybody join in?' and for several years the opening-day Festival highlight appeared to be a private contest between the best of the Irish hurdlers. England, it seemed, simply could not produce a horse to rival the Irish over the smaller obstacles. One year the first nine in the ante-post betting were trained in Ireland, and in 2005 there was only one English-trained horse in the first seven home. Even that one, Intersky Falcon, came from the yard of Jonjo O'Neill, who is not exactly Home Counties-bred!

As former jockey-turned-trainer Dessie Hughes put it at the

kitchen table in his yard on The Curragh: 'There was a time when everyone in Ireland had money and they weren't selling their horses. In the seventies and eighties most good horses won a bumper here and then went over to Walwyn or Winter or whoever. In the nineties they weren't for sale. There were some terrific years at Cheltenham.'

The pattern was confirmed in 2004 when Hardy Eustace, owned by Lar Byrne, trained by Dessie Hughes and ridden by Conor O'Dwyer scored a shock Champion Hurdle win at 33-1. Rooster Booster was up against him but was not allowed to dominate. Rooster joined the Irish horse at the last but had no more to offer. Hardy Eustace scooted away again in the hands of the 38-year-old Conor O'Dwyer to win by five lengths, with Intersky Falcon in third. Amid the Irish joy there were a few tears shed too. Race fans recalled that when Hardy Eustace had won the Sun Alliance Hurdle at the previous Festival he was ridden by Kieran Kelly, a promising young jockey. Sadly he had provided a reminder of the perils of the sport when he was killed in a fall at Kilbeggan the previous August.

That Sun Alliance victory too had marked a change of fortunes for trainer Dessie Hughes. It was twenty-one years to the week since his previous Cheltenham winner, Miller Hill. In the meantime he had suffered a ten-year hell while his stables were ravaged by the Aspergilus fungus, inducing a virus that affected the horses' kidneys and coats, and of course their racecourse performances. His winners and his owners dwindled before the Irish Equine Centre's microbiologists cracked the problem. Now with a Champion Hurdle victory he was back in the big time, and he admits, 'To be honest, Hardy Eustace lifted us up to a different level. He was a star.'

Although he had thought long and hard before going for the Champion rather than a handicap at the Festival, Dessie Hughes was surprised at the 33-1 price for his horse. 'We had no great worries about the trip. Like Monksfield [whom he had ridden to victory] he was a two-and-a-half mile horse but he had great pace. He could make the running and stretch it with a good, strong two miles from start to finish and he'd finish up the hill. We knew he could gallop.'

When they left the parade ring Dessie had second thoughts about the instructions he had given his jockey. Had he over-emphasised Hardy Eustace's front-running capabilities? He urged his son Richard, the Flat race jockey who made such a great fight of it for the championship in 2010, to dash off and tell O'Dwyer not to go too mad on him 'in case he thought he ought to blast them up in front'. Richard vaulted the rails and passed on the message. Dessie admits: 'You wouldn't really have to say it to Conor but when I'm in the stands I always think of something I ought to have said to the jockey.'

There had been another problem already. Hardy Eustace wore blinkers, but not the all-enveloping kind that give a horse tunnel vision. His had cut-down cups with a slit 'so he's not claustro-phobic, just for concentration'. But when his jockey came out to the parade ring the blinkers could not be found, only a huge blue pair with highly restricted vision. It was again son Richard who on a last-minute scramble through the weighing room found the correct blinkers in another jockey's bag.

Connections felt Hardy Eustace had not been given due credit for his victory but he was back to show his fighting qualities and win again the next year in a race that will long be remembered. He led at the last, but easing seemingly effortlessly alongside him up the run-in was Noel Meade's Harchibald. Most watching felt it was only a question of when his rider Paul Carberry would press the button and go past to win. But when he did there was no answer from Harchibald. The resolute Hardy Eustace battled away to hold him off, with another Irish runner, little Brave Inca, only another neck away in third.

A few in the crowd, unfairly, booed Carberry, feeling that he should have come sooner to challenge and ought to have won the race under a horse so patently full of running. The winner's trainer Dessie Hughes admitted: 'I though we were cooked when Harchibald cruised alongside.' But never was it so obvious that horses are not machines. Both Carberry and trainer Noel Meade were adamant that there was no other way to ride Harchibald. His jockey's only regret was that he hadn't made his challenge even later: 'He's a bridle horse. That's the only way you can ride him. If he hits the front, he stops.' Later he said of the talented but complicated Harchibald that he was 'Like an aeroplane. But the trouble with this aeroplane is that he hijacks himself.' Noel Meade also felt that Harchibald had a breathing problem which prevented him giving of his best at crucial moments.

As for Hardy Eustace's owner Lar Byrne, he looked at the list of finishers and declared: 'I don't think there's been a Champion Hurdle like this with seven Irish horses, and it's great to be able to say I had an argument with all of them and won.'

Much of the same cast were back in 2006. This time it was Brave Inca who triumphed. His previous jockey Barry Cash had been replaced by champion Tony McCoy and Brave Inca lived up to his name under an uncompromising ride from McCoy which showed how tough the pair of them were. They were perfectly suited; as the veteran trainer/commentator Ted Walsh put it, 'The horse would have to be dead two days to stop battling and McCoy would carry on riding if he had no arms or legs.' Brave Inca was not one of those horses to go ten lengths clear in a race. But when anything came at him, he responded. Said trainer Colm Murphy: 'He sticks his head out and anything that went by would know he's had a race.' This time Hardy Eustace was relegated to third and Mac's Joy, trained by Jessica Harrington and ridden by Barry Geraghty, was second, improving on his fifth place the year before.

Come 2007 and it was Ireland again, but this time not with one of the familiar names. Perhaps because it was only his second run of the season and only his sixth hurdle race, few had given much attention to John Carr's Sublimity, ridden by Philip Carberry. It was only after he had run out the 16-1 winner from Brave Inca, with Afsoun in third and Hardy Eustace fourth, that most people recalled that Sublimity had had good Flat form when with Sir Michael Stoute and that he had been an unlucky fourth at the previous year's Festival in the Supreme Novices' Hurdle. Sublimity was travelling so superbly well that he could be called the winner from half a mile out, and while Brave Inca stayed on stoutly he was never going to have the speed to cope with Sublimity.

Ireland still provided the favourite for the race in 2008 with Sizing Europe, and coming down the hill he and Sublimity were both very much in contention. But this was the year in which English trainers reasserted themselves. Little Katchit, trained by Alan King and ridden by Robert 'Choc' Thornton, was the winner, beating two more English candidates in Osana and Punjabi. Many experts used to argue that five-year-olds couldn't win the race but both the winner, Katchit and the third, Punjabi, were only five.

Katchit, who was not seen as the season began as a Champion contender, was one of those horses who just keep on improving. He had cost just £30,000 in a deal struck in a Salisbury racecourse bar between his trainer and Mick Channon, who had handled him on the Flat. Mick told his purchaser that the horse might win him 'a couple of little summer jumps races'. In fact Katchit won five out of his first six races on the Cheltenham track and his prize for that year's Champion Hurdle was worth £157,000. At Aintree later somebody made a disparaging comment about Katchit and Alan King interjected: 'Hang on, I bought him', only for his wife to add, 'Only because you were drunk at the time.'

Nicky Henderson has the best Cheltenham record of any trainer still in business and there was a reminder of the glory days of See You Then as he brought back Punjabi to win in 2009. The surprise for the Cheltenham crowd was that Punjabi was only a 22-1 shot while the horse he beat into third, Binocular, ridden by Tony McCoy, was the 6-4 favourite. The horse who divided them by a neck and a head was Paul Nicholls's Celestial Halo.

The betting exchange company WBX had offered a £1 million bonus for any horse winning the Champion Hurdle, the Fighting Fifth Hurdle at Newcastle and the Christmas Hurdle at Kempton. Punjabi had achieved the first two but sadly had fallen in the Kempton race when, in the words of his owner Raymond Tooth, 'he was cantering'. After the Champion Hurdle victory Punjabi's trainer ruefully called it 'probably the most expensive fall in the history of racing'.

Punjabi responded bravely to the urgings of jockey Barry Geraghty and lasted better up the hill than his two challengers. But after the race Nicky Henderson warned: 'Binocular is a year younger and I still think he is a horse with a big future. A.P. said he might just have had a bit of a blow from the horse but the horse is young and I wouldn't be surprised if he had his day.'

They were prophetic words because in 2010 McCoy did score on a horse for which he and his trainer and owner J.P. McManus seem to have a special affection. This time Celestial Halo faded earlier and the only one giving Binocular a race of it at the last was Nigel Twiston-Davies's Khyber Kim. Binocular had run some poor races during his preparation for the Festival and was nearly scratched from the race, so the good news for Henderson followers was that his price on this occasion was a more generous 9-1. McCoy, sometimes wrongly seen as an unemotional winning machine, was so overjoyed that he actually hugged the horse.

After the race he admitted that Binocular's performances through the season had had him 'tearing up his ticket'. The horse had been taken to see a series of vets and physios, even having a bone scan in Ireland as they attempted to find out why he was not sparking. But no physical fault had been revealed and when McCoy had been to school him the week before he knew Binocular had come right. 'I rode him as fast as I've ridden any horse schooling. I frightened myself we went so fast.'

The Champion Hurdle victory was one of the performances – along with his Grand National victory on Don't Push It – which helped to see Tony McCoy, the fifteen-times champion jump jockey, score a first for racing when the incomparable rider was voted as the BBC's Sports Personality of the Year 2010.

Nicky Henderson also won that year's Triumph Hurdle with Soldatino. The race was sponsored by the heavy equipment company JCB and when Henderson received a model JCB as part of his prize he remarked jokingly that in heavy winters he could do with a real JCB digger at home. Not long afterwards, courtesy of the grateful J.P. McManus, the real thing arrived at his Seven Barrows yard in Lambourn. That's style for you.

It is not only the Champion hurdlers who provide the speed at Cheltenham; there were stirring performances too in the Queen Mother Champion Chase through the late nineties and into the twenty-first century.

Chapter 29

The Champion Chase:
These We Have Loved

'He must have been watching too much Flat racing. Frankie
Dettori he ain't.' (Trainer Jessica Harrington on Barry
Geraghty's 'flying dismount' from the victorious Moscow Flyer)

One of the best-loved horses among jumping crowds through the past two decades was the exuberant fencer One Man, owned by John Hales and trained in Cumbria by Gordon Richards. His victory in the Queen Mother Champion Chase was probably the most popular in the history of the race.

A flamboyant grey like Desert Orchid, One Man seemed, like Dessie, to run below his best form in the Cotswolds. He was beaten when favourite for the 1994 Sun Alliance Chase and failed in both the 1996 and 1997 Gold Cups, looking like holding a winning hand coming down the hill to the last bend only to be exhausted by the final climb.

One Man was undoubtedly a class horse, winning the King George VI Chase over Kempton's easier, flatter three miles in both 1995 and 1996 for Richard Dunwoody. In 1998 however, his connections determined to show that he could win at Cheltenham too and dropped him back to the two miles of the Champion Chase.

Richard Dunwoody, who had ridden One Man to many of his

successes, was unavailable so the ride was given to stable jockey Tony Dobbin. When he fractured his thumb on the first day of the meeting the Greystoke stable's number two Brian Harding was given a chance to step up on the world stage. He did not squander his opportunity.

The decision by owner and trainer to drop One Man back to two miles proved to be a brilliant move. One Man was able to go with the pace and test the others with his jumping skills, with no fears about lasting the trip. Coming round the final bend Brian Harding was able to put daylight between One Man and his pursuers, and this time the grey did not run out of gas on the hill, winning comfortably from Or Royal and Lord Dorcet. It was, however, the horse's last success. Sixteen days later he went to run at Aintree, his patently ill trainer being applauded by racegoers lining the paddock rail.

Harding kept the ride, but this time it was to be tragedy, not triumph. Before the ninth fence One Man veered right, failed to get height and ploughed through the obstacle, breaking his leg and having to be put down. Trainer Gordon Richards, a countryman with an eye for a sheep or a bullock, and a man who, as he put it, 'had his coat off all his life' died of lung cancer that September.

Since then there has not been a year, apart from the foot-and-mouth epidemic of 2001, when the Queen Mother has not thrilled with its sheer quality.

In 1999 Paul Nicholls performed his own See You Then-style miracle by producing the glass-legged Call Equiname to win the Queen Mother, ridden by his then brother-in-law Mick Fitzgerald. Call Equiname's training programme had been frequently interrupted by sore shins but Paul had him absolutely right on the day. Mick Fitzgerald eased him into the action coming down from the turn at the top of the hill and sat ready to pounce at the last. An untidy jump then let Edredon Bleu and Direct Route get first run up the slope to the finishing line but Call Equiname had the class to get by and win by a length and a quarter. The horse owed his trainer. In earlier days the aggressive Call Equiname had almost certainly been responsible for the putting down of his most exciting prospect, See More Indians, by kicking him and shattering his leg when they were turned out together in the orchard of yard sponsor Paul Barber.

Paul loves the Queen Mother as a race. 'It's brilliant, terrific – great horses jumping at speed. Jumping's the name of the game and we spend a lot of time getting these horses jumping. It's a big plus. They don't have to be that quick but they have to gallop. Some of them are actually quite slow but they need to be able to gallop two miles flat out.'

The year 2000 produced another epic, one of those 'Were you there when . . .?' contests, this time featuring Henrietta Knight's Edredon Bleu and Northern trainer Howard Johnson's Direct Route. Champion jockey Tony McCoy, Edredon Bleu's rider, wanted this prize above all else and this was the year he secured it. Edredon Bleu, who ran in the Aston Villa stripes of Jim Lewis made famous by Best Mate, now had the quick ground conditions that suited him and they went pretty well flat out all the way. Said McCoy: 'I didn't worry coming down the hill at Cheltenham flat out at thirty-eight miles an hour – it never occurred to me that this fella might not take off.' Direct Route, ridden by Norman Williamson, had been put under pressure by Edredon Bleu's jumping earlier on but as the two began to shake off Flagship Uberalles at the last, Williamson came upsides. Fifty yards later Direct Route, on the far side, was a head in front. Both riders and horses really went for it, heads down, locked together up the hill in the ultimate nostril-to-nostril duel. With seventy yards left, the knot in Williamson's reins came undone. But nothing made any difference, says McCoy, whose television replay button gets more constant use than any in the country. Neither horse ever changed its stride pattern and at the line McCoy and Edredon Bleu had it by a short head.

Deputising for his regular paddock companion Best Mate,

Edredon Bleu went on to win the 2003 King George over three miles. But for many the Champion Chase was his finest hour.

In the Queen Mother in 2002 it was the turn of Flagship Uberalles, a big, strong horse built like a battleship who was owned by Americans Michael Krysztofiak and Elizabeth Gutner. Running in star-spangled colours, Flagship had won the Arkle Chase for them when in the Ditcheat yard of Paul Nicholls, giving the then still up-and-coming trainer his first Festival winner. But after he finished third in the Queen Mother behind Edredon Bleu on ground that didn't suit, his owners transferred him first to Noel Chance and then to Philip Hobbs, another of the West Country trainers who have been such a massive force at the Festival in recent times. It was for Hobbs that Flagship won his Queen Mother. Ridden by Richard Johnson, Flagship Uberalles had to be pressed to stay in touch in the earlier stages but was going so well as they came to the last that his rider was certain of victory.

But at the same Festival of 2002 a new Irish star trained by Jessica Harrington and ridden by Barry Geraghty, a horse by the name of Moscow Flyer, had taken the Arkle and he was to be a major player in the Queen Mother for the next four years. Winning the Arkle and going on to take the Queen Mother Champion Chase was becoming a predictable career path – one followed by Remittance Man, Klairon Davis and Flagship Uberalles and, a year later, by Azertyuiop.

In the 2003 Queen Mother Champion Chase, Moscow Flyer was facing the regular team. Edredon Bleu was there, and so was Flagship Uberalles, who had been tried over three miles in the King George VI Chase at Kempton and found wanting. Tiutchev could be a threat but Cenkos and Kadarran, Florida Pearl and Native Upmanship were seen as lesser rivals by Moscow Flyer's trainer. Moscow got a little close to the water and didn't quite meet the fourth last as his jockey wanted but was going best of all. Jockey Barry Geraghty, with a sixth sense, pulled out from behind the leaders Seebald and Latalomne before the second last and was glad he did so since both clipped it and fell. It was over the last and away, with the crowd's cheers encouraging Moscow Flyer to prick his ears as he coasted to victory. All that was left was for Barry Geraghty to do a flying dismount in the winner's enclosure. His trainer commented: 'He must have been watching too much Flat racing. While he remained upright, he wouldn't have got more than 4.5 or 5.0 from a gymnastics judge. Frankie Dettori he ain't.'

Moscow Flyer, however, did not have the cleanest sheet when it came to completing the course. He had fallen on his very first outing, and dumped his rider at Punchestown at the end of his first Queen Mother season. There was talk of a 'three-wins-and-a-fall' pattern emerging. His trainer's reaction to that was to point out that, like most horses, Moscow couldn't count.

Jessica Harrington was more worried about Azertyuiop in 2004 than she had been about any of the opposition in 2003, and because Moscow Flyer had suffered from the sniffles early in 2004 she hadn't given him the prep race she would have wanted to before Cheltenham. He was, she agrees, too fresh for the race and when he fell at the fourth that was part of the reason. She doesn't exactly blame the horse or Barry Geraghty, who couldn't believe that his mount was galloping on riderless after such a big mistake. It was one of those things. But Moscow Flyer's chance was gone and Azertyuiop was the new champion. Simple as that. They took Moscow's saddle off in the also-rans enclosure at the side of the weighing room. As his candid trainer agrees: 'When a horse ends up chucking his jockey on the deck, you know that something has gone wrong. It's difficult to isolate one thing. It's probably a combination of several things . . . A lot of the times it was when he was getting a bit bullish and thinking, "I can do things my way."'

The confidence of trainer, jockey and maybe horse were rapidly restored over two and a half miles at Aintree and then at Punchestown. But the Queen Mother Champion Chase of 2005, when Moscow would be eleven, was what mattered. And there was glorious redemption.

Early on, it did not look easy. Martin Pipe's Well Chief was the new kid on the block. The Paul Nicholls team were well content with Azertyuiop. Would Moscow Flyer still have the speed or was this the time to try him, with a pedigree that would give hope of him lasting such a distance, over three miles instead? All three top contenders went to Sandown for the Tingle Creek Chase and Moscow crushed his rivals. As his trainer said, he was telling the world that he was still the best two-mile chaser around, so no more thoughts of the three-mile King George. Instead there was a pipe-opener in the Tied Cottage Chase at Punchestown and he went on to Cheltenham.

This time Moscow Flyer had nothing to prove. He had won an Arkle, a Queen Mother Champion Chase and two Tingle Creeks, and in the event, Azertyuiop proved no threat while Timmy Murphy was working a long way out trying to get Well Chief to challenge. Moscow was cheered over the third last, the second last and the final obstacle before he beat Well Chief by two lengths to the line. He was back as the champion. Not since Royal Relief in 1974 reclaimed the two-mile championship after losing it had anyone performed that feat. Barry Geraghty tried the flying dismount again, and this time ended up on his backside. Said Jessica Harrington: 'You'd think he'd have perfected it by now. He needs to take lessons in elegance.' With Kicking King taking the Gold Cup, Hardy Eustace the Champion Hurdle and Hedgehunter triumphing in the Grand National, the Irish had a clean sweep of the top four spring races for the first time ever.

Moscow Flyer, says his trainer, was a character. He knew when he was at Cheltenham or Sandown. He went out in the field every day but refused to go when it was wet. 'As for going out in the snow, you must be joking. He just stood in the yard and refused to move.'

It was Ireland's turn again in 2006, with Newmill winning the Queen Mother for John Murphy and jockey Andrew McNamara after an incident-packed race. Well Chief and Azertyuiop did not run and a promising young chaser called Kauto Star fell, not only bringing down the well-backed Dempsey but hampering Moscow Flyer too. Other casualties were Fundamentalist and the French mare Kario de Sormain. When it was suggested to her trainer Jean Paul Gallorini that it was a tough ask bringing her to Cheltenham for her first race in England he replied romantically, 'She will take to the English fences like a young girl discovering love.' Alas she fell at the first fence.

In a race in which quick, clean fencing is the key, Oneway and River City both unseated their riders too, and it was his jumping which won the race for Newmill, who had spent most of his season chasing Brave Inca over hurdles. Moscow Flyer plugged on to finish fifth but was not the force of old and was retired after the race.

The 2007 contest was won by Voy Por Ustedes in the familiar pink check colours of Sir Robert Ogden, a great patron of the jumping game. This time Dempsey and River City stayed on their feet to finish second and third behind Alan King's charge. Once again it was a case of an Arkle Chase winner the previous year stepping up to win the Queen Mother. After that we were back into dual-winner territory with Paul Nicholls's precociously talented Master Minded, owned by Clive Smith, winning in both 2008 and 2009.

Master Minded was the first five-year-old to win in the history of the race. But he did not merely win – he destroyed a high-class opposition including the previous year's winner. Voy Por Ustedes was the only horse to give him any kind of a race but while his jockey Robert Thornton was hard at work from four fences out, Master Minded was merely coasting, and Ruby Walsh could have extended his winning margin of nineteen lengths if he had needed to.

Paul Nicholls brought the awesome Master Minded back in 2009, and although the trainer reckoned his charge was only ninety-five per cent ready, the race was put to bed from several fences out, although the winning margin of seven lengths was less comprehensive. It was the veteran Well Chief, back on the racecourse after a 698-day absence, who came closest to giving him a race this time although things might have been different if Big Zeb, who was going well at the time, had not fallen four out.

The common expectation was that Master Minded, the 5-4 on favourite, had only to turn up in 2010 to match Badsworth Boy's record and become only the second horse ever to win the race three times. But these are horses, not machines. In the event it was Big Zeb, who might have beaten Master Minded in a previous clash at Punchestown had he not clouted the last fence, who gave the jumping display while Master Minded never looked happy and could do no better than fourth. Winning jockey Barry Geraghty, formerly Moscow Flyer's regular partner, had chosen to ride Big Zeb for Colm Murphy rather than the previous year's Arkle winner Forpaddydeplasterer, and while they say that jockeys make the worst tipsters his judgment was proved right. As for Master Minded, his jockey Ruby Walsh blamed the ground, but his trainer wondered aloud if the horse was now past his peak despite being only seven. None of Master Minded's family, noted Paul Nicholls, had 'trained on'. 'He has won two and they will never take them away from him, but he may not win another.'

Chapter 30

How to Ride Cheltenham

'If you have to think about going into a gap at Cheltenham the gap has closed and you are too late.' (Former jockey Mick Fitzgerald)

Cheltenham is not an easy course to ride, certainly not at Festival time. Some horses cannot cope with the undulations, some become unbalanced racing down the hill to the lowest point before the uphill finishing straight. Some, used to easier park courses, find that final rise too stiff and their stamina gives out. And at Cheltenham everything happens a little bit faster than many horses, and their jockeys, are accustomed to doing things. Under pressure, mistakes are made.

We are probably blessed today – thanks partly to the opportunities for self-analysis provided by video-recording – with the fittest, most talented and professional corps of top jockeys there has ever been. But Cheltenham has helped to create other legends. Before the Second World War, George Duller revolutionised hurdles riding, while Dick Rees was a street in front of most of his contemporaries. After it came greats like Tim Molony and Fred Winter; in the sixties and seventies Pat Taaffe and Tommy Carmody; in the eighties the determined Jonjo O'Neill and the coolly elegant John Francome, a recruit from the showjumping scene who had no equal at presenting a horse to a fence. Then too we enjoyed the skills of that great judge of pace Peter Scudamore; the dashing Jamie Osborne, with his record five Festival winners in 1992; the smart tactician Charlie Swan; and the ultimate professional Richard Dunwoody.

Over more recent years the Cheltenham Festival stars have included Mick Fitzgerald, associated with so many Nicky Henderson winners; Robert 'Choc' Thornton; and Richard Johnson, stable jockey to Philip Hobbs's consistent Somerset yard. 'Dicky' Johnson, who would have been champion jockey several times in any era except one in which he has had to compete with fifteen-times champion Tony McCoy, is in fact the only current rider who has won all the big three at the Festival: the Gold Cup, the Champion Hurdle and the Champion Chase, with a fourth-day top race, the World Hurdle, to boot.

But it is three Irish riders – Ruby Walsh, Tony McCoy and Barry Geraghty – who now head the all-time lists. The remarkable record seven wins achieved by Ruby Walsh in 2010, following three the year before, put him top of the all-time list with twenty-seven victories, two more than Arkle's partner Pat Taaffe. Ruby's total can only grow, since he is retained by the most powerful stables either side of the Irish Sea, those of Paul Nicholls and Willie Mullins.

Then with twenty-three Festival victories comes Tony McCoy, one-time stable jockey to Martin Pipe, now retained by the sport's biggest owner J.P. McManus. In third place with nineteen is Barry Geraghty, supported by powerful Irish stables as well as riding for Nicky Henderson, who tops the Festival list for current trainers.

What that tells us for a start, apart from the fact that it helps to ride for a top stable, is that riding Cheltenham winners is not down to a particular style. Their former colleague Mick Fitzgerald says that we are blessed to have two such good jockeys as A.P. McCoy and Ruby Walsh to watch. But he notes their styles are very different: 'Ruby is very quiet. You see a lot more movement with A.P. but both are just as effective. Ruby is brilliant at what he does.

He rides a very different race to A.P. He's a lot quieter, he allows the horse much more time to get into it. He does little things that you can't actually see. If you watch Ruby you'll see him make little moves, he'll sit down a little bit lower on a horse, he'll ask a horse to quicken a little at a particular time because he wants to get into a position he wants the horse in. A.P. is a bit more aggressive in attitude.

'I've ridden against Richard Dunwoody. I found Woody to be the best that I've ever seen. He was brilliant at what he did. He was good in a finish, strong, he was brilliant at presenting a horse at an obstacle. A.P. has taken that and he's found a little bit more aggression, he's a real winner, A.P. Anybody who backs him, you know you're going to get a run for your money. Somebody said to me, 'If I was skint, down to my last tenner and I wanted a jockey to ride a horse for me there wouldn't be any question, it would have to be A.P. every time.'

Martin Pipe concurs: 'A.P. does like to win *everything*. He's got the determination, no matter what kind of race it is. Dunwoody was a very good jockey, very stylish, perhaps he improved in big races. Scu [Peter Scudamore] was a natural, a great front-running jockey. He went out, knew the pace, knew the horses would jump, and got them jumping and going.'

There was no better example of the 35-year-old McCoy's determination than his ride on Alberta's Run to win the Ryanair Chase in 2010. Earlier he had taken a kick to his head when Jered fell in the first, and needed four stitches in his jaw. His neck was stiff and sore, but he noted, 'I picked myself up and I wasn't dead. Nothing was broken, so I carried on.' In the Ryanair he then rode a perfectly judged race setting a gallop to draw the sting from his main rival Poquelin, and setting sail from the top of the hill to see off the pack. He was limping painfully after another fall on Song of Songs later that day but never even contemplated giving up his ride on Denman the next day, when they finished second in the Gold Cup.

Curiously, a dozen of McCoy's Festival winners came in his first four years, and he hasn't been champion at the Festival since 1998. But then he hadn't won a Grand National either until his universally acclaimed victory in 2010.

With his father Ted's encouragement, Ruby Walsh initially modelled himself on Richard Dunwoody. Then he came to admire Charlie Swan even more, rating him the best jockey tactically he had ever seen. In his autobiography Ruby says: 'Charlie was better tactically than everyone. He was ahead of every jockey he ever rode against. Maybe there were stronger jockeys over a jump and maybe there were jockeys who looked more stylish but nobody was better than Charlie for winning a race when he had no right to.' Swan, he believes, won races with his head because he knew instinctively what to do and Ruby insists that while physical strength may win you one race in a hundred it is what goes on in your head as a jockey that wins you the rest. Trying to correct a horse physically too much he believes can be counter-productive, leading to crossed wires. Better to let him find his own way of popping a fence. Part of his job, he reckons is reducing stress for the horse. 'The good ones find something from the occasion. The horses who are mentally strong are usually the good ones. It's as important as talent.'

He acknowledges that at Cheltenham coping with the pressure is key. 'It's the making and breaking of your year. There's relief when you ride a winner. It's where you want to perform and where you want not to make mistakes. You have to be consistent for four days, every half hour or forty minutes. If I go to Cheltenham and draw a blank do you think the headlines are not going to say 'Disaster for Walsh'?

Says Paul Nicholls: 'Ruby's probably got it all. He's worst on the first race on the first day. It's a good thing that the Gold Cup is on the last day and he'll have ridden a few winners, whereas if the Gold Cup was on the first day I wouldn't say he wouldn't be as good a jockey but he wouldn't be as relaxed. He does get wound up about Cheltenham and it takes him a ride or two to get out there and relaxed. Once he's done that there's no better jockey. He's brilliant on those big occasions.'

Jessica Harrington, for whom he won two Champion Chases on Moscow Flyer, says much the same of Barry Geraghty: 'He is a very good rider but he rides another ten per cent above himself on the big days. His great expression is, 'Pressure? Pressure is for tyres.''

Others too have their admirers, like the sometimes turbulent Paul Carberry, rider of eleven Festival winners, who is supported by Noel Meade for his sheer instinctive talent. Says Noel: 'A.P. is an unbelievable man, he's so dedicated. He's actually better than ever he was. He and Ruby are just so brilliant – brilliant hands, brilliant judge of pace. Barry Geraghty might not have as much natural talent but in ways he has more talent – he eyes the whole show up very well. If he rides one for you he will know everything in the race that has a chance. Paul wouldn't, he'd ride on instinct.

'Paul is up there with any of the good jockeys we've had as long as we can remember. He's had his ups and downs. He has struggled with a lot of injuries – whether that's partly because he was a big drinker, I don't know – whether he didn't heal as well or hurt himself more when he hit the ground. He has the talent, he has the natural ability, he has uncanniness in his head that he can do the right thing easier than the wrong thing. My grandfather, a good footballer, said "the ball finds a good player". They're in the right place. It's the same with jockeys. His father was exactly the same.'

Fellow-trainer Edward O'Grady seems to agree. He rates a Tommy Carberry ride on Tied Cottage at the Festival one of the best he ever saw: 'He made the horse pop his fences throughout to conserve his energies. Most jockeys look for a big jump here and a big jump there. It was just an outstanding piece of horsemanship. Get up close, pop every fence and then bring him through to win over the last two.' In 1999, son Paul Carberry rode Bobbyjo, trained by father Tommy, to win the Grand National. It was the first Irish-trained winner of the race since L'Escargot had won twenty-four years before, ridden by Tommy Carberry. Carberry senior too had a reputation for knowing how to enjoy himself. Some fellow jockeys claim that he had been out all night before riding L'Escargot to Gold Cup glory.

From Noel Meade too there is praise for two more Irish riders: 'I would say Charlie Swan was as good a jockey as ever was, and Tommy Carmody the same. I don't think Charlie ever lost a race for me he should have won, and he probably won one or two more than he should.'

But, general qualities apart, how do the best jockeys ride Cheltenham? Tim Molony, winner of four consecutive Champion Hurdles, once told Tim Fitzgeorge-Parker how to tackle Prestbury Park: 'Two or three miles, hurdles or chases, I rode Cheltenham like this. First you must get a close-up position before the water jump [up the back hill]. This is vital. Then you can hold that position, sitting into him nicely on the bridle up the hill to that ditch on the top. If you are pushing there, off the bridle, you are in trouble, and then, as Lord Mildmay used to say, "That can be the worst fence in England, even if your horse has got his second wind." Now you can give him a breather, freewheel down the hill. But you must have your race won at the second last. You must ride for that. The second last has always been my winning post. If you haven't won at the second last you are not going to win anyway.

'From here you have two options. If you are going well enough you can give him a breather round that bend before wriggling into the last and home. Or you can ride like hell into the last and all the way home to the winning post.'

Martin Pipe's advice to his jockeys in the highly charged atmosphere at Cheltenham was always the same: 'I always told my jockeys, even A.P., "Mind you get the start right." It's most impor-tant. Once you've got the start right and jumped the first hurdle you're in the race and you should be in the right position. Then the race will come your way. If you get it all wrong, make a mistake at the first, and you're struggling from then on, you're really in trouble. I always used to tell the jockeys, from Peter Scudamore on, the only two hurdles that count are the first hurdle and the last. Whatever happens in between, those are the ones that count. If you jump those you'll gain ground and win races. Of course they all count but I just try to emphasise that the importance of jumping the last is that the winning post comes to you easily.'

Choc Thornton gave readers of the *Racing Post* in 2009 a tutorial in how to ride the two Cheltenham courses, the old and the new:

> You'll always get an end-to-end gallop. On the new course the pull from the second last is a lot stiffer than on the old course, but the old course is still plenty stiff enough and if you come off that bend in front it can take a week to get to the line, especially if you've been at the front for a while and you can start to feel the others eating into your lead. There's no worse feeling in racing but it's a fair test for man and beast and if you're on a horse that stays every yard you've got a chance. It's what festival racing should be about.'

He argued that you ride differently at the Festival, quoting Steve Smith-Eccles's advice to line up one or two off the rail. 'If you're on the paint and you get boxed in there's only one way to go and that's out. Start going out and you keep going out and can lose an awful lot of ground.' Sitting two or three places off the rails, he argued, gave you the chance of escape if you encountered traffic problems. 'I like to be quite handy so you can keep tabs on the leaders but also have options.'

In the Champion Hurdle, said Choc, you should keep handy (in close touch with the leaders) then freewheel to the second-last hurdle to allow your horse to fill up so he can get up the hill. As Katchit's successful rider put it, 'Works for me, why fix it?'

Thornton counsels that the old track for the first two days rides sharper. 'You always seem to be on the turn and if you let them run away from you at the top of the hill they'll be gone. You've got to be handy. If you are a few lengths back they can get away from you.' On the new course on the third or fourth days you have a bit more latitude. 'You've got more time to catch those in front over the last three or four.' The new course, he says, is more of a galloping track than the old but 'whatever the race they are going a good clip'. That, plus the size of the fields, and you need a bit more luck than normal and a bit more heart.

Finally he warned that the Cheltenham undulations will unbalance a horse, and if they are not travelling well because they have got unbalanced you have problems. It's OK if you can get your horse on an even keel. 'But if you're on something that shouldn't be there it's the worst and your race ends up being all about survival.'

The biggest debate, hinted at there by Choc, seems to be about whether it is best to take the shortest way round the left-hand track by sticking to the inner rail or not.

Mouse Morris is precise with his jockeys about where on the course he likes to see them make ground and where they should not attempt it, though he wasn't telling me where. Former rider Charlie Swan says: 'It is always on a slight curve and the hills make it even tighter. Mouse impressed on me not to go round the inside. If I did I would be pushed about and run the risk of being knocked back. He felt it was OK on the inner if we were on the heels of the leaders but if further back you must be towards the outer. "You will lose ground on the turns but nothing like what you would lose if you were interfered with."'

But most of the horses Charlie Swan rode at Cheltenham he did keep to the inside, while Conor O'Dwyer, for example, who won the Gold Cup on Imperial Call and War of Attrition, and the Champion Hurdle on Hardy Eustace, used to be adamant that a few places out was best. He insists that commentators who criticise jockeys for going round the outside at Cheltenham don't realise that its constant turns make it a comparatively tight track. 'If you are on the inner and something falls in front of you, if it doesn't bring you down you are baulked or get stopped completely. You've got to get your momentum going again and it costs you a lot. When you consider the pace these races are run at it isn't easy to get back the distance you've lost. For the bit that you lose [by choosing to go] on the outside, at least you never lose momentum and you can keep going at a nice steady, easy pace.'

Dessie Hughes, rider of Gold Cup winner Davy Lad and both rider and trainer of Champion Hurdle winners, says that's a reasonable argument if you are riding the best horse in the race, but not if you are on a 14-1 shot. 'In races like the Arkle or the RSA Chase there's not much between six or eight horses, so if you can sneak a length here or a length there from the time you jump off, you go the sharpest way, and if you can avoid making a bad mistake, nip half a length here or there with a good "lep". Then, by the time you get to the line, if you win half a length you'll say: "I wouldn't have won it by going any other way."'

Willie Mullins says of Festival jockeys: 'I've watched all of them, and lots of times you have to take into account your horse. Charlie was riding Istabraq and a few other fast horses like that which you can afford to have on the inside, and they're quick enough to take a break. Whereas Conor with Imperial Call, a slow myopic chaser, I think he probably wanted to make sure he had a better chance of keeping his rhythm up and keeping his jumping, going – going around a bit wider so he didn't get into any messy situations. Hardy Eustace was a galloper. He didn't want to get into trouble with the horse. But you've got to take every race and every horse as you find it. You can't make a general rule.'

He is echoed by Martin Pipe: 'It all depends what position you are in the race. That's why the jockeys like to follow good jumpers. There's no better way round than the shortest way round, really, but you can get in trouble. I like horses to be handy, providing they're not going too fast. If they're going too fast then you probably have to pull off three or four out, whatever. It's important to go the right pace.'

Mick Fitzgerald is another pragmatist. 'When Richard

Dunwoody rode, it was as if his inside leg had a hook on it that ran along the inside rail. He would be on the inside always. But when it got to Cheltenham you would predominantly find Woody on the middle to outer because he had that worry about horses coming back to you once they haven't been good enough up front or there were traffic problems. There's no hard and fast rule. Charlie Swan was nine times champion in Ireland and he very rarely left the rails, very rarely.

'You can't have hard and fast rules about Cheltenham. It depends on the horse you are riding. If you've got a horse with a lot of speed, tactically you can go where you want. It doesn't matter whether you are inside or outside, you will get the breaks. If you have to think about going into a gap at Cheltenham the gap has closed and you are too late.'

Dunwoody himself says of riding at Cheltenham: 'I wouldn't like going round the inner, especially at the Festival. One day I went down the inner and got stopped. I always like to give myself an option – be about one off, make good use of them, make sure I don't go too soon. They can all get very excited and start racing too early. You need to try and get a bit of a blow on them as they head up the back hill, then start to run again down the hill.' And all these years later there are echoes of Tim Molony when he argues: 'Those two or three horses that have made it to the second last in a challenging position are not going to stop. You can only make up so much ground after the last.'

The key for trainers, says Noel Meade, is to employ a good jockey and leave it to them to make the decisions. 'I would say, "He's better coming late" or, "Make use of him through the race" but basically I would leave that to themselves. If a jockey is worth his salt he's the one who should make up his mind.'

What the jockey needs, of course, is a willing partner, and the horses have to be looked after by the course planners as well as by those who tend to and train them. In the modern world, responsible racecourses put the safety and welfare of the horses above fogeyish demands that everything be left alone to continue the same historic tests; riding the Cheltenham course well also requires adapting to changes on the course itself.

The Jockey Club and National Hunt Committee agree these days that racing is part of the entertainment industry, and that the layman's views have to be taken into account. It is all very well for trainers and jockeys to argue that racehorses live, comparatively, the life of Riley and that the price for staying in five-star equine hotels is occasionally being driven hard to exert yourself on a racecourse. As Tony Balding once put it, 'Racing is about competition, and competition is about pain. Let's not delude ourselves. We are asking athletes, who happen to be horses, to exert themselves to their fullest, and to do that they sometimes have to go through a pain barrier. And the whip is what generates their innate ability. Without its motivation most of them would not bother.'

But some of the old-time jockeys who almost filleted a horse in their efforts to drive it first up the Cheltenham hill to the winning post would hardly recognise today's cushioned whips. Nor would they be allowed to ride remotely as they did. There are strict rules now about where a horse may be hit and how often. Richard Dunwoody, one of the all-time greats in his sport, now cringes when he recollects how he drove the often unsound Charter Party, brilliantly trained by David Nicholson, from the last fence to the winning post. 'I should have been hung, drawn and quartered for being far too hard on him. It was a question of, "I'm not going to get beat, I'm not going to get beat."'

The Cheltenham executive is highly conscious of public concern about the safety and welfare of horses running at the Festival, and it constantly monitors the course to ensure that the casualties which are, alas, inevitable in jump racing, are kept to a minimum. In 2006 they suffered something of a public relations disaster. Through the four days of the Festival nine horses suffered injuries which resulted in them dying or having to be put down, and a further two had to be put down later to avoid further suffering.

Investigations swiftly followed but after taking evidence from jockeys, trainers, course officials and everybody concerned, the Horseracing Regulatory Authority report published that July concluded that there was no single factor or combination of factors that could be blamed for the large number of deaths. The report confirmed that the going was no quicker than good and that 'contrary to popular belief' the course was not over-drained. Indeed it noted: 'Much of the track has no installed drains whatsoever.'

It found no evidence of bunching, or no-hopers getting in the way, nor of off-track distractions. All obstacles had been prepared in the usual way and there were no bad ground 'hotspots'. None of the horses who died had a record of injury, all had run at least three times in the previous year and none were bad jumpers – in their previous 116 runs collectively there had only been three falls. Only one of the nine injuries occurred in a race where the time was faster than normal. The huge casualty list, it seemed, was down to sheer bad luck. There had, after all, been no equine fatalities at the three Cheltenham fixtures that season prior to the Festival.

Ferdy Murphy, the experienced trainer of a good few Festival winners, possibly put his finger on a contributory factor when he said: 'The track was in fantastic shape but they go very quick at the Festival and any horse coming to the meeting with a small injury like a stress fracture that goes undetected will get found out.'

Media attention at the time focussed on the three deaths in one race, the National Hunt Chase. Noting that it was the longest race at the Festival and one confined to amateur riders, pundits pointed out that the race conditions had been changed to allow hurdle winners as well as chase winners to participate, effectively opening the race to better horses, but also to faster ones not necessarily suited to four miles. For four years before the change there had been no fatalities but in the five runnings of the race from 2000–2006 (one year Cheltenham was cancelled) seven horses had died, including three in 2006.

Cheltenham itself looked long and hard at the race conditions and the British Horseracing Authority, noting that Cheltenham's long-term fatality rate was twice the national average and that faller rates were higher at the March meeting than at its non-Festival equivalents, recommended a pre-race veterinary review of Festival runners not meeting certain criteria, a recommendation that was implemented. Cheltenham also reduced the safety limit on runners to twenty-eight in handicap hurdles and twenty in the National Hunt Chase. They also ensured a further five yards of fresh ground on the new chase course was available for future Festivals.

Director of Racing and Clerk of the Course Simon Claisse, who rode in the Foxhunters' Chase himself the last time it was the race before the Gold Cup, looks with the Cheltenham team every year to see if they need to make changes. In 2010 the second last fence, a fence that was jumped just as horses met the rising ground approaching the finishing straight and which had claimed a number of horses' lives over the years, was re-sited about 80–100 yards further on off the last bend in the finishing straight, closer to the last fence. It left a longer run downhill between the third-last and second-last but with two fences in the straight gave the crowd a better view. The move was supported by most trainers and jockeys, some of whom were consulted in advance and who would have been aware of the statistic showing that horses were seven times more likely to fall at that fence. Because of where they started, the re-siting meant there would be an extra fence to jump in two-mile and two-and-a-half mile chases on the old course.

Said managing director Edward Gillespie: 'Safety of the horses is the important thing for us, and the key with that fence was that horses were falling without making mistakes. Many appeared to jump the fence well, only to knuckle on landing with their back end going faster than their front end. It tended to be horses in contention which fell, rather than those dropping back, and that was what got us asking, "Is there an alternative location?"'

Cheltenham has also persevered with the 2010 Festival change which moved the final flight of hurdles seventy yards closer to the finishing line. Previously the run-in from the last hurdle to the finishing post was 220 yards; this cut it to 150 yards. Bringing the jumping action closer to the viewing public, the hope was that the move would also result in fewer whip bans for jockeys driving their mounts home up the hill. It also meant, however, that mistakes at the last obstacle would be more heavily penalised because there was less recovery time. Some critics said that the re-siting would thus increase the chances of the best horse getting beaten by bad luck. But is making a poor jump bad luck? It is called 'jump racing', after all. And whip offences at the 2010 Festival did reduce by seventy-one per cent.

Chapter 31

Ireland's Successes and
Ireland's worries

*'The Irish love horses and racing and they pack the place. When
one of their own, particularly a well-backed runner, begins to get
the upper hand in a race it is as though they are picking
Cheltenham up and banging it on the ground.' (Former jockey
Mick Fitzgerald)*

It was Vincent O'Brien who started it. His Gold Cup victories
with Cottage Rake in the early post-war years were the first by
an Irish trainer, and the Anglo-Irish rivalry which runs
through the four days of the Festival like the lettering in a stick of
Blackpool rock has been with us ever since. But what constitutes
an 'Irish' victory? The tallies kept by the Cheltenham authorities
are compiled on the basis of where a horse is trained. Thus the
Gold Cup victory for Imperial Call, trained by a patrician Old
Etonian who had served in the Guards, went down on the slate as
one for Ireland because the courageous Fergie Sutherland had
moved from Newmarket to his mother's estate in Ireland. Horses
trained at Jackdaw's Castle, Temple Guiting are cheered home by
Gloucestershire folk as local 'English' successes from just up the
road although the establishment is owned by J.P. McManus and
the horses, many of them running in J.P.'s colours, are trained by
Jonjo O'Neill, a man whom no one could listen to for a minute

without being clear about his Emerald Isle origins. And what about the horses and jockeys? According to the convention we use, seven of the twenty-six winners at the 2010 Festival were 'Irish victories', that is they were horses trained in Ireland. But fifteen of those twenty-six winners were bred in Ireland and twenty of the twenty-six races were won by Irish-born jockeys.

Irish fortunes have varied over the years. In both 1987 and 1988, Galmoy, trained by the late John Mulhern, was the only Irish winner and in 1989 the Irish had none. In 2006 there was a record haul of ten Irish victories. Not only did they hit double figures, but for the first time there was an Irish-trained 1-2-3 in the Gold Cup. The winner of the Queen Mother Champion Chase was trained in Ireland, and so were the first four home in the Champion Hurdle.

Certainly there are some races which Irish punters planning their Festival strategy normally reckon to 'belong' to their side of the water. Irish entrants have a formidably high strike rate in the Champion Bumper, a Flat race without obstacles for horses bred to jump them later. The invaders generally fare well too in one of the more recent Festival innovations, the cross-country 'banks' race, although it has to be said that their winner of the race in 2010, A New Story, took some finding. The twelve-year-old hadn't won a race since 2005, in forty attempts.

Enda Bolger, one of many trainers to benefit from the patronage of J.P. McManus, is the acknowledged master of training horses to win over the endurance courses of banks and walls, ditches, rails and bushes. The seven-times Irish champion point-to-point rider, who won the Foxhunters' at the Festival on Elegant Lord in 1996 for J.P., learned his trade under Paddy Mullins and P.P. Hogan before taking out his own licence in 1986. His veteran Spotthedifference has won six times around the Cheltenham track.

We looked earlier at the stars trained by Vincent O'Brien and Tom Dreaper. Those two departed giants of Irish racing are the only ones to have trained more Festival winners than the eighteen accumulated by Edward O'Grady, whose father Willie trained three Festival winners in the 1960s.

Edward O'Grady's total of Cheltenham Festival winners would have been much larger than that were it not for his decision to follow the O'Brien pattern and switch to Flat racing in the early 1980s. There were, he says, good economic reasons for doing so. On the Flat he made more money from fewer winners, but he did not get enough top-calibre horses to compete at the highest levels, and after ten years he came back to jumping, insisting that while it brought greater heartaches it was better for the soul at the end of the day. 'Training jumpers may be a 24-hour-a-day occupation but it has a calibre of satisfaction and reward you can't find elsewhere.'

He has won some of Cheltenham's most traditional races, taking the National Hunt Chase, for example, with Bit Of A Skite and Mr Midland but almost certainly the best horse O'Grady has trained so far was Golden Cygnet. He won the Supreme Novices' Hurdle in 1978 in a time faster than the Champion Hurdle was run in that year. Some Cheltenham veterans like former Clerk of the Course Philip Arkwright say they never saw a better horse. Golden Cygnet then ran in the Scottish Champion Hurdle and had the great Night Nurse and Sea Pigeon stone cold and well beaten behind him when he fell and broke his neck. Edward O'Grady will never forget him. The horse, he says, originally used to gallop with his head between his legs, cutting his knees with his teeth. But no sooner had he consulted with showjumper Harvey Smith on the construction of a protective boot than Golden Cygnet ended the habit. 'He was an extraordinary horse in that most horses tend to pull at the start of a race and come off the bridle at the end of a race. He was the opposite. He started off 'off the bridle' when you dropped him in but the further you got into a race the more he pulled. I can still see him between the third last and the second last at Cheltenham doing this [he weaves his clasped-together hands from one side to another], coming down like a snake. He was pulling so hard before he got to the second last where he left

Western Rose behind him. He was a beast. I was very young when I had him, the world was at my feet and I thought like the number six bus there would be another one coming along, but sadly there was only one.'

O'Grady's first Cheltenham winner was Mr Midland, who won the National Hunt Chase in 1974. Not a lot of horses went from Ireland in those days, he recalls. 'We'd sold most of them.' It was the pre-corporate age. 'It was very civilised – purely racing people, six races a day for three days – and the winners' enclosure was terribly special. The horses used to walk down and come into this little amphitheatre. I had never seen people with bowler hats and umbrellas, people with walking sticks and pushchairs – if they weren't running they were certainly going at top speed to get there to welcome back the winner. It was very intimate and very special. The only people who went into the winners' enclosure were the direct connections of the horse.'

So was it less important to have a Cheltenham winner then? 'It was terribly important to have a winner at Cheltenham but people managed to survive without it. It was important but it didn't have the hype it has now. There was no television in Ireland, for starters. Maybe some people used to get a bit of BBC so they could probably watch a bit in black and white – with snow.'

When O'Grady returned to National Hunt racing it took him a while to get back to the top and it was crucial he had winners at the Festival of 1994 to signal his return to the top. He was convinced that Gimme Five and Sound Man, both ridden by top jockey Charlie Swan, were going to win on the first day but both disappointed. 'Because he was such an outstanding jockey I didn't bother giving Charlie Swan any instructions. But for whatever reason on Tuesday night I was very deflated and I didn't think Charlie had covered himself in glory on my two horses so I decided, "Bugger this, there are going to be instructions tomorrow." We fancied Time For A Run in the Coral Cup and I wanted him to produce the horse late so I told him I didn't mind if he came too late and got beaten but I would not be best pleased if he came too soon. He was therefore to ride with "balls of steel".'

Charlie Swan timed his run to perfection, working his way through the field and only taking the lead in the dying stages of the race. He also won the bumper that same day on Mucklemeg, the favourite, by three lengths. 'She was one I bought,' says Edward. 'I'd never run her before she ran in the bumper at Cheltenham but that day she would have won the Ascot Gold Cup. She was just outstanding.' The double duly signified O'Grady's return to the jumping heights and shortly afterwards, from the workshops of Matty Ryan, jeweller to the racing fraternity in Ireland, there arrived at Charlie Swan's home a couple of round metal objects tastefully mounted on a green baize background with the inscription: 'Balls of Steel. Time For A Run and Mucklemeg. Cheltenham Festival 1994. Thanks, Edward.'

The one man who lost out on Time For A Run, unusually, was owner J.P. McManus. He had instructed his brother to place some large bets, but not at less than 10-1. Unfortunately his brother, betting on credit, was restricted to a few bookies who knew him, and they wouldn't take the sums involved at better than 8-1 (the horse had opened at 14-1 and started at 11-1). He arrived in the box with the bad news that he had refused all offers and there was no bet, just as Charlie Swan wove his way through the field to win.

Second time around, Edward O'Grady reckons the competition has hotted up. With the precocious French-breds coming in, Irish horses are now having to be broken (prepared for riding) earlier. As for the racing: 'It's much sharper. The owners are more demanding. The amount of training gallops that people can go to, the amount of schooling hurdles that people can go to now, you don't have horses coming out pretty unfit and using the racecourse as a training ground, which used to be par for the course. Those days are long gone. It's a bit like musical chairs now. Get out of your chair for a minute and somebody else is sitting in it.'

O'Grady sums up the approach and experience of many when

he says that at the start of every season half the yard is Cheltenham-bound and they have no point-to-pointers. By March he has too many pointers and hardly a horse left for Cheltenham. One difficulty is persuading would-be owners of Cheltenham candidates to pass up some of the cherries on the way, as you have to in order to peak at the right time.

For one thing all racegoers should be grateful to Edward O'Grady. He it was in 1982 who trained the first Cheltenham winner for J.P. McManus, the greatest individual supporter jump racing has ever seen. When Mr Donovan that year won what is now known as the Neptune Hurdle his owner was reputed to have taken £250,000 off the bookies in backing him down from 6-1 to 9-2. It obviously helped to increase his appetite for the game. He now has some 300 horses at a time, spread across a wide swathe of trainers large and small. But J.P. had had to show patience. His early attempts to win the National Hunt Chase with the heavily backed Jack of Trumps (1978) and Deep Gale (1979) both ended in expensive failure when the horses fell.

In Ireland it sometimes seems that trainers earn as much respect for their prowess in the betting ring as they do for the quality of the horses they send into the parade ring, and one of those in the wave succeeding Vincent O'Brien who was especially loved by the punting public was Mick O'Toole. He began as a greyhound trainer, and sent Marjorie over from Dublin to win the English greyhound Oaks in 1965. Mick had two uncles, one of whom trained horses and the other greyhounds, and the next year he started training horses too, beginning with a five-box yard near Phoenix Park. In all, he trained 800 winners from Maddenstown on The Curragh, and he had eight Festival winners including the 1977 Gold Cup winner Davy Lad. In fact Mick O'Toole had nine first past the post at the Festival. Chinrullah was a runaway winner of the Champion Chase in 1980 but, like Ireland's Tied Cottage in that year's Gold Cup, he lost the race afterwards in the dope-box because a batch of horse-feed had been contaminated. Minute traces of theobromine and caffeine were found in his urine. The authorities were sympathetic because it was clear that no blame attached to the stables concerned but the technical offence forced them to disqualify Chinrullah. O'Toole was philosophical, reflecting: 'We had our fun on the day. The horse won by twenty-five lengths and we were reimbursed for the prize-money because the horse-feed people took responsibility.'

Chinrullah's 1980 success in the race occurred the year that the Champion Chase became the Queen Mother Champion Chase and Mick O'Toole was one of a small group of people whom she asked to be invited to a celebratory lunch organised for her at the English Garden restaurant in London by Peter O'Sullevan. The normally loquacious trainer – any thoughtful donkey would be checking his hip joints after encountering him – was nervous of being seated next to the star invitee but they got on so well that he became a regular participant as the lunch became an annual occasion.

There was no doubting the Queen Mother's affinity with racing folk and sometimes she was a practical help too. Once her regular jockey David Mould called her in desperation because his badly broken leg was so infected most people would not touch it. She put him in touch with her personal surgeon Sir Henry Osmond Clarke. Although it was touch and go, Sir Henry saved both the leg and the jockey's career.

One Festival winner for whom Mick O'Toole had special affection was Bit Of A Jig who won the Stayers' Hurdle. The horse, he says, was a bit of a family pet because he was sold to America after winning a bumper and a few hurdles but had to be brought back because his dam was unregistered. Bit Of A Jig though probably owed him one. There is still a note of rueful horror in Mick's voice as he tells you of the horse's first bumper success: 'He won without our knowledge.' Ireland's bookmakers would testify that O'Toole horses that were ready to win didn't often set off unbacked. As a horse buyer and a gambler, says Dessie Hughes, his long-time stable jockey O'Toole was 'brave as a lion'. 'He made a lot of money gambling and he lost a lot of money gambling.' He was popular 'because he's a supreme optimist, he enjoys a good craic and he was a very good trainer.' He was also a man with a formidable eye for a horse. Hughes recalls: 'He went to Doncaster sales one day and came back with two box-loads, ten horses. They were mostly £600, £800 or £1,000, no horse cost more than £15,000, and every one of them won. It was just incredible. Our Albert won the Galway Plate. Coffee Royale was a hell of a horse, Bit of A Jig won at Cheltenham and Wild Irish won three bumpers . . .'

The two trainers with the strength in depth to dominate the Irish jumping scene in recent years have been Noel Meade and Willie Mullins. Both have won Irish championships, whether decided on winners or prize-money totals, but Mullins has had the better of it at Cheltenham. Noel Meade thought he had his first Festival winner with Heighlin, only his second runner at Cheltenham, in 1978. Everyone was congratulating him, and then it turned out Heighlin had been beaten a short head. There were more frustrating seconds with Heist, Hill Society and Tiananmen Square before he finally laid the bogey twenty-two years later with Sausalito Bay. When he came into the winners' enclosure he kissed the turf like a visiting pope and declared, 'I can die a happy man now.' In the very next race his Native Dara looked all over a winner – and was caught on the line by What's Up Boys. That's racing.

Says Noel Meade: 'To get your name on those trophies is a big thing and you'd better make the most of it when you do because you know that every week in this game will bring you another kick in the teeth.' He certainly had his frustrations with Harchibald, discussed in the Champion Hurdle chapters. One of the best hurdlers never to win a Festival championship, Harchibald was still the winner through his career of more than £500,000.

Noel Meade says of the Cheltenham Festival: 'It's a fantastic place and it's fantastic to be involved in it, but it's heartbreaking as well. For a long time it wasn't my favourite place but to us in

Ireland and to everyone in jumping it is the pinnacle where you want to win those Grade 1 championship races. My first memory of it is rushing home from school to see Cheltenham on TV. At that time it was black and white. Tom Dreaper, who trained Arkle, was my hero – I had a scrapbook on him – and I remember pedalling very hard on my bicycle to get home from school and see Arkle on the telly.

'It's not a particularly great track but it's a great theatre. It's a sharp track. OK, when they come up the straight they have a run up the hill, but other than that you're on the bend all the time and it's very undulating. A lot of horses don't act at Cheltenham, they don't come down the hill and they don't travel round it that well. I suppose it's a bit like what they say about Epsom: it's a good trial of the thoroughbred but if you went out tomorrow to build it again you wouldn't build it like that. But it's there, it's where the championships are, and whoever wins the Grade 1 races there is the champion. History is something you can't get away from. It's everyone's dream to train the winner of the Gold Cup at Cheltenham, and I would give anything to train the winner of the Champion Hurdle or the Gold Cup. I wouldn't give you tuppence to win the Grand National – it's not a championship.'

Willie Mullins too has a great record of success. He won the Grand National with Hedgehunter and then ran second with him in the 2006 Gold Cup. He saddled Florida Pearl to win four Hennessy Cognac Gold Cups and he has a unique record in the Cheltenham Festival Bumper, having won it six times with Cousin Vinny, Missed That, Joe Cullen, Alexander Banquet, Florida Pearl and Wither or Which. But his Cheltenham successes began as a rider for his father – the much-loved Paddy Mullins, who died in 2010 – when he won the historic National Hunt Chase on the 8-1 shot Hazy Dawn in 1982.

That first Cheltenham winner was, he says, a wonderful experience, but it was a scary one too: 'She galloped and jumped very well, she stayed all day, but I remember turning for home in front and getting the fright of my life because I couldn't see any fence. Though I had walked the course in advance I thought, "Cripes, am I after taking the wrong course?" The one thing Jonjo O'Neill had said to me was that you can't take the wrong course because it's railed the whole way. How did this happen? There was no fence in front of me and this whole thing went through my mind. It was probably about three seconds but it felt like ten minutes. I think it was the way the sun was shining off the stand or there was a shadow that just blocked my eyesight and then suddenly the fence appeared and I jumped it. But it had given me the fright of my life. She then pinged the last and it was just a magical feeling for a rider to have his first Cheltenham winner on his first ride there. I was absolutely delighted.'

There was extra Irish celebration because Hazy Dawn's owner was Roly Daniels, the country and western singer. 'His brother in law was Terry Casey [later to train Rough Quest to win the Grand National], then my father's head man, that was the connection. I think Roly might have sang a bar or two on the winners' rostrum.' Indeed he did, according to reports on the day. And it was probably not the first time 'Danny Boy' has been sung in that winners' enclosure.

Two years later, Mullins father and son repeated the dose with Mack's Friendly, owned by John Mulhern, who later trained on his own account. Willie recalls: 'He bought the horse the day before the race and it ran in his colours. Very pleasing. He was by the sprinter Be Friendly so it was a freak that he could stay four miles. He needed a trip.'

Paddy Mullins, who bred a racing dynasty of three trainer sons, was a great family man, and it was said that Willie's success on Hazy Dawn gave him greater pleasure than Dawn Run's great Gold Cup victory, after the altercations with her owner over who should ride the mare. Willie says tactfully: 'I know of all the winners that I have had at Cheltenham, legging up my own son Patrick in the bumper on Cousin Vinny (the winner in 2008) was as good a feeling as I can get. You know how tough it is to train and ride a Cheltenham winner so it is very satisfying to put your own son or daughter up. Patrick gave him an excellent ride on the day. That gave me huge pleasure. But Cheltenham winners give you a huge buzz anyhow.'

Willie Mullins also put himself up in earlier days, both training and riding Wither or Which to win the bumper in 1996. While some were surprised he did not choose a top professional he says, 'It wasn't a decision. I rode all the bumper horses and that was it. We would always put amateurs up in the bumper in Cheltenham. I would always try and give my own amateurs first choice or second choice.' He reminds you that Ruby Walsh, with whom he has shared so many successes since, got his first Cheltenham rides that way. He did, however, put up Richard Dunwoody the next year to ride Florida Pearl to success in the bumper, but only because he had just retired from the saddle and Ruby, who won for him in 1998 on Alexander Banquet, was not yet ready. Willie Mullins firmly supports the Irish practice of having bumpers confined to amateur riders, and he would like to see English courses adopt the practice too.

He says: 'Wither or Which was special because he was an Irish banker. Tourist Attraction the year before was my first Festival winner as a trainer – she won the Supreme Novice Hurdle. I got a huge boost from that, I enjoyed that. However Wither or Which, which was a horse we made ourselves, coming over as favourite and winning, was hugely beneficial to us from a training point of view. It immediately showed we could buy, make and train a horse to win at the top level.'

Florida Pearl of course was a Cheltenham regular, though his best successes were achieved elsewhere. 'He was a huge horse, about seventeen hands and with everything built in proportion. He was very precocious. Even at that size he was probably as good at four as he was in the rest of his life. He always had gears, which probably just accounted for the fact that maybe he might not just have stayed that extended trip in the Gold Cup [i.e. three miles two furlongs rather than three miles]. He flew around Kempton when he was there, a different kind of track. He was a perfect racehorse, size-wise, though he was not everyone's cup of tea. Some don't like horses that big but I thought he was good. He was a very sound horse too. I don't think he ever missed a season.'

Ironically, though Florida Pearl was one of the best horses Willie Mullins has ever had, winning eighteen of his thirty-three races between 1996 and 2004, including a King George VI Chase and four Hennessy Gold Cups, Willie's top jockey through the period, Ruby Walsh, never ever won on the horse he says always felt like a superstar on the gallops.

Other trainers who have impacted on the Irish racegoers' consciousness have included Arthur Moore, son of Dan, who follows the tradition his father began when L'Escargot took the Grand National by putting his trilby between the ears of big race victors in the winners' enclosure.

Then there are those who are lucky to be associated with horses who have been wrapped to the collective Irish bosom like Dorans Pride and Danoli. It took Michael Hourigan, the handler of Dorans Pride, six years to train his first winner but he went on to win ten Grade 1s with Beef Or Salmon, named in honour of the regular query from the waitress at a County Limerick restaurant. Sadly for Hourigan, Beef Or Salmon never performed well at Cheltenham; indeed he never won a race outside Ireland.

The best Dorans Pride managed in the Gold Cup was two thirds. But he did win the Stayers' Hurdle, since renamed as the World Hurdle. In all, Dorans Pride, who started out being called Padjo until he was sold to Tom Doran, won twenty-seven of his sixty races for Michael Hourigan. What racegoers loved about him as much as anything was his sheer pluck. In December 1995 Dorans Pride developed colic, an affliction that can kill a horse in half a day. He suffered badly for forty-eight hours, and his life was in peril during two emergency operations. But he still came back after that to score some of his finest successes. Because he enjoyed it so much, Dorans Pride was still competing at Cheltenham at the age of fourteen when he sadly had to be put down after breaking a leg at the second fence in the 2003 Foxhunters'.

Another popular hero was Danoli, trained by Tom Foley. He was the 9-4 favourite when he won the Sun Alliance Novices' Hurdle in 1994, thanks to a massive gamble by J.P. Mcmanus. McManus had lost £30,000 on Edward O'Grady's Gimme Five the day before, and after Stephen Little paid him out the £155,000 to his £80,000 bet on Danoli, J.P. famously declared, 'That put the wheels back on the bike.'

Danoli was the horse they called 'the people's champion', the epitome of the small man's dream and one of those horses who took racing off the back pages and into the news. Trainer Tom Foley was a farmer who dabbled in a few horses and who got to train Danoli because he went to his bone-setter owner Dan O'Neill for treatment for his back. The horse's name came from Dan and his daughter Olivia – Dan-oli.

On Tom Foley's advice the first-time owner bought him for £3,000 less than the price sought at Goff's sales. Before he won the Sun Alliance he had won three hurdles in the 1992–3 season and three more the season after, as well as finishing second in the Irish Champion Hurdle. When he came to Cheltenham it was the first time Tom Foley had been in a plane, and the media picked up on the man who insisted on staying not in a plush Cheltenham hotel but in the hostel reserved for stable lads.

When Danoli won the Sun Alliance, coolly ridden by Irish champion Charlie Swan, the popular veteran reporter George Ennor reported: 'They cheered him down to the start. They cheered him as he started. They cheered more loudly as he took the lead and they raised the roof as he passed the winning post in front.'

Danoli won races like the Martell Aintree Hurdle at Punchestown and the Hatton's Grace Hurdle at Fairyhouse. But the Sun Alliance was his only Cheltenham victory. In 1995 he finished third in the Champion Hurdle behind Alderbrook and then went to Liverpool where he won the Martell Hurdle in April. In doing so he broke a fetlock joint, showing considerable courage in getting past the winning post. Some feared his life was in danger and it was reported that there had even been a note from Rome saying that the pope was including the stricken horse in his prayers. The fractured cannon bone was pinned with two metal screws and Danoli was racing again by January the next year, but he was never quite the same force over fences. In all he won seventeen of his thirty-two races and never finished worse than fourth in those he completed. Sadly he was not destined to have a long retirement. Retired to the Irish National Stud in Kildare, where he became the inseparable companion of Vintage Crop, the Melbourne Cup winner, Danoli died from a bout of colic in 2006.

Ireland's smaller-time Cheltenham heroes include people too, and none more so than Oliver Brady, the man who puts the ex into extrovert and is sometimes known as the 'bard of Monaghan'. He trains at what he calls a 'little place just outside of Ballybay' on land paid for by the £100,000 won on a series of cross doubles and a treble at Cheltenham in 1981 with Sea Pigeon (6-1), Willie Wumpkins (13-2) and Little Owl (7-4), despite suffering from stomach cancer and a heart condition that required a quadruple by-pass. He says he is 'drawn to the glory of the little man', though he is clearly not that at all. With his Kenyan partner Rita Shah he runs a recycling company employing seventy-six people and is busy too raising around £500,000 in charity projects for African orphans. Like J.P. McManus, he likes to spread his good fortune.

When Brady's Baron de Feypo achieved third place in the Coral Hurdle in 2009 he sprinted to the winner's enclosure and stripped off his suit to reveal a Monaghan Gaelic football jersey. It was a day when the English had won five races, mitigated only by Jessica Harrington's Cork All Star winning the bumper with Barry Geraghty, but Brady sent them all back across the water with a smile on their faces. Conducting crowd celebrations he declared:

'I know I only finished third but, sure, it was like a winner coming here. When you can come from County Monaghan to Cheltenham and finish third in the Coral Cup your health doesn't bother you. I leave my health in the hands of God. I've finished my treatment. If he wants me up there, I'll be up there. If he wants me down here, I'll stay.'

Not long before, medics had fixed monitors on Brady to check his heart rate over two days. It was fine for 47.5 hours and went berserk for the other 30 minutes. Said Brady: 'I'd just had a winner at Clonmel and it was my first for a while so I got a bit excited.' If the horses threaten to kill him, they also keep him alive.

Ireland's big men enjoy Cheltenham just as much, like Ryanair boss Michael O'Leary. He says that he worked solidly for twenty years, made a few quid and wants to have some fun. Though there is little sign of the work rate dropping, he too gets that fun from racing. Under the banner of the Gigginstown Stud he has some fifty horses in training, spread across twenty yards. He says: 'Only half of them cover their training bills. That's why I have to work Monday to Friday.' The great thing about jump racing, he says, is that everyone can live the dream. 'It's very hard to do that on the Flat but over jumps all these horses are freaks. A syndicate paying ten or twelve grand for some crooked beast at the sales could fall on the next Dunguib.' (Dunguib was the outstanding bumper horse of the 2009 Festival.)

And if the Irish love Cheltenham, then there is no doubt that the feeling is reciprocated. They are very much made to feel welcome. Says Willie Mullins: 'Cheltenham are always very helpful, very good. Any time we seem to have a problem they immediately set about rectifying it. Every year after the Festival they send someone over to Ireland to chat to all the trainers just to find out are there any grievances they didn't air at the time, and they are proactive in promoting better relations with the trainers and owners for the following year. They're always trying to improve and to head off trouble at the pass. They're always trying to improve the way we get on over there and they bend over backwards to help us.'

That is echoed by Edward O'Grady who dates it back to Philip Arkwright's time. 'They spend a lot of time and effort trying to get it as right as possible for everybody, whether it be the ground, the siting or the fences. They are wonderful in that they welcome constructive criticism and always consult the trainers. They ask after every Festival how they can tweak it or improve it for next time. That's a testament to their success.'

What worries many though is whether the problems with the Irish economy will see a sharp drop in Irish attendances at the Festival and sharp cutbacks in the whole horse-racing industry across the Irish Sea. Says Willie Mullins: 'It's going to be huge in a couple of years, the impact. There's very few locally-owned horses going to Irish trainers. There are many more trainer-owned horses running in bumpers than ever before. That has to impact down the line. The next two or three years there's a lot of political rhetoric but it doesn't look good for any Irish business, not just racing.'

Hard times indeed, and Mouse Morris said to me not long ago as we watched his horses exercising in the morning sun at Everardsgrange, County Tipperary. 'We have to be bloody good salesmen, because we're selling something nobody needs.' But hopefully in Ireland there will be stern resistance to such a thought.

Chapter 32

You've Never Seen So Many 'Readies'

'It was duck or dinner, sink or swim at that stage. Most of the Irish had their last zee on to try and get the price of the boat home.' (Trainer Edward O'Grady on his Staplestown winning the 'getting out stakes', the last race of the meeting, in 1981)

Most people who go racing enjoy a bet. Hazarding money on a horse gives you a temporary share in ownership, a sense of belonging, an extra right to cheer on a particular set of colours. At Cheltenham the betting too is on an altogether different scale to what you will encounter on most racecourses. Those who venture down among the bookmakers in front of the stands will probably see more money physically changing hands than they have ever done in their lives before as wads of 'readies' are unfolded from back pockets or scooped from bookies' satchels. Says Edward Gillespie: 'It's the sheer strength of the market. Put on several thousand pounds at Cheltenham and a bookie doesn't flinch.' Try that on the average course on a mid-season Saturday and you'd be lucky if he allowed you £100 each way.

The turnover is colossal. Over the four days of the Cheltenham Festival off-course punters on-line and in betting shops hazard an average of £150 million a day on the outcome of the races. Another £1 million in cash is gambled on every race by those in attendance. More than £40 million is wagered on the outcome of the Gold Cup alone, and over last year's 26-race card the average was about £24 million per race, taking total turnover to around £600 million. Around £1.2 million is withdrawn daily from the twenty cash-points around the course to refill depleted wallets and handbags. It can have a significant influence on bookmakers' annual profits. In 2003, when favourites won half the races, several bookmaking companies blamed the Festival for profits falling short of their forecasts. There is a jumping fixture list of more than a thousand races, but the four days of the Festival account for around ten per cent of the Tote's annual on-course betting turnover.

People back their fancy in the championship races as a declaration of allegiance, but on racecards dotted with multi-runner handicaps they are tempted too to find long-odds winners offering significant reward.

It is not by any means a new phenomenon. Huge sums were wagered on the outcome of the races for amateur riders back in the nineteenth century, and many family fortunes were lost, and a few occasionally won, on the racecourse.

Some of the greatest Cheltenham gambles, inevitably, have involved the Irish contingent. Ireland is as famous for its gamblers as for its playwrights and poets. The legendary Barney Curley once trained for the priesthood but gave it up for training and gambling, famously winning £300,000 in the Yellow Sam sting at Bellewstown, when he got a large friend to occupy the only phone box on the course so bookmakers could not get through to the track and reduce the odds being set there. Curley set off to the Cheltenham Festival in 1971 with £700 in his pocket and came back with £50,000, declaring: 'At the Festival that year I was so red hot I was in danger of spontaneous combustion.' The Australian horse Crisp, in the Queen Mother Champion Chase, was his banker bet at odds of 3-1 and better. But while Curley is a shrewd gambler he admits he is an indifferent businessman. With his 1971 Cheltenham winnings he bought a pub next to a Catholic church and added a cabaret lounge. In a couple of years it cost him £120,000. He still did better than the small Irish punter who won enough on the Champion Hurdler Istabraq to pay off his mortgage and then invested so heavily and unsuccessfully on Danoli in the Gold Cup that he lost the whole property. 'To be sure,' he is alleged to have said, 'it was only a small house anyway.'

The Irish carpet millionaire and world class poker player J.J. Furlong, known as 'Noel' because he was born on Christmas Day, is another who has made the bookies quake. In 1991 he paid off £360,000 to settle a VAT wrangle with the British tax authorities, in effect as an entry fee to be allowed to come to Cheltenham. There he struck significant bets with Ladbrokes and others on his own horse Destriero, trained by Andy Geraghty. Destriero netted him around £2 million by winning the Supreme Novices' Hurdle but Furlong also had more bets, coupling the horse with The Illiad, who was running in the Champion Hurdle. Furlong had backed the Illiad down from 36-1 to 6-1 when he won the Ladbroke Hurdle at Leopardstown two months earlier, picking up another £1 million plus there. Had The Illiad won the Champion Hurdle, Furlong stood to pick up several millions more on his doubles. He said: 'I was £2 million in front of the bookmakers as The Illiad went to post and the double bets were a bonus if they came off.' Said Mike Dillon, the imperturbable Mancunian who is the public face of Ladbrokes: 'Noel Furlong took on the ring on his own that day.' When The Illiad trailed in nearly last in the big race after ruining his chances by hitting the fourth hurdle hard, Dillon described the result as 'an advertisement for the power of prayer'.

Furlong only plays poker occasionally at a few top tournaments but he was good enough to walk away with £1 million from the tables in the World Series poker championships in 1999. Not one for telling the media a lot about himself or his horses, he once declared: 'You can ask me about them if you like but I'll probably end up telling you lies.'

Bookmakers' prayers are not always answered. Dillon, a popular figure with an incomparable contacts book – he introduced

Manchester United boss Sir Alex Ferguson to racing – is sometimes called the best-informed bookmaker in the world. One of his key roles is in helping to set the odds for his company.

Back in 1990 he wasn't much impressed with the prospects of Kribensis, the only jumper trained by Flat trainer Michael Stoute, in the Champion Hurdle. On his advice Ladbrokes went 6-1 to other layers' 5-1, and when Kribensis won, the extra point cost them a million pounds. You win some, you lose some. Sometimes you do both at the same time. The year that Carvill's Hill was favourite for the Gold Cup, Mike Dillon did not rate his prospects on the Cheltenham track, despite the fact that the Welsh Grand National winner was trained by Martin Pipe and ridden by Peter Scudamore. On fast ground and an undulating track he reckoned Carvill's Hill to be fallible. Ladbrokes went over the odds – pricing him at evens when everyone else had the horse odds-on – and took in fortunes. Mike Dillon recalls that somebody literally did bet their house that day on Carvill's Hill, coming in with a draft for £50,000 from the Halifax Building Society. When Carvill's Hill flopped and Cool Ground won the race, Ladbrokes thought they had a great result, only to discover a few minutes later that at one of their betting shops in Portsmouth an unemployed joiner called Dick Mussell had spent about £7 in 10p doubles and trebles, and that the last leg was Cool Ground at 25-1. His £7 netted him around £600,000.

Dillon consoles himself that even the big losers for the bookies, like all Red Rum's Grand National victories, Frankie Dettori's seven winners in a day at Ascot and Desert Orchid's victories, including the Gold Cup, are good advertising for the industry! But even he has been burned on occasion. He went for breakfast with Irish trainer Mick O'Toole at his Maddenstown base shortly before Carrig Willy won the 1980 Sweeps Hurdle. O'Toole and the owners persuaded him to give them odds of 40-1 and they picked up £64,000 between them. O'Toole later told Dillon, who took it all with his usual good humour: 'There are some lessons in life that have to be learned the hard way and one of them is that bacon and eggs do not come cheap on The Curragh.'

Probably the most famous of all the Irish gamblers, certainly the most popular with the Festival crowd, is the international financier J.P. McManus. The green and gold hoops of his colours are the most familiar on the jumping racetracks and when a 'J.P. special' takes the lead at the second last, an Irish roar will almost certainly accompany it.

The unfailingly polite McManus started life driving diggers for his father's construction business and had to go back there once or twice working double shifts to pay off debts incurred when he first set himself up as a bookmaker. Now J.P. has more than 300 horses in training with a wide range of handlers in Ireland and in Britain. A true sportsman, he often leaves expensive purchases with the smaller trainers who have nurtured them and uncovered their talent, and he is respected too for the way he looks after his old horses when their racing days are done, taking many of them home to enjoy a happy retirement at his Martinstown stud.

J.P. rarely talks about his bets, certainly not to the jockeys riding the horses on which he has gambled many thousands, but friends say that he lost £200,000 on a single bet when Finnegan's Wake, who was still going easily, fell at the Festival in 1997, and he still kept smiling. J.P. enjoyed jousting with the late Freddie Williams, an adventurous bookie whose readiness to accept McManus's massive wagers made him too the stuff of legend (and probably explained why armed robbers were waiting for him one night when he drove back from the races, ambushing the car and stealing his winnings and stake money).

McManus had £100,000 each way with Williams on a horse called Lingo, which won at odds of 13-2. When he then asked the layer, who also ran a Scottish bottling plant, for a bet of £500,000 on another race Williams reminded him wryly that it was Highland water, not whisky, that his company bottled. But he still accepted £100,000 of McManus's bet.

Another well recognised owner is City financier David Johnson, who has had the bulk of his horses first with Martin Pipe and then with his son David. Johnson made no secret of the fact that he collected £500,000 when his Well Chief won the Arkle Chase in 2004. 'Everyone was on big time,' he said. 'We backed him down from 33-1 to 12-1 and then we ran out of money.'

There is an intriguing tale to one of Johnson's successful bets on his own horses. Carol Pipe, Martin's wife, was so struck with a horse she saw winning at the French track of Auteuil one day when Martin was off at the races that she instructed their agent to buy it. The grey, called Champleve, became one of David Johnson's string. The horse showed early promise and Martin Pipe called David Johnson and said he would talk him through a schooling session there and then. Said Martin in mock commentator-style, 'He's jumped the first fine. Good jump at the second. Really nice at the third. He's jumped the fourth really well and,' he added with a rhetorical flourish, 'he's won the Arkle.' (The Arkle is the two-mile race for novices at the Festival.) Pipe did not realise it at the time but Johnson thought his trainer was predicting his horse would win the Arkle next spring. He rang his bookie there and then and had a large bet at the odds he was offered of 33-1.

Champleve progressed nicely, was duly entered in the Arkle and he and the Irish horse Hill Society stormed up Cheltenham's finishing slope for a photo finish. Martin Pipe and Irish trainer Noel Meade embraced each other amicably after the race and Martin declared, unawares: 'It doesn't matter who won, it was a great race anyway', only to have his biggest owner remonstrating with him that at 33-1 the result mattered very much to him, thank you! Luckily for the Pipes and for David Johnson, the photo went their way.

Some yards are well known for their nerve and finesse in landing large bets for a horse's connections. There was a big stable coup, for example, when the Jimmy Fitzgerald-trained Forgive 'n' Forget won the Coral Hurdle Final of 1983. The English-based trainer, who came from the County Tipperary village of Horse and Jockey, had invested heavily himself at 8-1. The next year he and the horse's connections backed him heavily again to win the Royal & Sun Alliance Chase but Forgive 'n' Forget could only finish second. Unabashed, Fitzgerald backed him there and then for the 1985 Cheltenham Gold Cup, and duly collected.

In 1981, Irish punters at the Festival had had a terrible time, with all their favourites failing. In the County Hurdle, the last race on the last day of the meeting, Edward O'Grady ran a horse called Staplestown, who had appeared the previous Saturday at Navan. He had shown snatches of form but only had one win and one place to show from twelve appearances on the racecourse. In the highly competitive handicap Tommy Ryan's mount opened at a price of 12-1. But everyone who had enough Irish in them to know a shamrock from a four-leaved clover seemed to know what was coming. They all piled in and Staplestown's price rapidly tumbled to just 11-2. Says Edward O'Grady: 'It was duck or dinner, sink or swim at that stage. Most of the Irish had their last zee on to try and get the price of the boat home or whatever. Commentaries have improved enormously since those days. It was the last race, it was getting a bit murky, there was a maximum field and it wasn't easy to see. He wasn't mentioned until they were coming down the hill. When the commentator said that Staplestown was coming on the outside the crowd gave an enormous roar and the roof of the stand virtually lifted off. Sure enough, he came through and he won quite well. Last race, last day, it was great.'

If the Irish owed Edward O'Grady for that one, all jumping fans probably owe him for helping to kindle the enthusiasm of jump racing's greatest benefactor, J.P. McManus. When Edward trained Mr Donovan to win what is now the Neptune Hurdle, it was the first Festival winner to cross the line in J.P.'s colours, and there too lies a story.

As a judge at the Derby sales, O'Grady chose Mr Donovan as champion in the pre-sale show and then backed his judgment by buying him. Six months later when he passed him on to a good client, the purchaser insisted on a vet's inspection, despite the one he had undergone at the sales. 'It turned out he had a frightful heart murmur, so much so that the vet ran out of the stable saying that he was afraid he might fall on top of him. I was left with the horse but he turned out to be a very good bumper horse and he ran in some good hurdles before Cheltenham. He got beaten by a good horse of Arthur Moore's called Irium and so went to Cheltenham as a maiden, losing his maiden status in the Sun Alliance Hurdle. It was an important win for me but it was important for J.P. as well.'

Britain's champion trainer Paul Nicholls is not by any means a regular punter. But he does sometimes take a view about some of his own horses. Approaching the 1999 Cheltenham Festival he was yet to train a single Festival winner. But that did not stop him backing three of his entries that year in a series of doubles and trebles. The banker was Flagship Uberalles in the Arkle Chase at 11-1. Paul also had 25-1 on Call Equiname in the Queen Mother Champion Chase and 33-1 on See More Business in the Gold Cup. When all three of them won he totalled up his winnings and found he had £36,000, which he blew at one go on a Mercedes for his then wife Bridget.

There was another significant profit for the Ditcheat trainer when Kauto Star regained his Gold Cup crown in 2009. Nicholls had put £1,000 on Big Buck's when he discovered bookmakers offering 20-1 against his chances of winning the World Hurdle. When Big Buck's came home he then reinvested the winnings on his Gold Cup favourite Kauto Star, and when he won too picked up a cool £40,000.

Paul has no wish though to gamble on the scale of Denman's one-time part-owner Harry Findlay. He was there in his owner's box at Cardiff Arms Park when Harry, having invested heavily on New Zealand in the Rugby Union World Cup and persuaded all his friends to go in heavily too, saw the All Blacks fall apart in the second half. Findlay, once memorably described by his trainer as 'an interview waiting to happen, an open mouth in search of a microphone' lost £2.6 million on that result and probably a friend or two as well. But race crowds and the media love him, and he wins and loses with style. Asked by the media if he had, as reported in some quarters, won £2,078,000 on Denman when he won the Gold Cup, Harry put the media right. 'Oh no,' he said, 'it was only just under £1 million.'

Perhaps we should leave the last word on the subject to Nicholls's Irish stable jockey Ruby Walsh. When Ruby rode Big Buck's to win that World Hurdle it followed expensive failures by two of the meeting's banker bets for many, Dunguib and Master Minded. By winning when he did, he was told, he had been the punters' saviour. With a douche of cool reason he replied: 'Politically I should say that is good. But the reality is that I ride for myself, the trainer and his owners. I suppose it has been hard for the punters but the bookies always have the money. It has always been that way.'

Chapter 33

The Start of the Four-day Festival

'Whatever the conditions you could always rely on the horses to bale you out. If the ground was a bog or whatever it was. The horses always came to your rescue.' (Philip Arkwright, former Clerk of the Course, Cheltenham)

Cheltenham is big business. Around 220,000 racegoers attended the four days of the Festival from 16–19 March 2010, some 67,000 of those arriving on Gold Cup day. With ticket prices ranging from £20 to £75, the gate receipts were around £7 million. Ryanair stage an extra twenty flights from Ireland in Cheltenham week, and Cross Country Trains, First Great Western and Virgin all run additional services. Typically 30,000 cars, 2,000 coaches and 50 stretch limos converge on the course, while the 650 helicopter landings make Cheltenham the busiest temporary airfield anywhere in the country.

Gloucestershire Tourism reckons the value of the Festival to the wider local economy, with 10,000 beds booked each night (even if some, held for the more inveterate all-night gamblers, are little used) to be around £50 million. At the racecourse itself there is a massive shopping village with eighty stands selling everything from wine to wellington boots, binoculars to bedsocks, silverware to Spanish villas. While true *aficionados* comb the shelves of the Arkle bookshop for volumes missing from their racing libraries or commission portraits of their favourite horse or jockey, the fashion-conscious can acquire fur hats spectacular enough to stop the traffic at fifty paces – I know, because Mrs Oakley has done it.

Shooting coats, gleaming brogues and elegant tweeds are temptingly on offer and there is nothing safety first about the display. Tweed skirts are available on some stalls in the kind of mini lengths once known as 'pussy pelmets', a positive danger to the blood pressure of elderly gents who catch a glimpse of the leggy fillies prepared to risk them.

On course, 36,000 racegoers are looked after in the 240 private boxes and chalets, seven restaurants and twenty marquees, with around 12,000 enjoying a three- or four-course sit-down meal. All tickets (at £600 a head) for the 300-seater Panoramic Restaurant sell out for the entire Festival the previous autumn. Overall it is the biggest catering operation of its kind in the racing world and it has been calculated that the supply of sandwiches, burgers and hot dogs, if laid end to end, would stretch 3.2 miles, the distance run by the Gold Cup contenders.

To help judge the effort required to cope with such numbers, the racecourse caterers, Jockey Club Catering, supplied 18,000 bottles of champagne, 30,000 bottles of wine and, of course, 220,000 pints of Guinness. Using 30 kitchens and 53 mobile catering units, 3,000 staff, including 250 chefs, prepared 3 tonnes of smoked salmon, 2 tonnes of fillet and sirloin of beef, and 25,000 beefburgers and hot dogs.

There were some 500 equine guests to cope with too, a quarter of them travelling over from Ireland. The average racehorse drinks between 10 and 12 gallons of water a day (still, not sparkling, even at Cheltenham) and consumes up to 25 pounds of dry food, so that too requires organisation. That is one of the multifarious tasks which fall under the remit of Simon Claisse, Director of Racing and Clerk of the Course. An average Festival day for him starts before 5.00 a.m. when he walks the course for the first time to send out the first official report on the going at 6.40 a.m. The first walk is a safety check too, to make sure there has been no overnight damage: 'You have to give yourself enough time to allow for that – particularly if there has been snow or rain or substantial winds, that you can formulate some sort of plan in advance of having to say anything.

'Wildlife probably causes us as much grief as the weather, whether it is badgers, foxes or deer. We have muntjacs here which rub their tusks into the ground and make funny little curls in the ground . . . we just have to live with them really.'

Simon's team put out ground updates on the radio and also through the British Horseracing Authority's administration site. At 7.00 a.m. Simon Claisse grabs a cup of tea with the head groundsman to check through the schedule for the day, including activities other than horse-racing happening on the track. At 7.30 he goes down to the stable-yard to talk to the manager there. 'At the Festival we can have up to 300 horses on site at any one time. We can have forty, or fifty or sixty coming out onto the gallops in the morning.' (They have a round six-furlong all-weather track and a straight five-furlong for the visitors to get a blow.) He checks in too with stable security. 'Because if I have to go there during an emergency in the course of the day I can't just rush in. Even as an employee of the racecourse I have to sign in with the BHA stable guards who look after it.' He also checks out Hunters Lodge, the hostel where stable staff are fed and sleep. 'In terms of stable staff we are probably talking about 160, 170. We have accommodation normally for 124. We install ten little things called 'Kip Cabins', little portakabins which have two single beds in them plus a shower and toilet and a telly.'

Does the accommodation allow for the fact that many stables have more lasses than lads these days? 'In the main area we are still four to a room. We have fallen rather behind the pace there, but that will come. We have girls in girls' rooms and boys in boys' rooms but what happens after dark is up to them.'

Back to the office then and another important duty. 'When I

come back off the course I open up the weighing room and switch on the sauna. It's no use the jockeys arriving early to make use of that and finding it stone cold.

'By 10.00 a.m. the racecards arrive With them comes all the paperwork needed for the officials, the clerk of the scales, the judges. I have to prepare my racecard for racing, timing all the schedules – when horses have to be in the pre-parade ring [for saddling], when jockeys have to be called out, when the jockeys' bell rings [for mounting]. All that is on a tight schedule so that we can get every race off within three minutes of the official time. For each race I note the standard time so I can measure my ground conditions. I also note things that need to move – rails and tapes that have to be shifted during the race. That gap should be open . . . those rails should be shut. We have intersections all over the place.

'That takes me to 11.00, and people are arriving, and then I go on an official course walk with the chairman of the stewards. By the time we are back we are within an hour of racing. Because of the scale of the Festival, we have a briefing with all the key BHA officials on what we would do if there was a bomb scare etc. Half an hour later we have a briefing with all the officials and handicappers who come from Ireland. We run through the card – it's a liaison between the stewards and handicappers on what might happen so that if it doesn't, they know what questions to ask and can decide which horses have a dope test. That also gives me the chance to pick up information if a trainer has asked for a horse to go out first or last or be mounted on the course. Before we know it we are racing . . .'

In 2008, Cheltenham's organisational capabilities were put to the ultimate test. Fierce winds blew down temporary structures overnight and made it too dangerous to race on the Wednesday. Not only did the Cheltenham team pass the test, they turned it into a public relations coup for the course. Other racetracks might have shrugged their shoulders and said, 'Maybe we can save a couple of races and run them over the next two days, so let's decide which ones we have to scrap.' Cheltenham determined to save the whole programme and run every single race. While those who had made their way to Cheltenham for racing that Wednesday contented themselves with card schools, lengthy pub lunches and shopping around the spa town's boutiques, the racecourse staff worked feverishly to stable more horses, rejig catering arrangements and rearrange the programme. The sister racecourse at Warwick opened its stables, and local volunteers, who temporarily jammed the switchboard with offers of help, provided more equine lodging space. Not a race was missed. Over the next two days Cheltenham staged a glorious bonanza — nine and ten-race programmes accommodating the full Festival programme and earning plaudits all round for their can-do attitude.

A key question for the clerk of the course is the state of the ground. Drainage operations over the years have helped but 'all the drainage here does is make the wetter ground more consistent with the dry ground. The good-to-firm bits are the bits with no drainage. They drain naturally. It's a real challenge for us in a dry time to get those quicker bits of ground where we want them. If we didn't have drainage in the rest of it we'd end up with some ground really soggy and the rest of it would still be quick. What we're trying to do is to produce a consistent surface.'

So how difficult is it repairing the ravages after five hundred horses have galloped round the track for four days? 'It's an enormous job but we're lucky here for two reasons. We have two courses. So although we're racing seventeen days a year we're on two sets. The old course that we run on in October and November, we don't run on that again until March so we know through the middle of the winter when not a lot of grass grows, at least we're not cutting it to ribbons in December and January. The new course we run on in December and January and then that does the second two days of the Festival. The trick here is that none of the ground we run on in the Festival are we setting foot on between March and March. So the inside five, six, seven yards on both hurdles tracks and both chase courses is railed off at the moment [October] and stays railed off except where the courses cross.

'What we did in preparation for running four days of the Festival, when we were adamant we wanted the Gold Cup to climax the four days, and to ensure we provided fresh ground for the blue-riband steeplechase of the season, was that we widened the steeplechase course. So the preserved ground on the inside of the chase course is about fourteen yards wide. We race on the right-hand side of that chase rail through December and January. On the third day of the Festival we open up five or six yards of fresh ground and on the Thursday night of the Festival we take all that rail down and open up another strip.

'On Wednesday night we're changing from old to new. This year [2010], not only were we changing from old to new so all the interchanges had to be measured and realigned, but we were watering overnight as well. It's a huge challenge. The ground staff were up until three o'clock in the morning and back at 7.00 am.'

One Gold Cup former Clerk of the Course Philip Arkwright won't forget in a hurry is the race of 1978. During the Festival meeting he normally slept at the course to be available early. Clearly not a superstitious man, he says: 'I used to stay in the mortuary – we had a mortuary in the weighing room, a stone slab. I used to put a sleeping bag on that. It was a perfectly adequate place to sleep and you didn't get bothered. The first two days of the meeting went well and on the second night I said, "Sod it, I'm going home for the night." Then I woke up in the morning to find everything blanketed in snow, and roads impassable. There were no mobile phones and I was forty miles away . . .' That year Gold Cup day was cancelled and the race won by Fred Winter's Midnight Court was run later, in April.

There is often plenty of debate about Cheltenham's progress-chasing, debate both external and internal. Philip Arkwright is not a fan of all the changes since his time: 'I'm against all this proliferation of races. When you had three days if you came away at the end of the third day and I said to you, "What horses haven't you seen here that you would like to have done?" you might think of half a dozen and that would be it. I look upon two and a half miles as the National Hunt equivalent of seven furlongs on the Flat. It's neither one thing nor the other. All it does is to dilute the Gold Cup and/or the Champion Chase.'

As for the cross-country race 'Don't talk to me about that. I didn't think it was necessary to muck up this lovely racecourse and turn it into a municipal park. In the old days you could sit here and look at two beautifully laid out racecourses. Now it's buggered up with all this abracadabra.'

Philip agrees though that the cross-country race has proved popular with the public, and while he may be the voice of conservatism he acknowledges improvements. 'The jockeys have become more professional. Fred Winter and Dave Dick would be on the piss until three o'clock in the morning. There wasn't a sauna in the weighing room in those days. Certainly the jockeys and the horses are fitter.'

A rider himself before he took up his admin duties, he suggests that the days of owners and trainers buying 'store' horses to be put away for three years while they developed has now pretty well gone, and that the lighter-framed jumpers we often see now are more likely to suffer leg injuries. 'They are good racehorses but they weren't really built for this sort of game. They are less intrinsically sound than the old type of National Hunt horses.'

Although in some ways a traditionalist, the former Major Arkwright made significant changes in his time as a Cheltenham official. 'The hurdle course used to go up behind the big screen. I got rid of that so that both courses went round the way they do now. There was a chute beside the lower stand and the fence on the course proper was the third fence. In the four mile National Hunt Chase you never jumped the same fence twice.' He too was willing to try things out. 'We did experiment in the mid-eighties with a shorter course eliminating the hill. The horses started at the 2½-mile start. They went round the stud bend and round which-ever course it was, cut in at the water jump and went back down to the start again. It was a little 2½-mile circuit, the idea being an easier race in the early part of the season for lesser horses. It didn't work and was abandoned after a couple of years.'

What Philip Arkwright has never lost is that neck-hair tingling as the crowd roars off the start of the first race at the Festival. And he reflects: 'Whatever the conditions, you could always rely on the horses to bale you out. If the ground was a bog or whatever it was. The horses always came to your rescue.' What he means, I believe, is that whatever the conditions, the equine participants in the Festival, with their spectacular efforts, their guts and their grace, always ensure that there are stories and memories to recall when racing folk gather in times to come.

Sponsorship of course has been key to Cheltenham's develop-ment, and there has never been a shortage of companies or indi-viduals eager to associate themselves with the Festival's obvious success. Companies like to be associated with winners, but getting your name into the Festival programme doesn't come cheap. Prize-money at the 2010 Festival totalled £3.4 million, an overall average of £131,346 per race, and £1.68 million of that came from commercial sponsors. In 2010 the Totesport Gold Cup was worth £475,000; the Smurfit Kappa Champion Hurdle £370,000; the Seasons Holidays Queen Mother Champion Chase £320,000; the Ladbrokes World Hurdle £260,000; and the Ryanair Chase £250,000. In 2011 the prize money for the Gold Cup was raised to half a million pounds for the first time and the Ryanair Chase prize increased by £10,000 to £260,000.

Some sponsors have lasted longer than others. The RSA spon-sorship at the 2010 Festival marked a fortieth year of involvement for the company previously known as Sun Alliance and then Royal & Sun Alliance. Christie's the auctioneers, who sponsor the Foxhunters' Chase, have been contributing for thirty-two years.

The Tote has sponsored the Gold Cup since 1980, taking over from Piper-Heidsieck Champagne.

Other companies come in and out for shorter periods, says Peter McNeile, the director of sponsorship. In days past, he says, sponsorship was 'patronal rather than commercial'. Now, in a faster-changing world, things may change swiftly because of take-overs or speedier personnel changes in companies. Sometimes the sponsorship is a short-term marketing strategy, sometimes it is a case of companies feeling they have squeezed the juice out of racing and deciding to try something else. But almost invariably when a sponsor has moved on, Cheltenham has found a replace-ment willing to put in a larger sum for association with such a successful brand.

To some extent you can measure economic trends from the sponsorship scene. Drinks companies and the media industry are doing less sponsorship in racing than they used to. Car manufacturers have almost disappeared from the scene. Certainly, strengths and weaknesses in the national economies of two nations affect the sponsorship scene. For the moment, Cheltenham's strong associations with Ireland are less obvious in the Festival programme. Irish banks, property companies and construction firms used to be queuing at the door. But long-time sponsors Waterford Crystal went off the list some years ago, and economic turbulence on the other side of the Irish sea saw the disappearance of Anglo-Irish Bank from the Festival scene. In 2010 two more major Irish companies, Ballymore Properties and Smurfit Kappa, pulled out of their Cheltenham sponsorship, the latter being replaced as sponsors of the Champion Hurdle by bookmakers Stan James. That put them on the Festival list alongside the well-established Coral Cup and the Ladbrokes World Hurdle, previously known first as the Spa Hurdle and then the Stayers' Hurdle, although the William Hill Chase has now gone from the Festival programme. At hunkering-down periods like the present there tends to be a proliferation of companies associated with the betting industry giving their name to familiar races. Says Peter McNeile: 'They tend to be quicker off the blocks than other brands in recognising the opportunities.' But of course not all sponsorship or commercial benefit to the course goes directly into sponsorship of named races. In return for 'pouring rights' (selling their products on the premises), Guinness pay the lion's share of creating the temporary grandstand in the Guinness Village, a very visible part of the Festival which gives Cheltenham space for more paying spectators. The *Sun* newspaper sponsors the Best Mate enclosure, using it to publicise its Saturday pull-out section which is normally focussed on the nation's number one spectator sport of football. 'It drives football to the racecourse,' says McNeile approvingly.

Fortunately for Cheltenham, Edward Gillespie and sponsorship director Peter McNeile have always insisted on Cheltenham retaining a series of sponsors for individual Festival races rather than having a single meeting sponsor, as Epsom and Aintree have tended to do. They have also tied in sponsoring companies for several years, not accepting one-off deals, so as to ensure continuity. That has made it less painful losing the occasional individual sponsor.

Cheltenham's biggest gamble in the Gillespie/Vestey years was that switch from a three-day Festival to four days in 2005. Many wondered if their livers and wallets would stand it. Others feared, and a few continue to fear, a dilution and downgrading of the Festival's championship quality. Edward Gillespie and his colleagues consulted widely before they made their decision. Among those who became deeply involved were the full Channel 4 racing team, who were as divided among themselves as the rest of the racing community about whether it was a good idea. None who were present have forgotten a dinner in a private room at a smart hotel in Newmarket where the Cheltenham team and Channel 4 dined long, loudly and rambunctiously to debate the question. So passionate were the feelings expressed, say participants, that at times it almost came to blows. Says Channel 4's Andrew Franklin: 'It was a classic example of how deep-seated the Festival is in our hearts.'

To meet the fears about dilution and downgrading, Cheltenham pushed the Gold Cup from Thursday to Friday and made the World Hurdle, a three-mile event for staying hurdlers, the focus of day three on the Wednesday along with the Ryanair Chase, the fifth most valuable prize on offer at the Festival. Once again the marketing was shrewd. In recent years a couple of star horses have given the World Hurdle genuine crowd appeal and the kind of year-on-year continuity of star names which helps to make the Festival what it is.

First there was the French hero Baracouda, whose trainer François Doumen once famously declared: 'His neck goes the wrong way. His hips are pointy. He's got a white eye and he won't even take a sugar lump. But he's good for my bank balance.' Baracouda won the World Hurdle in 2002 and again in 2003. He was back again in 2004 to be beaten into second place by Iris's Gift and in 2005 he was back again, finishing three lengths second to Inglis Drever. His final attempt to win back his title came in 2006 when the race was won by Alan King's My Way De Solzen. That race, after which he was retired to owner J.P. McManus's Martinstown Stud, was the first time Francois Doumen's charge had failed to finish first or second in twenty-six contests over six years. Baracouda won the Long Walk Hurdle at Ascot on four occasions. He was not an easy ride but, said Francois Doumen: 'He was not difficult to train. He needed to be fresh and for his morale to be intact.'

Inglis Drever, the horse who came to succeed him as a favourite with the Festival crowd, was trained in the North of England by Howard Johnson after being bought out of Sir Mark Prescott's Newmarket yard at Tattersall's sales in the autumn of 2003. Racing owes him a wider debt because he was the third horse bought by former computer tycoon Graham Wylie, and was his first

Cheltenham runner. Wylie went on to accumulate more than a hundred horses. A shrewd dealer in horseflesh, Sir Mark Prescott is said to utter an annual prayer for the continued existence of Mr Wylie, who on Inglis Drever's sad early death in 2010 declared: 'He instilled in me a passion for racing. He has left behind great memories and a great legacy.'

An honest and dependable racer, Inglis Drever had that touch of fallibility which helps to make Cheltenham heroes. He often had a 'flat patch' in his races when he appeared to be fading, only to come again and cause huge excitement as he reasserted himself at the finish. He ran four times at the Festival. The first time he was beaten half a length by Fundamentalist in the 2004 RSA Novices Hurdle. His other three visits all resulted in victories in the Ladbrokes World Hurdle. Said Howard Johnson on his death: 'He never let you down. He had guts and he was so brave. He was a hell of a horse.'

Of Inglis Drever's thirteen wins as hurdler, nine were gained at Grade 2 and three at Grade 1 under a range of jockeys. His partner when he beat Baracouda in 2005 was Graham Lee. After missing the 2006 race with an injury, he beat Mighty Man in 2007 partnered by Paddy Brennan, and in 2008 it was Denis O'Regan in the saddle as he beat Kasbah Bliss. He won seventeen of his thirty-five jump races and over £800,000 in prize-money.

As the switch to four days demonstrated, Cheltenham doesn't lack confidence. When Royal Ascot was forced to stage its 2005 fixture elsewhere during the rebuilding programme, Cheltenham made a bold, if slightly tongue-in-cheek, pitch to be the alternative venue, underlining its bid with a glossy 28-page presentation document. This argued that Cheltenham had a reputation built on wonderful horses, thrilling races and experience in handling visitors. 'We welcome this unique opportunity to combine the heritage, prestige and glamour of Royal Ascot with the elegance and passion of Cheltenham, the town and the racecourse. It is difficult to imagine a more natural partnership that will create the most impressive race meeting ever staged in Britain.' The Cheltenham pitch, which was viewed by the Queen when Lord Vestey stayed with her during Royal Ascot, said that racecourse and town were 'an essential economic driver to the region as well as a world renowned event'. 'In recent years £60 million has been reinvested in the course, 60,000 people have attended the festival each day and the benefit to Gloucestershire's economy is estimated at £44 million each year.' Cheltenham, it pointed out, was the festival town of England, with events celebrating music, literature, and jazz as well as the National Hunt Festival. 'For your guests, who are used to enjoying 350 acres of rolling parkland at Ascot, Cheltenham offers the opportunity to exchange one exquisite setting for another.'

Cheltenham's bid to become a one-year Ascot explained how extending the current course from the two-mile start would provide starts for races at five furlongs, six furlongs, seven furlongs, one mile and the Gold Cup. It admitted: 'At first Cheltenham racecourse may not seem like the obvious setting for the most famous Flat race meeting in the world. But thanks to major course restructuring and further proposed developments it will be the most natural venue.' Work on new sections would start rapidly and be suitable for Flat racing well before June 2005. As well as its reputation for horse care, the brochure pointed out: 'Cheltenham is synonymous with gambling, that is why we are the best in the business when it comes to meeting betting needs.' It boasted of Prestbury Park's 600 Tote windows and 226 bookmakers around the course. The pitch concluded that Cheltenham would find accommodation for the bandstand and make suitable arrangements for the royal procession.

Some long-time Cheltenham devotees thought that Gillespie & co had lost the plot. Even the word 'betrayal' was used about the jumping course's flirtation with the Flat. Even now, Irish trainer Edward O'Grady says of their bid to host Royal Ascot: 'That I don't commend one bit. Had they got it, it would have been the death knell for National Hunt racing. It is very important that Cheltenham and the Irish do everything they can to preserve National Hunt racing, otherwise I think it will go.'

I don't believe that Cheltenham ever seriously expected to win the bid battle, and to have to undertake the promised re-structuring. But it was another example of Cheltenham's PR flair. The pre-eminent jumping course in the country took the opportunity of the competition to remind a wider world that it was precisely that and, on the back of the Ascot bid, to advertise its own wares. Edward Gillespie says that as they went along they realised more about their own potential. 'There was a worrying moment when we thought we could actually win it.'

Ascot is busy building itself into a centre of international racing, and one thing some Cheltenham regulars would like to see, particularly when they recall the exploits of Francois Doumen with The Fellow and Baracouda, is more French runners at the Festival. Senior trainers, including those like Willie Mullins and Paul Nicholls who buy plenty of French-bred horses, say that is unlikely.

Says Willie Mullins: 'They have plenty of prize-money and a different season and their owners don't aspire to come to England like Flat owners do. If they have a good horse they don't look further than Auteuil. There's huge prize-money there. They seem to have an autumn and a spring/summer campaign and not much in the middle of winter. When we're getting ready for Cheltenham they're only having their second run back. In October they're gearing up for their autumn festival. Their fences are different too, more like a cross-country course.

Paul Nicholls says the French sell many of their best jumpers and have little interest in coming to Britain. 'The timing of their calendar doesn't fit in. Prize-money is terrific for their top horses, they're better staying over there. It's difficult for us to win races over there. Different ground, different style of racing, kind of obstacles. Run a chaser round Auteuil, you've got open ditches, bullfinches, walls, all sorts of things. Though you could probably win a good staying hurdle with a good staying chaser I am not sure about the chases. If owners here were given the choice of running for £30,000 at Newbury or £100,000 at Auteuil, most would choose to go for the Newbury race.'

Says Edward O'Grady: 'They have a big meeting in November, the next big meeting isn't until June, therefore it doesn't suit them to peak their horses in March when they want to peak at Auteuil in June. There's no incentive for French owners. With prize-money we can only envy, they can stay at home where the competition is much less.'

The Cheltenham Festival authorities have never believed in standing still, so what is the next development we can expect? Racing For Change, the body set up to help popularise the sport overall, is pushing for the Gold Cup to be held on a Saturday to make it available to a wider range of racegoers and to ensure maximum weekend TV coverage. In one sense they are pushing at an open door. Edward Gillespie and his team can see the arguments for ending the Festival on a Saturday. But that raises two immediate questions: would the Festival then become a five-day event, and has Cheltenham the facilities to cope with the size of crowd to be expected on a Festival Saturday?

In fact it raises more than two questions. Sam Vestey argues that if the Festival is to embrace a Saturday, the Gold Cup should still be run on a Friday, thus drawing a crowd of around 65,000 for both days. 'The advantage of Friday would be that the Gold Cup would still be run on fresh ground but the disadvantage is it wouldn't be the climax of the meeting. I'm glad I won't have to decide that one.'

Edward Gillespie said, in introducing Cheltenham's 2010–11 programme in October, that it could be five years or more before the Festival ended on a Saturday. While he appreciates that sporting authorities want more big fixtures at weekends to maximise attendance and exposure, he does not want to alienate a new class of potential racecourse regulars by disappointing them with Cheltenham's facilities. He says his 'master plan' hasn't changed much over the past five years but the financial circumstances have. In a sense Cheltenham has become a victim of its own success. The money it has generated has been used by the Jockey Club to underpin developments at other racetracks, along with borrowed money which now has to be paid back.

Says Gillespie: 'We take great pride that this muddy field has helped deliver the ambitions of Epsom, Newmarket and others. But the fact is that we need £20–£30 million spent here now and it is a question of when we are able to do it. We don't want to be holding Festivals on a building site.'

You can sense frustration, but the thinking is clear. Cheltenham has to remain a quality product. 'When we moved to a fourth day of the Festival, for the first couple of years I felt that we were attracting a different kind of racegoer than we were seeing on the other days of the meeting, and I think if we raced on a Saturday the situation would be the same. The issue at the moment is whether we would be delivering them an experience that they would recognise as being a world-class sporting event.

'We haven't ruled out including a Saturday in the 2012 Festival but we might have to wait five years or so until we are in a position to make the investment in our facilities . . . We hear comments that some of our buildings are looking a bit tired – as you would expect from those that date back to the 1920s and 1930s.'

Sam Vestey outlines part of the master plan, which envisages re-siting some key facilities on the track side of the parade ring, and building an additional stand below the present one. 'We started building from the top. We moved the weighing room from up at the top and moved the paddock round. We definitely need to rebuild from the royal box downhill and to change the press room and the weighing room. We want to build an owners' and trainers' stand with a press box and weighing room all in the same building. The slope means there could be six floors there, not just five.' The key, of course, in any further development is retaining the magic.

Chapter 34

The Magic of Cheltenham

'Every time you buy a horse you start with a dream. The owner who doesn't think of his horse as a potential Cheltenham Festival horse is rare indeed.' (Top Cheltenham trainer Nicky Henderson)

For jump-racing folk any year you miss Cheltenham is like having Christmas taken away from you. Ruby Walsh heads the chapter on Cheltenham in his autobiography 'The Love Affair Begins.' Mick Fitzgerald says, 'I've never been a footballer but I can imagine what it's like walking out at Wembley. When you walk out onto the track for the opening on Tuesday you look up to the stands and there's just a sea of people, and when you jump off you can hear that roar come down the track.'

What does make Cheltenham so special? Why is the Festival the phenomenal success it is? Regulars will give you a whole range of answers, but nearly all include the continuity of the cast list, the guaranteed presence of cherished performers. Like those audiences who pile into coaches for a trip to the West End to see their favourite sitcom performers in the latest revival of *Blithe Spirit* or *The Importance of Being Earnest*, Festival racegoers enjoy guaranteed quality and the comfort of the familiar. There is The Dikler running in his seventh Gold Cup or See More Business in his fifth. That's Willie Wumpkins winning his third Coral Hurdle, and good old Buena Vista in his sixth Festival appearance, at last making it to the winners' enclosure in the Pertemps Final.

Flat racing simply cannot compete with that. You get only one chance at the Classics – the 1000 and 2000 Guineas, the Oaks, the Derby – when you are three years old. Prove any good as a Flat racer and you'll be packed in cotton wool and whisked off to the breeding sheds for your owners to cash in on your stud value before the public at large have even learned to spell your name. It is the n-word again – narrative. In jump racing the good horses come back year after year, not least because, since most of them are geldings, there is no way of cashing in on their value except by running more races.

In one sense Cheltenham is fortunate. The Duke of Devonshire, who is chairman of the Ascot racing authority, perhaps Cheltenham's nearest equivalent on the Flat, points out a touch ruefully: 'We are competing with Ireland, France, Germany, Japan. Cheltenham virtually have jumping to themselves.' But at the same time he pays tribute to 'Edward Gillespie's great ability to put on a show' and concedes that, for example, Cheltenham gets added value out of the shopping facilities it provides in a way that Ascot and the Flat courses have yet to emulate. Cheltenham has what feels like several acres of country fashion emporiums under canvas, while other courses have a few scattered trade stalls selling mostly racing memorabilia.

Putting on a show and playing to the emotions is what Cheltenham does so well, and it is no coincidence that Edward Gillespie is almost as well steeped in the theatre as he is in horse-racing. When he came to Cheltenham from his previous role running Epsom (where the elegant innovator helped to rescue the ailing Derby by moving it from the Wednesday to the Saturday), his spare time often found him at the Everyman Theatre pitching into the local amateur dramatic scene. He has been heavily involved, not just in Cheltenham's racing Festival, but its literary festival too.

Everything about the Festival seems to add to that sense of

theatre; after the horses have passed the winning post they have to turn back and walk past the stands, allowing the crowd to salute their heroes. While those who have turned out to be bit-part players head for a less distinguished ring, the leading lights walk back down the chute to the winners' enclosure.

Says Willie Mullins: 'The walkway from the racecourse back past the stands and back to the parade ring [and winners' enclosure] is fantastic for any jockey and whoever is leading up the horse. For anybody going down that chute the atmosphere is incredible. A lot of the punters rush there to say "Well done" and people you haven't met for years come out of the woodwork to give you their regards. Lots of jockeys take their time and just savour it.'

Once their heroes are in the winners' enclosure a tiered amphi-theatre allows hundreds to crowd in to see victorious jockeys exulting and clusters of 'connections' hugging, smiling and occasionally crying with joy at their moment of elation. All of that, of course, against the glory of Cleeve Hill and the Cotswolds, a backdrop Cecil B. DeMille would have died for.

Cheltenham brings together an understanding audience and people at the top of their sport. The sheer chemistry of the place helps both make the best of it. Edward Gillespie says 'It's a very genuine camaraderie – people gathering to share something dear to their hearts, something they almost dare not identify. It's not just the racing, but staying in Gloucestershire, going out in the evenings, and completely without rank.' Enjoyment is the key word, whether it is riding or training a winner, bringing off a bet or simply soaking up the extraordinary atmosphere. As Irish trainer Jessica Harrington puts it: 'Everyone knows in jump racing how hard it is to get a good horse, keep him sound, get him to the races and not make a cock-up. When you get the good times you've got to enjoy them because you don't know when the next one is going to come.'

As far as the racing spectacle goes, Gillespie and his team see their role very much as one of stage management: 'You've got to provide a sense of theatre and get the spotlight in the right place. Our job is to prepare the stage and let the real heroes tell the audience.'

The layout, the building programme and the race scheduling are all designed to help them do that, and the Cheltenham team have the comfort of knowing that the stars will turn up. Aintree and Punchestown, for example, have very real attractions to offer. But they are not full-scale championships in the way that Cheltenham has become the Olympics of jump racing. At Cheltenham every race counts. They scarcely have to do any publicity-seeking – the jockeys and trainers do it themselves through the jumping season, pronouncing anything that wins a reasonable race as a 'Cheltenham prospect'.

Such pre-eminence could be a recipe for complacency but the Cheltenham authorities these past twenty years have been careful not to fall into that trap. They accept that they don't have a God-given right to go on staging the championships just because they have done it so well up to now. As Edward Gillespie points out: 'A predator could buy a racecourse and do the same as we do – it would be cheaper than buying a football club.' The Cheltenham team like to feel that they are feeding down into the racing pyramid. They want the Carlisles and Newton Abbots to feel involved in their success. 'We've always been very inclusive.' The money that Cheltenham makes for Jockey Club Racecourses has been responsible for huge developments elsewhere.

Talking partly with a wider Jockey Club hat on and emphasising how much Cheltenham's development and profits have helped the wider world of racing, former chairman Sam Vestey says: 'When I started we were making well under a £1 million a year. Now it is more like £10–£11m. We've built Kempton, we've built Aintree, though Aintree has started to make some money now. We've built Sandown. We bought Wincanton, Exeter. We've bought Carlisle. We've put money into Market Rasen, and that's all really through Cheltenham. If anything happened to Cheltenham . . .

Cheltenham alone makes half of the net profit of Jockey Club Racecourses.'

Cheltenham's co-operative policy stretches across the water too. Says Edward Gillespie: 'We have helped out some Irish courses, sending over experts to help them reconstruct their fences, because we need them to have winners here.' But Cheltenham is jealous of what makes it special. They have been prepared to take legal action to stop others calling their efforts 'festivals'.

Too much continuity, when tradition becomes pickled into ritual and formality, can be a danger, and there Cheltenham has succeeded in getting the balance right. For some the rites of Cheltenham are welcome reassurance that the vision of rural England which they fear each year is about to disappear has survived for another twelve months. If ever a preservation park is needed for the trilby and the Barbour, Cheltenham will provide it. There is no shortage still of tweedy ladies who appear to drink, drive, dine and possibly even sleep in their sheepskins. You can still meet men around the parade ring wearing their grandfather's tweeds. But these days the crowd is morphing into something younger and less rural. Stretch limos roll up alongside the four-wheel drives. Sharper-suited young men from the City sporting this month's hair-gel and the latest iPhones are cutting deals in the hospitality boxes. The spreading of wealth through society has brought in owners and spectators from a far wider sphere, without ever affecting Cheltenham's basic tenet that it is the quality of the sport, not who you are or what you own, which is the thing. Unlike some grand Flat meetings, says Ryanair chief Michael O'Leary, Cheltenham is for everybody. 'It's culturally different, there's none of the pomposity of Ascot.' One ex-military owner with a traditional trainer described a recent Festival as 'the best all-ranks event around'. Adds Edward Gillespie: 'You see people standing next to each other here who would never do it anywhere else.'

If there is a casualty in the sheer weight of numbers that has marked Cheltenham's success, it is perhaps the loss of intimacy at the four-day modern Festival. Edward O'Grady is one who acknowledges the need for the course to develop the corporate hospitality market but regrets that loss. 'It's becoming bloody difficult to eat and drink anywhere. It's easier to train a winner there than to meet your friends before, during or after.'

Says Jessica Harrington: 'It is harder work now. Four days is hard work. It used to be cosier, we all knew the bars. The corporate world has sort of split things up. People go off to boxes and unless you go up there you don't see them because they tend to hibernate because of the crowds.' And Willie Mullins too warns of the danger: 'Cheltenham, as a three-day Festival was fantastic. As they go out in time it's going to lose its allure. It's four days now, and there's talk of another day. So Irish people already go now for two days, for the first two days or the last day, they're not interested in doing four days . . . I wonder if it's in danger of losing its allure by having more racing, much as trainers would want more racing because it's more chance of a winner at the Festival. It's got to guard against just becoming one of the other festivals, but like most racetracks these days the accountants tell them what should be done.'

Cheltenham was never as smart as Ascot. The horse was, is, and will continue to be king. You don't go to Cheltenham to be seen. Despite the prosperous shopping village at Festival time, fashion has never intruded.

Cheltenham makes a virtue of not making any dress demands on anybody at any level. Edward Gillespie explains: 'Somehow it has never been an issue. We've fought off pressure from a few people. Basically everyone is made to feel comfortable. It is all one enclosure at Cheltenham, apart from five days a year. Nobody feels anyone else is a threat. Chairmen of multi-nationals choose to dress down at Cheltenham, and they enjoy the company of people who don't know who they are.'

The same lack of fuss applies when it comes to accommodating the royals. Queen Elizabeth the Queen Mother was a true jumping fan who had more than 400 winners in her own colours. She came to the Festival every year from the late 1940s and the respect and affection the Cheltenham crowd felt for her was properly reflected in the renaming of the Champion Chase. But as Lord Vestey points out: 'At Ascot and Epsom the royal box is controlled by the royal family. They take initiatives and issue the invitations. The royal box here is our box and the Queen is our guest. They always used to put bookmaker Joe Coral at lunch next to the Queen Mother because they got on so well together.'

The Queen is less of a Cheltenham regular but she did attend the Festival in 2003 and in 2009 when Barbers Shop ran in the Gold Cup.

Zara Phillips, who was an item for a long time with leading jockey Richard Johnson, is president of Cheltenham's 16–24 Club, and she and her cousins come regularly. They tend to treat it as a dress-down event. Prince William and Prince Harry go in the tented village with their mates as if they were going to the polo.

Racecourses everywhere have been benefiting from the introduction of ladies' days. Some have gone completely overboard with the concept. Cheltenham had to move too. Says Edward Gillespie: 'We like to celebrate our heritage and enjoy an element of tradition but we haven't got where we are by denying changes in public taste.' But again Cheltenham has adapted without compromising its identity as a racing temple. The course, he says, did not want to have dressiness making others feel unwelcome. They therefore linked their Ladies' Day to awards for women who had brought benefits to racing and combined it with charity fundraising. In came some fun and fashion, but 'We are not shoving it in your face and it is all over and done with by the time racing starts.'

'Evolution not revolution' is the Cheltenham motto. According to Edward: 'You've probably got to change five or ten per cent every year. But we are not afraid to try and say it didn't work if it didn't.'

One element that helps to make Cheltenham special is the cult of the amateur. The whole Festival, after all, dates from the days long before the Gold Cup and Champion Hurdle existed when the National Hunt Chase, or the 'Amateurs' Grand National' as some used to call it, was the very centrepiece of the action. Not only is the National Hunt Chase still going strong, along with the Foxhunters' Challenge Cup, Cheltenham is one of those rare events – perhaps golf could be included – where the talented amateurs not only have their own reserved events but can compete alongside the professionals too. There are three amateur races still on the Festival card, probably one more than the authorities would plan if starting again today, and there is a race too confined to 'conditional' jockeys – probationers still in receipt of a weight allowance when competing against their seniors. They don't have an apprentices-only race at Royal Ascot.

At the 2010 Festival the amateurs made some of the happiest headlines. Few in the media will forget the sight of Gold Cup-winning trainer Nigel Twiston-Davies halting the celebratory press conference to cheer on his son Sam, then an amateur rider, as he won the Foxhunters', the next race, with a perfectly judged ride on Baby Run. Said the proud father: 'Imperial Commander winning the Gold Cup was amazing but this has to take the biscuit. It's been a hell of a forty minutes. Maybe I'll die soon.'

There was, too, the demonstration of girl power. There were sixteen male riders and three women competing in the four-mile slog of the National Hunt Chase over twenty-four fences, and the finish was fought out between two flatmates, Katie Walsh on Poker de Sivola and Nina Carberry on Becauseicouldn'tsee. Nina is the sister of top jockey Paul Carberry, Katie the sister of the leading Festival rider Ruby Walsh. Just to complete the connection Nina was engaged to Katie's brother Ted.

In a furious driving finish both women were suspended for several days for excessive use of the whip, but the delighted Katie was scarcely contrite, declaring, 'When I'm riding, the last thing on my mind is possible suspension. You want to win. The horse would have got three more cracks if it had made the difference between winning and losing.' Nina Carberry was already the leading woman rider at the Festival with four wins to her name. Before it ended Katie had closed the gap further by riding Thousand Stars to win from the professionals in the Vincent O'Brien County Hurdle.

The brilliant publicity the Festival received from Katie Walsh's successes was a suitable recompense for the Cheltenham authorities' deft footwork and readiness to keep looking at ways of improving both horse safety and the race programme. After the multiple horse deaths of 2006, the Gillespie team looked long and hard at the future of the National Hunt Chase, the race which began as the very heart of the Festival. They examined and adjusted the race conditions. The rehabilitation of the race began when Cheltenham turned a near-disaster in 2008 (high winds caused the cancellation of a day's Festival racing) into a bonus by staging nine and ten-race cards for the next two days, with the National Hunt Chase heading the card on the first of those days. Good horses of the calibre of Butler's Cabin and future Grand National winner Silver Birch were attracted, and the race was re-branded with Sir Peter O'Sullevan's name attached. Girl power proved to be the icing on that particular cake.

The Gillespie style has led to some sharply taken breaths and the occasional ceilingward ascent of some more traditional eyebrows. One idea, for relay races, definitely bombed. But it is not just the Gillespie Factor. An adaptable racecourse committee, he reckons, has proved itself remarkably open to fresh ideas. 'With the peculiar cross-country course, for example, we were taking on something totally non-core but felt there was something here that people might like. They were initially back-of-the-envelope calculations but we did it well, levelled the land, did the drainage and brought in a top eventing man as course designer. We did our homework and persuaded people here to make the investment. Sporting Index did the right thing at the right time in sponsoring it. Some still hate it, but it has given an opportunity to horses like Spotthedifference and MacGregor II [and Garde Champetre]. Another board at another course might well have turned down the idea but ours took a leap of faith.'

Racing in general, its efforts led by Racing For Change, is struggling to modernise in an effort to widen its customer base. Its chief executive, Rod Street, is clear about the role of the Prestbury Park team: 'The first stage of Racing For Change – getting the bigger stories out to a broader audience – has happened largely because of the brilliant narrative Cheltenham provides. We've got the stories, we just need to be better at telling them.'

If much of Cheltenham's success is down to good management, they have some luck running for them too. They stage their festival at a time of year when the sporting landscape is short on competition. There is the Six Nations Rugby, some Premier League football (though not involving local sides) but the calendar is relatively light on alternative attractions. Says Edward Gillespie: 'The timing is perfect. It is the end of winter, a shining light.'

Prize-money levels are important, stresses Edward, and they make sure they remain competitive even when sponsors are thinning out. But at the end of the day Cheltenham is a class apart. And they have confidence in their product. 'There is nowhere like it and the best way of appreciating this place is to go to some of the others.'

The Festival attracts people who are looking for something they can rely on, for genuine quality. In an age of spin we have grown cynical. But at the Cheltenham Festival you know that every horse and every rider is trying. Strength, courage and stamina are all tested at a greater pace than the participants have faced elsewhere. As trainer/commentator Ted Walsh puts it: 'It's the race meeting that's going to answer all the questions. Every horse is prepared with Cheltenham in mind all year long and this is the place where you get the answers.' At the Festival there is no hiding place. Every achievement is real and there is probably no sporting crowd with a better appreciation of what it takes to get there and to win.

Edward Gillespie puts his finger on it best though when he argues that the honest character of National Hunt racing works in Cheltenham's favour: 'As other sports become more obviously commercial, with their agents and transfer fees and footballers cynically kissing badges, jump racing is incredibly grounded. The jockeys go out for comparatively little reward riding barely tamed wild animals. They are people at the top of their sport going out for £110 a ride, not £80,000 a week. What they do runs so in the face of what most people confront in their lives. They are real heroes, modest people with the courage of round-the-world sailors, who have to be brave however good their boats may be.

'This place has got soul. The horses don't ask for double wages. They are so generous. They ask for nothing more than their next meal and the spectators can tell the difference between a special championship race and an ordinary race.' As ever, the Festivals of the last few years have given us vivid evidence of that, with two stars trained from adjoining boxes in the same yard.

Chapter 35

The Decider that Wasn't

'I was close to breaking down as Kauto Star crossed the line, yet I was so elated with Denman the tears never came.' (Trainer Paul Nicholls)

P aul Nicholls probably knew he had the 2007 Gold Cup in his grasp, barring accidents, when he saw the wide grin on stable jockey Ruby Walsh's face as he rode towards the winner's enclosure at Haydock Park after the Betfair Chase on 18 November 2006. Ruby had already suggested Kauto Star could win a King George VI Chase. Paul had trumped that by telling his jockey he could win a Gold Cup. But that was the day they tested their theories by running him over three miles for the first time in a Grade 1 chase against a cluster of top horses. They were lured to Lancashire by the £1 million bonus Betfair were offering to any horse who won their race, plus either the King George or the Lexus Chase in Ireland and the Gold Cup.

Kauto Star did not just win that day against the likes of Kingscliff, L'Ami and Beef Or Salmon. He demolished them to stride home seventeen lengths clear of Beef Or Salmon. In so doing, says Paul Nicholls, he changed the landscape of steeplechasing.

The trainer wanted to go straight to the King George at Kempton then on to the Gold Cup. But suddenly his owner said

314 | THE CHELTENHAM FESTIVAL

he wanted instead to run Kauto Star a fortnight later against the crack two-milers lined up for Sandown Park's famous Tingle Creek Chase. The initial reaction from Paul Nicholls and from Ruby Walsh was that it would be unwise to rev the horse up by taking him back to two miles just when they had taught him to settle over three. But they changed their minds, and Kauto Star demonstrated his versatility by winning that race too by seven lengths from Voy Por Ustedes, the horse who was to go on and win the Queen Mother Champion Chase at Cheltenham. The King George duly followed. But twice in that race, and once in his Cheltenham prep race in the spring, Kauto Star alarmed his connections by making jumping errors – not just small ones but mistakes which would have led to many other less well-balanced horses falling as a result. In particular he seemed to panic a little at the final fence and dive through it. Being the star that he had rapidly become, this foible was given ample coverage in the media. Once again the public had what they liked best – a spectacular hero with just a hint of fallibility about him, enough to turn every race he ran into a drama.

In the Gold Cup itself, Kauto Star did not disappoint his admirers or his detractors. With an electric acceleration round the final bend he went clear of his pursuers, but then he lost concentration, got too close and launched himself at – rather than over – the fence. Somehow he got through it, and somehow Ruby sat tight. They were pursued up the hill by McCoy on Exotic Dancer but once Kauto Star had found his feet the result was clear. He duly collected the £1 million bonus for his owner, trainer, jockey and stable staff. Quite a nice little addition to the £242,335 first prize.

So when did Denman, a massive great brute of a horse whom his then part owner, the gambler Harry Findlay, called 'the Tank' and who needs a huge amount of work, begin to look like a rival Gold Cup candidate? For sure at that same 2007 Festival, when he won the Sun Alliance Novice Chase. With his huge ground-devouring stride and seemingly boundless stamina he dominated the field and won by ten lengths.

The two Nicholls champions took different routes to their Gold Cup destiny match in 2008. They were never tested against each other at home, and there was no point running them against each other in any other race. Meanwhile a third super-star had appeared in the Ditcheat yard. The two-miler Master Minded, bought from Guillaime Macaire, had arrived and was to win the next year's Champion Chase in a style which had the handicapper raising him to a mark of 186 compared to 182 at the time for Denman and 179 for Kauto Star.

Though hugely respectful of Denman, who sometimes needed working even before the day he raced to keep him in trim, Paul Nicholls didn't envisage anything beating Kauto Star in 2008. But Denman, before his trainer reckoned he had him fully racing fit, and under the hefty burden of 11st 12lb, had demolished a talented field to win the 2007 Hennessy Gold Cup at Newbury by eleven lengths, a week after Kauto had won another Betfair Chase. With Ruby Walsh out with a shoulder injury, Denman was ridden by the stable's number two Sam Thomas. It was a performance of stunning authority.

Under the barely recovered Ruby Walsh, Kauto Star went on to win another King George on Boxing Day. He remained Ruby's choice of ride for the Gold Cup although Denman had won the Lexus Chase in Ireland, and remained undefeated over fences. As he said, 'How do you get off a Gold Cup winner?' And he didn't change his mind after partnering Regal Heights for Donald McCain to finish a remote second to Denman in his prep race, the Aon Chase at Newbury, although there was a scare for Kauto when he was briefly lame after winning his prep race at Ascot. That fortunately turned out to be no more than pus in his foot.

The first Kauto Star v. Denman battle took place in the Gold Cup on Friday, 14 March 2008, with the Cheltenham executive encouraging supporters of both to wear scarves in the appropriate colours. It was not quite the all-the-way epic battle expected. As Denman made the pace, Kauto Star made mistakes at the two fences approaching the stands on the first circuit. The normal imperiousness, the majesty, wasn't there.

Denman was dominating, Paul Nicholls's other runner Neptune Collonges, the grey, was hanging on, and Kauto appeared to be struggling to close the gap. He did close it to a degree but the ruthless Denman was away and gone. In the end Kauto only took second place from Neptune Collonges by the narrowest of margins. Manor Farm, Ditcheat still housed the winner, but there was a new champion, his ownership then shared between the Odd Couple, the voluble gambler Harry Findlay and the prosperous dairy farmer Paul Barber, the restrained epitome of the rural élite.

Nicholls himself could be enormously proud of having trained the first three home in the most important jumps race in the calendar but he had mixed feelings. It was almost like a parent learning in the same telegram that one son had won a Victoria Cross and the other had been lost in action. Denman had proved even more brilliant than he had realised but he was sad that Kauto Star's colours had been lowered by his stable companion. At the time he was inclined to believe that at Cheltenham over three miles two furlongs Denman would always prevail from then on, but would be beaten by Kauto in the King George on the sharper, flatter Kempton track. But Denman, who put everything into his races, took two hours to cool down that day; perhaps his Gold Cup exertions had taken more out of him than was realised at the time.

Everyone in racing was agog for the return match. But the next August, when Denman returned from his summer break, it was clear that all was not well. He was permanently hot, had little interest in his work and occasionally blood in his nose. It turned out that he was suffering from atrial fibrillation of the heart, an irregular heartbeat. He was sent to Newmarket for treatment, and Kauto Star, his next-door neighbour and stablemate, seemed to miss him. Though the treatment worked, Denman lost a crucial two months of activity. When he came back it was more a question of nursing him back to confidence rather than imposing the formidable work regime that had previously been required to hone his raw strength to lean competitiveness. Meanwhile Kauto Star, despite his defeats by Denman and then at Aintree in April by Our Vic, was returning to his best on a slightly lighter programme.

Come the 2009 Festival the re-match was on, though Ruby Walsh too had had his trials, this time having half his spleen removed after a bad fall. In his absence the able Sam Thomas had endured a nightmare, being unseated by Kauto in the Betfair Gold Cup and coming off Big Buck's while he was in with a big chance in the Hennessy. Then, with Ruby back on board, Kauto won his third consecutive King George. Denman meanwhile had been nursed back from his illness but did not appear to be the force he had been, especially when he was beaten twenty-three lengths by Madison du Berlais in his comeback race. Lacking enthusiasm at home, he was nearly scratched from the Gold Cup but suddenly began to improve ten days before the big meeting. Paul Nicholls warned his owners that it would be a miracle if he could finish in the first four.

In the 2009 race Nicholls was confident that Kauto was back to his best, and the horse proved him right with one of the most imperious performances in the history of the race. He not only became the first Gold Cup winner to regain his crown after losing it, he did so in regal style, winning by thirteen lengths. What pleased his trainer – and the Cheltenham crowd – so much was that the horse in second place was Denman, not quite the force he was but clearly on the way back. Said Paul Nicholls: 'I was close to breaking down as Kauto Star crossed the line, yet I was so elated with Denman the tears never came.' Many true sportsmen felt the same. And Neptune Collonges was there again too to stamp the form, this time in fourth place, with Nicholls's My Will in fifth. Not so very far off the Michael Dickinson record.

Look, when you get the chance, at the pictures of Ruby Walsh standing up in his stirrups, waving his whip to the crowds after that victory. Yes, there is contentment in his look. But there is more than a smile. The teeth are bared too in an expression which conveys something far more basic, something angrier too, from this essentially friendly and thoughtful man. It is a look which says to those who had dared to contemplate his defeat: 'Don't you ever doubt this horse's quality again.'

With both the big two in training, and no hospital visits in the 2009–2010 season, we had it all to hope for once more in the 2010 Gold Cup. But this time there were hiccoughs along the route to Prestbury Park for both horses. Perhaps we should have taken more notice too of Imperial Commander, the horse who gave Kauto Star such a test in the Betfair Cup at Haydock that he won by only a nose, and of his sporting jockey Paddy Brennan who rode over to pat Kauto on the neck after the pair of them had duelled down the straight, twenty-four lengths clear of the field.

That had been a narrow squeak but there was no mistaking the majesty of Kauto's victory on Boxing Day in the King George. He won that by thirty-six lengths, from Madison du Berlais, the horse who had the previous season handed a twenty-three length defeat to the still-recovering Denman. Top-class horses were struggling behind his imperious cruising speed even before the first circuit was done. He was ready for the big one.

Denman started in November with a victory in a Grade 3 chase, ridden by Ruby Walsh. With Walsh determined to ride Kauto Star at Cheltenham, and Paul Nicholls believing that Sam Thomas's confidence had been undermined by his run of bad luck, Denman's owners Paul Barber and Harry Findlay decided that Denman would not be reunited with the man who had ridden him to Gold Cup victory but that champion jockey Tony McCoy would replace him. He rode him too for a prep race at Newbury which ended in disaster as the 6-1 on Denman, normally a dependable jumper, made a mistake at the second fence and then ejected his jockey as he landed squarely on top of the third.

His trainer reckoned that Denman had finished second when only half a horse the previous year, and that he had the 'miserable, grumpy bastard' back to full fitness. But as the two headed to Cheltenham for their fifth year running he still did not give him a chance of beating the stable's undoubted number one Kauto Star, whose tenth birthday fell on Gold Cup Day, 19 March.

That was how we entered the ultimate decider. The 2010 Gold Cup, many expected, was to be the race to end all races between the two superstars. This was to be the contest that answered all the questions. Instead, racing being racing, it simply opened up a new one and introduced a new star. It may have been Kauto Star's birthday but he did not give his followers a present. Having coasted to that point, he hit the eighth fence hard and lost his rhythm. Jockey Ruby Walsh was working hard from then on to keep him in the race. If you don't jump, you don't win.

The front-runner Carruthers was taking them along, with Denman handy, when at the fourth fence from home Kauto Star barely rose and took a terrible-looking fall, pitching onto his head and turning over. Urged on by McCoy, Denman took the lead down the hill. But he did not look quite like the invincible automaton of old, and he was being stalked by the horse that had run Kauto Star so close in the Betfair Cup at Haydock, Imperial Commander, trained by local hero Nigel Twiston-Davies and ridden again by Paddy Brennan, a man whose time had come.

Stamina had always been Denman's strong suit but this time he did not have anything more to give. Imperial Commander touched down first over the second last and went steadily away to score a thoroughly deserved victory by seven lengths. His rumpled trainer, who had been irked by all the pre-race attention for the big two in the Gold Cup, reminded us then that a horse he felt had been unduly neglected in the hype was actually winning his sixth race at the course. Imperial Commander had, for example, won the Ryanair Chase at the previous Festival, and won it by staying on up the hill.

With all the attention given these days to marketing and media hype, Ian Robinson, the head of the 'Our Friends in the North' syndicate who own Imperial Commander, criticised the track for selling scarves in the colours of Kauto Star and Denman. He said: 'It introduces a level of tribalism to the sport that isn't necessary. The only black spot on my Gold Cup day this year was when someone standing near to me wearing a Denman scarf punched the air after Kauto Star fell.' Sadly, with bets at stake, it isn't only people wearing scarves who do that sort of thing. Cheltenham countered that the scarves were harmless fun, helped to engage casual racegoers, and contributed to the sense of occasion. Fair enough. It seems to work for other sports. But I won't be wearing one, not even in the black and white of Imperial Commander's colours.

Nigel Twiston-Davies, who won three of the 2010 Festival's last four races as well as sending out the second in the Champion Hurdle, reminded us you don't actually have to spend a fortune to get a Gold Cup winner. On behalf of the six-strong syndicate he secured Imperial Commander for just £30,000. Twiston-Davies is another quintessentially Cheltenham man. Perhaps more in his element at the celebration party at his local, the Hollow Bottom, than facing the media in the parade ring, Twiston-Davies has that typically British combination of quiet pride in his success and slight embarrassment at the attention it brings. He is occasionally morose but capable too of riotous celebration.

Expectations – though not those of the Twiston-Davies team – were confounded in 2010 but we still saw great horses, talented riders and a perfectly judged training performance from a man who represents the very core of National Hunt racing. All had their consolations. For Denman, the recovered invalid, there was another honourable second. Because it was Cheltenham and the Festival, even for Kauto Star there was still something worth having: the heartfelt cheer from the crowd when he scrambled to his feet after the fall, bruised and sore but living to fight another day. But it was Imperial Commander's day. It was not quite 'The king is dead, long live the king', but in the moment of his triumph Imperial Commander became the new target, the new number one who must repel the challenge of the next wave of top-class steeplechasers. Once again, the Festival had demonstrated both its affection for past heroes and its capacity for finding new ones. Against the perfect backdrop, Cheltenham has the precious power of constant renewal.

Bibliography

Bateman, Charles, *Cheltenham Champions of the Eighties*, Federation of British Racing Clubs, 1989

Bromley, Peter, *The Price of Success: The Authorised Biography of Ryan Price*, Hutchinson/Stanley Paul, 1982

Clower, Michael, *Champion Charlie: The Authorised Biography of Charlie Swan*, Mainstream, 1997

Clower, Michael, *Kings of the Turf*, Aurum, 2007

Colley, Declan, *Mouse Morris: His Extraordinary Racing Life*, Collins Press, 2008

Corry, Eoghan, *The Irish at Cheltenham*, Gill & Macmillan, 2009

Cottrell, John and Armytage, Marcus, *A-Z of the Grand National*, Highdown, 2008

Curling B.W.R., *British Racecourses*, H.F. Witherly Ltd, 1951

Fitzgeorge-Parker, Tim, *The Ditch on the Hill: 80 years of the Cheltenham Festival*, Simon and Schuster, 1991

Fitzgerald, Mick, *The Cheltenham World of Jump Racing*, Racing Post, 2010

Foley, Tom and Taub, Michael, *Danoli, the People's Champion*, Robson Books, 1997

Gill, Peter, *Cheltenham Races*, Sutton Publishing, 1997

Harrington, Jessica, with McClean, Donn, *Moscow Flyer*, Highdown, 2005

Herbert, Ivor and Smyly, Patricia, *The Winter Kings*, Pelham Books, 1989

Humphris, E.M., *The Life of Fred Archer*, Hutchinson, 1923

King, Peter, *The Grand National: Anybody's Race*, Quartet, 1983

Lee, Alan, *Cheltenham Racecourse*, Pelham Books, 1985

Lee, Alan, *Fred: The Authorised Biography of Fred Winter*, Pelham Books, 1990

Nicholson, David with Powell, Jonathan, *The Duke: The Autobiography of David Nicholson*, Hodder and Stoughton, 1995

O'Neill, Peter and Boyne, Sean, *Paddy Mullins, the Master of Doninga*, Mainstream Publishing, 1995

Peters, Stewart, *Festival Gold: Forty Years of Cheltenham Racing*, Tempus, 2003

Pinfold, John, *Gallant Sport: The Authentic History of Liverpool Races*, Portway Press, 1999

Rickman, Eric, *Come Racing with Me: Reflections on His Life as Robin Goodfellow of the* Daily Mail *1929–49*, Chatto and Windus, 1951

Sarl, Arthur J., *Horses, Jockeys and Crooks: Reminiscences of Thirty Years Racing by 'Larry Lynx' of the* People, Hutchinson, 1935

Saville, John, *Insane and Unseemly: British Racing in World War II*, Matador, 2009

Scally, John, *Them and Us: The Irish at Cheltenham*, Mainstream, 1999

Seth-Smith, Michael, ed., *Steeplechasing and Foxhunting*, New English Library, 1977

Smith, Raymond, *The High Rollers of the Turf*, Sporting Books, 1992

Smith, Raymond, *Vincent O'Brien, the Master of Ballydoyle*, Virgin Books, 1990

Stevens, Peter, *History of the National Hunt Chase 1860–2010*, Peter Stevens, 2010

Walker, Jimmy, *Richard Dunwoody: Bred to be Champion*, Sporting Books, 1993

Walsh, Ruby, *Ruby: The Autobiography*, Orion Books, 2010

Welcome, John, *The Cheltenham Gold Cup*, Constable, 1957

Index

Hardy Eustace 135, 233–5
Harrington, Jessica 83, 84, 117,
 235, 242, 243, 244, 251, 304
Hartigan, Frank 38
Hastings, Aubrey 33, 38, 39
Hatton's Grace 73, 76–7, 78, 79,
 92, 134, 136
Hayward, Emma 13
Hazy Dawn 269–70
Head, Alec 136
Head, Willie 136
Height of Fashion 124
Henderson, Johnny 109–11
Henderson, Nicky 94, 96, 139,
 163, 164–6, 170–1, 180, 219,
 237, 238
Hennessy Gold Cup 124, 160
Hennessy, Peggy 96–7
Henry, Miles 139
Hill, Charmain 2, 3–4, 6, 7
Hill House 130
Hill, William 78–9
Hilly Way 119–20
Hobbs, Philip 232, 242
Hobbs, Reg 67
Hollins, H. 38
Holman, Alfred 26
Holman, Frederick 26
Holman, George 14
Holman, William 13, 14, 15–16,
 22, 26, 67
Holman, William (Junior) 26

Hors de la Loi III 230, 231, 232
Horse and Hound 76
Hourigan, Michael 224
Hoy, Andrew 208
Hughes, Dessie 135, 146, 147,
 154, 232–4, 255, 267–8
Hughes, Richard 234
Hughes, Robert 152–3
Hurst Park 83
Hyde, Timmy 71

Imperial Call 213, 214, 216, 261
Imperial Commander 319–21
Imperial Cup 37
Inglis Drever 296–7
Inkslinger 119
Insane and Unseemly (Saville) 60
Insurance 37, 46–7, 50, 56–7, 135
Intersky Falcon 232
Irish Cambridgeshire 73
Irish Cesarewitch 73, 74, 77, 79
Irish Horse 72–3, 79
Irish Lincoln Handicap 77
Irish National 70, 133
Irish Sweeps Hurdle 142, 143
Istabraq 9, 134–5, 228–33

J.L.T. 50
Jack Finlay 71
Jay Trump 97
Jenks, Bill 168
Jockey Club 109–10, 305